INTERPRETING TRADITION

THE ART OF THEOLOGICAL REFLECTION

INTERPRETING TRADITION

THE ART OF THEOLOGICAL REFLECTION

Edited by Jane Kopas

The Annual Publication of the
College Theology Society
1983

Volume 29

SCHOLARS PRESS   CHICO, CALIFORNIA

Library of Congress Catalog Card Number: 84-71053

Interpreting Tradition, The Art of Theological Reflection.
    (The Annual publication of the College Theology Society, ISSN 0276-2064; 1983, Volume 29)

ISBN 0-89130-621-8

Published by Scholars Press, California 95926

Typeset at Saint Joseph's University Press, Philadelphia 19131
Printed in the United States of America

TABLE OF CONTENTS

PREFACE

This compilation of essays, *Interpreting Tradition: The Art of Theological Reflection,* continues the spirit of reflection initiated in the preceding volume, *Foundations of Religious Literacy.* In that book, the Annual Publication of the College Theology Society for 1982, the articles addressed the topic of literacy, exploring conditions for religious literacy and the role of the classic. The annual volume for 1983 continues the series and consists of eleven articles that explore further the resources and challenges of the interpretative process. All the papers were originally presented at the 1983 national convention of the College Theology Society at Cabrini College in Radnor, Pennsylvania, with the exception of one which was delivered at an earlier convention.

Foundational insights and experiences of a religious tradition are kept alive in a variety of ways — through re-enactment in ritual, through representation in doctrine and teaching, through reappropriation of values that shape morality in concrete decisions. But all of these forms take shape in contexts that add not only light but also shadows to their meaning and at times even call it into question. Thus, in order for tradition to be understood, it not only needs to be handed on, but it needs also to be interpreted in changing contexts which have their own resources and their own problems. The authors represented in this volume take up the challenge of exploring ways that tradition is preserved and vivified through interpretation. The interpretation of tradition, as they demonstrate, is a process which requires both art and technical skill, both sensitivity to one's own experience and that of others and mastery of the tools by which one comes to grasp the issues that are at stake in living tradition.

Monika Hellwig's piece, "Theology as a Fine Art," which opens this volume, devotes sensitive attention to a neglected perspective, the practice of theological interpretation as an art. After discussing what theology is not, Hellwig explores the essential elements in a theological attitude that is truly "faith seeking understanding" — contemplation, empathy, and reason. Her analysis and description of her own practice of the art bring to life the process of uncovering the richness of tradition alive in the present.

The second article, J. Patout Burns' "Variations on a Dualist Theme: Augustine on the Body and the Soul," painstakingly examines a dimension of Augustine's thought while questioning the interpretation that has been attributed to it. Burns demonstrates, particularly through his use of Augustine's study of number, that the apparent dualism of body and soul in Augustine is actually a conflict within the soul. He shows that Augustine's interpretation of the human condition moves beyond the traditional dualism defined by polarities of body and soul, and he offers suggestions as to why Augustine's effort were not wholly successful. Gary Macy's "The Theological Fate of Berengar's Oath of 1059: Interpreting a Blunder Become Tradition," represents a careful study of a struggle between interpretations. Macy discusses the oath imposed on Berengar, showing how successive interpreters disputed the assumptions behind it and turned to an interpretation of the Eucharistic presence they regarded as more faithful to tradition. In the process of examining the topic he uncovers the pluralism that has characterized theological interpretation.

The role of narrative as interpretation is considered by William Loewe in "Myth and Counter-Myth: Irenaeus' Story of Salvation." Loewe presents Irenaeus' version of the Christian myth as *recapitulation*, emphasizing the narrative elements in Irenaeus' approach and juxtaposing it against the Gnostic myth he was concerned to refute. Loewe maintains that narrative elements rather than doctrinal ones are the key to understanding the efficacy of Irenaeus' interpretation and his creativity. Only a myth of considerable scope and comprehensiveness, Loewe states, was adequate to meet the Gnostic challenge.

Interpretation of the biblical tradition is considered in two articles. Alice Laffey's "Biblical Power and Justice: An Interpretative Experiment," questions how the texts that reflect biblical views of power and justice might foreshadow a new way of structuring political and religious society. After thoroughly exploring the perspectives of Hebrew Scriptures and Christian Scriptures on power and justice, Laffey underscores the ways the two notions are inextricably related. Power is meant to be used for justice, and correspondingly the exercise of justice frequently requires the redress of wrongs caused by the misuse of power. The biblical views are shown to offer a resource for a non-hierarchical and non-patriarchal approach in contemporary theology.

In "Kingdom Speaking and Kingdom Hearing: Matthew's Interpretation of Jesus' Kingdom Tradition," Gary Phillips explores the evangelist's method of presenting the kingdom tradition that Jesus expressed in the parables, particularly the Parables Discourse of Chapter 13. Phillips argues that Jesus' approach to the proclamation of the kingdom was taken up and interpreted by the evangelist who provided a commentary that highlights the dynamic character of tradition. Matthew provides an interpretative model of the way the reader of the text may come to participate in the development of tradition. Thus, the first part of this volume focuses on examining classical sources of tradition to discern new dimensions within them that aid understanding.

Part Two focuses on the discovery of new avenues for enhancing our understanding of tradition. It opens with Ewert Cousins' "Interpretation of Tradition in a Global Context." Cousins sees tradition as an archetype exemplified in various religions and notes that study of spirituality provides an effective, though neglected, means for theology to deepen its understanding of the archetype of tradition. He observes that this is especially important today because of a shift to global consciousness which is characterized by a convergence of traditions and encounter between world religions. The shift to a global context demands that one see one's own tradition as participating in the global archetype shared by the human community and that one cultivate an empathy toward other religious traditions for a deeper understanding not only of the other tradition but also of one's own.

The selections that follow offer other examples of the use of new resources to interpret tradition. Diane Apostolos-Cappadona offers a study entitled "Images, Interpretations, and Traditions: A Study of the Magdalene." She examines the question of the identity of Mary Magdalene and the symbols that underlie visual representations of her, and she analyzes various depictions that have appeared through history as Mary Magdalene emerged from being part of a narrative to standing as an individual in her own right. Apostolos-Cappadona observes that the image of the Magdalene is a classic that has survived the centuries through interpretations that have made her character an exemplar of redemptive and transformative love accessible in different contexts.

Michael Gallagher's "Toward Doctrinal Consensus" examines the rise of ecumenism through the Faith and Order movement and considers the new light that has been shed on statements of faith as a result of the ecumenical movement. Gallagher explores the meaning and purpose of consensus statements, identifies the conditions for conciliar fellowship these statments make possible, and points out the limits as well as the complexities that attend them. He concludes by drawing out the implications the movement has for the rediscovery of tradition and for forging the beginnings of a new development of tradition.

In "Original Sin and Psychoanalysis" James Forsyth addresses the problem of re-interpreting an important element of the doctrine of original sin so as to make it more comprehensible to the contemprary believer. The issue at stake is the transmission of original sin through generation, not imitation. The conceptual framework enlisted in interpretation is psychoanalytic theory with the aid of the category of generativity. After examining situational and personalist views of original sin, Forsyth analyzes psychoanalytic theory and the process of generativity as the medium of transmission. He then offers an interpretation of original sin which attempts to respond to some of the problematic issues he has raised.

The book concludes as it began with an article that focuses on interpreting tradition in a teaching context. Keith Egan in "The Return to the Classroom of Thomas Aquinas" makes a case for including a course on Thomas Aquinas in the theology curriculum so as to give students first-hand sustained contact with the mind of a great Christian thinker. Though this section of the volume highlights shifting horizons and the utilization of new resources for theological reflection, Egan's article which documents the absence of courses on Aquinas, offers a complementary view. He suggests approaching Aquinas both as a classic figure and as a model for new inquiry. Egan also relates his own experience in presenting such a course and offers some recommendations that flow from his conviction.

Though admittedly these essays draw upon different sources in the past and reflect different concerns and methods, one may identify certain general trends or characteristics that mark their attitude toward tradition and their practice of interpretation. The articles demonstrate that the interpretation of tradition requires the art of discernment. As Ewert Cousins observes, "not all of the past is worthy to live in the present." Concern for the practice of discernment is reflected also in the work of J. Patout Burns, Gary Macy, Keith Egan, and James Forsyth. The art of discernment depends upon the cultivation of sensitivity to experience and to the central issues at stake in the formulation and communication of tradition.

Another characteristic that stands out in this collection of essays is the conviction shared by the contributors that classic texts, events, and symbols come alive in the present through a process of interpretation that is inherent in tradition itself. The articles of Gary Phillips, Diane Apostolos-Cappadona, and Michael Gallagher reflect this view in various ways. The idea that interpretation does not stand outside of tradition makes it possible to accept pluralism as an aspect of the richness of tradition rather than an aberration of it.

Finally, the authors, though engaged in a task that requires considerable use of critical reason, give witness to the conviction that interpretation is not merely a rational exercise. In particular the articles of Monika Hellwig, William Loewe, and Alice Laffey draw upon aspects of human understanding which show meaning embodied in and communicated through religious experience, narrative structure, and moral claims. The interpretation of tradition and the reception of tradition are shaped by these dimensions of experience as well as rational factors.

Special thanks are due to many generous readers who assisted the editor in the evaluation and selection of articles and offered helpful suggestions to the authors. Thanks are likewise due to the authors for their openness to suggestions and their maintenance of inclusive gender-related language. Thanks to these colleagues, it has been the editor's experience that to witness the art of theology dynamically operative in the interpretation of tradition is one of the aesthetic delights of participating in a community of inquiry.

Jane Kopas
University of Scranton

ACKNOWLEDGEMENTS

In *A History of the College Theology Society* (1983) Rosemary Rodgers recounts the story of the Society's annual publication series. Initially known as the Society of Catholic College Teachers of Sacred Doctrine, the Society was born in 1954. It held its first national convention in 1955 which resulted in the first volume of *Proceedings* (1956). Published by the Society, this new series followed the strict proceedings format which reflected all the activities of the annual meeting, including papers, the presidential address, accounts of business meetings and reports, etc. But this pattern was dramatically altered with the publication of the twelfth book in this series. Emanating from the 1966 convention, this volume — *On the Other Side* (1967), edited by Katharine T. Hargrove — was published as a trade book which contained a collection of selected papers but excluded the formal organizational and business material from the national meeting. This departure, consequently, pointed the Society's Annual Publication Series in a new direction which it has followed ever since. Therefore, this present book, *Interpreting Tradition,* is the 29th volume in this series.

Its appearance provides an opportunity to thank some of those persons who contributed to the Annual Meeting at Cabrini College in Radnor, PA in June of 1983 at which the contents of this book essentially took shape. Sister Eileen Currie, M.S.C., president of Cabrini College, provided the hospitality and graciousness of the beautiful Cabrini campus and facilities. Mary L. Schneider, of Michigan State University, served as chair for the Annual Meeting; Margaret Reher, of Cabrini College, was the local chairperson. Members of the national board of directors were Vera Chester, of St. Catherine's College, Paul Misner, of Marquette University, Walter Conn, of Villanova University, Robert Kress, of Catholic University, Joseph LaBarge, of Bucknell College, Sonya Quitslund, of George Washington University, William Loewe, of Catholic University, Robert Masson, of Marquette University, Joann Wolski Conn, of Neumann College. The officers of the Society were George Gilmore, of Spring Hill College, treasurer; Suzanne Toton, of Villanova University, secretary; and Kathleen McGovern Gaffney, of Xavier University, LA, vice president. Gratitude is expressed to these, and to all others who contributed to this highly successful meeting of the Society.

Jane Kopas, of the University of Scranton, has capably edited this volume. Robert Masson, chairperson of the committee of research and publication, and Joseph Gower of Saint Joseph's University, managing editor for the committee, also deserve thanks for their work in bringing the book into publication.

Villanova University   Rodger Van Allen, President
                                                        College Theology Society

I

THE THEOLOGIAN'S CHALLENGE – REVISITING THE CLASSICS

THEOLOGY AS A FINE ART

Monika K. Hellwig

Our contemporary experience of religious and cultural plurality demands of us rather urgently that we reflect in some depth on what it is that we do under the name of Christian theology. I think this is a wholly fortunate development. It is not only so that we may give an answer concerning ourselves to those of other traditions, that we need to reflect deeply. It is also necessary for our own sakes, so that what we do may be authentic and coherent, and that we may be at ease with one another.

At the outset it may be well to set aside immediately and quickly the descriptions of some activities that are not "doing theology." Most obvious and most tempting among these to college theology professors is the repetition and explanation of what others have written. I say, "most tempting," because one can so easily impress students and make a course outline look very respectable by plodding through difficult works of major theologians, contemporary or classical in the tradition. Because this is such a respectable procedure it may be necessary to consider carefully why it is not adequate.

College undergraduates concentrating in other fields usually have no special need to know particular theologians. If they desire to read them and we want to introduce them to these authors, the only good reason must lie beyond the authors themselves. The students want to learn how to deal with religious questions in their own lives, and their reading of masters in the field should serve them as an apprenticeship in learning how to theologize creatively in their own social, cultural, and historical contexts. In the case of undergraduates whose concentration is in theology, it may well be that they must be introduced to particular authors or texts in order to complete their training or prepare for the next stage of that training. But even here we must ask why it is essential or important in their training to have acquaintance and mastery of the material. Again, the real reason lies beyond the specific texts and authors. Ultimately what is important is to have a critical grasp of a tradition of thought so that one may profit from it in order to think better and to be better able to share and exchange thought with others.

In order to teach in this way, so that the reading of the masters becomes an apprenticeship in thought rather than an exercise in memory and endurance, one must be engaged oneself in the process of reflection rather than repetition, of course. In other words, the teaching of theology cannot be carried on outside the process of the doing of theology. And this means that we are all challenged to clarify further for ourselves what that doing of theology really means.

At a time when religious and cultural plurality was less in evidence it may have seemed that theology was a science in the modern sense of the term. It may have seemed that we were investigating evidence in order to be able to reason from it and infer facts not subject to direct scrutiny. The facts that constituted the data or evidence would have been "truths of revelation" as formulated and officially taught in the tradition. The method of theology might have been thought of as simple rational argumentation from evidence to conclusions. As in detective work the aim would have been to identify and prove the true solution and to show that all other solutions were false. In such a frame of reference it might make sense to try to identify the one true church of Christ, thereby showing that all other churches were false claimants to be the church of Christ. Or it might have made sense to argue whether transubstantiation or consubstantiation is the correct explanation of what happens in a Christian Eucharist, thereby showing the other to be incorrect. Yet again, it might have made sense to argue very carefully in order to arrive at the truth of what happens to a human being beyond death, other answers being thereby shown to be untrue.

It has become increasingly clear that in some such questions truth is not black and white as in detective stories, and the matter for study cannot be dealt with after the manner of collection of evidence and inference of further facts. It has also become clear that in other such questions, such as that of human destiny beyond death, there must indeed be a factual answer, but no ingenuity of reasoning from collectable data will provide us with that answer. Yet to say that we cannot arrive at a determination of factual truth is by no means to claim that we are not dealing with a quest for truth. It is only to claim that truth is larger than the principle of contradiction, far larger than the empirically verifiable, and certainly larger also than the logically necessary.

This takes us further in the attempt to understand what it is that we do when we do theology, though it takes us by a path of negation. It may seem that the only option left is to understand theology as the continuing explanation of a religious tradition and the account it gives of its beliefs in story, ritual, iconography, and systematic explanation. Thus the formulations made in Christology in the fourth and fifth centuries should be explained in language clear to the reader or listener today. Or the Lord's prayer should be explained with reference to its context in Jewish worship of the time of Jesus, and with reference to its subsequent uses, elaborations, and commentaries by Christians. Again, the sacraments of Christian worship should be explained by tracing the historical unfolding of the rites and of the explanations that were being given of the rites, and placing this historical unfolding in its changing contexts as much as possible.

It seems to me that this is indeed a part of the work of theology but by no means the whole or even the central part. This uncovering of the past has a purpose beyond itself, and that purpose is not to bind or subject us to the past but to place the past at the service of our present and future. Therefore, to profit from the exploration of the past, and not to get lost forever in the archaeological excavations, we must try to achieve some clarity of expectation concerning the way a knowledge and understanding of the past might serve our present and future. This means that we must be clear about the questions to which we are seeking the answers. It may be difficult. For the most part, we who are now teaching theology to undergraduates have spent much time and energy assimilating answers to which we never experienced any questions.

Theology is, when all is said and done, an attempt to find ultimate meaning in life, to find a purpose that makes it all worthwhile. Theology does not set out to invent that meaning and purpose but to discover it, and the road to discovery is essentially a road inward into the subjective dimensions of human experience as well as outwards into interpersonal and intramundane history. We cannot really disagree with Feuerbach that the theological enterprise is necessarily an anthropological enterprise, for we can but seek for the ultimate in our own experience. Yet this does not imply that there is no ultimate or that our quest does not move towards it but runs into blind alleys of our own projections. There is indeed a reciprocity between the doctrine of creation in the biblical traditions and Feuerbach's insight. From the point of view of the doctrine of creation, the human is the best available image of the divine, and to search human consciousness, explore human longings, reflect on what is noblest in human behavior, is indeed the way to glimpse the divine. From the point of view of the conviction that all theology is really anthropology, the inquiry that is pursued by projection is constantly probing reality where it is to be found and therefore must be moving towards what is ultimate.

This is another way of saying that theology is the interpretation of the reality of our own experience in ultimate terms. Yet one might pause here to notice another temptation to settle for an inadequate definition of the task. Just as repetition of authors or repetition of the past is not theology, so a simple reflection upon the experience of the participants in a particular discussion is not yet Christian theology, even if the participants happen all to be Christians. We are all familiar with students who arrive in college innocent of any acquaintance with the figures, stories, and imagery of the Bible, not to mention the elaboration of any of these in Christian tradition or the attempts to arrange them systematically into a world-view. What must be obvious to any classroom teacher is that those who are thus deprived of the cumulative experience, vision, and wisdom of their tradition, are very inadequately equipped to reflect even on their own immediate experience.

We are all very dependent on the imagery and symbolism built up by those who went through our world before us. After all, even when we say that we have fallen in love or been scared out of our wits, we are able to express it because we inherit the delightfully earthy imagery of a tumble to suggest the disconcerting suddenness and helplessness of the situation, or borrow the symbolism of an eviction to hint at the indignity and alienation attached to the emotion of fear. To try to bypass the heritage of symbol and image and story and even the legacy of ponderous systematic explanations thereof, is to impoverish oneself and one's students to a point of destitution at which little personal reflection can happen.

The fine art of theology seems to me to lie in the simultaneous cultivation of contemplation, empathy, and reason, it being taken for granted that one does not become a professional theologian without life-long study of the tradition in all its dimensions. By contemplation I do not mean in the first place a form of prayer but something much wider in its application. Just as the talent of the graphic artist is not primarily in manual skill but in a habit of vision, so it seems to me that the talent of the theologian is not in the first place in mastery of argument but in vulnerability to experience. And even as the power of the poet does not reside mainly in the craft of the wordsmith but rather in a certain immediacy of presence to the reality that gives itself to human perception, so it is, I think, that the persuasion carried by a theologian is not founded in the rational or literary finesse of the presentation but in the quality of the theologian's own experience of reality.

The essence of a contemplative attitude seems to be vulnerability — allowing persons, things, and events to be, to happen, allowing them their full resonance in one's own experience, looking at them without blinking, touching them and allowing them to touch us without flinching. It is a matter of engaging reality in action, allowing it to talk back to us and listening to what is said. It is a constant willingness to be taken by surprise. It is a deep existential grasp of the truth that all our theory is a critique of our praxis and that evasion of experience means distortion or alienation in our theory. This applies to theology as it does to aesthetics. But perhaps it is more difficult in theology because there is so much at stake and because we always tend to cling to a kind of certainty which we cannot have in matters ultimate.

Our Trinitarian and Christological doctrines are an example both of the difficulty and of the high stakes involved. These doctrines are so central and everything else depends on them to such an extent that we are continuously tempted to keep them severely separate from our fluctuating experiences and perceptions, and to guard orthodoxy by the literal preservation of classic verbal formulations. Yet the process of alienation is evident. Both the semantic drift apparent in the vocabulary and the cultural obsolescence of the imagery and philosophy involved in the formulations, make it gradually easier for Christian believers to ignore these central doctrines in their efforts to find ultimate meaning in their own lives.

We need the courage and the conviction to approach these and all the traditional doctrines with the whole force of the contemporary human question about the meaning and purpose of life, and this depends in the first place on total openness to one's own experience in the world. The Gospels of the New Testament present Jesus as one who did precisely that. They show him as one who could spend long periods alone experiencing the harmony but also the conflict in nature, seeing the splendor and spontaneity but also the transience and fraility of flowers and birds. The Gospels introduce Jesus as one who entered into immediate, shockingly unconventional relationships with people, not evading the human encounter by the choreography of the socio-cultural role definitions. The Gospels also reveal Jesus as one who faced the structures of society, seeing everything that is there and entering into the raw experience of the frustration, the anger, the fear, the dashed hopes that are engendered by institutions that embody a many-faceted heritage of sin. Finally, the Gospels record for us in the teachings of Jesus and the answers he gave to questions put to him, a clarity of vision that sliced straight through all the sophistication and complexity of the conventional theological debates of his time.

Contemplation is an attitude pervading all aspects of life, all experiences, activities, and relationships. It is also a way of prayer. It is a way that allows the ultimate to reveal itself in the immediate that is given to us when we do not try to escape the silence at the roots of our own consciousness or the emptiness at the center of our being. The ultimate reveals itself when we do not try to escape the immediate or to distort it in self-defense or to subvert it to our pettiness. That dimension of contemplation that turns explicitly to the divine must not be glibly named without being experienced in its essential namelessness. Whenever that happens, there is a note of inauthenticity in the discussion.

Nevertheless, to speak out of the practice of contemplation is certainly not enough, if contemplation does not spill over into the keenest empathy. Empathy is required not only to read the contemporary questions aright and to make an effective presentation but in order truly to theologize. What I mean is that it is necessary on the one hand to take up ultimate human questions in a depth in which one may not oneself have experienced them yet, and that it is necessary on the other hand to be able to read the images, stories, and rituals of the tradition, truly entering into the human experiences and longings out of which they come. Good scribes are, after all, householders who know how to bring both old things and new out of their treasuries. In the wedding of the two there is true wisdom.

Our present culture, with its emphasis on critical thinking, abstraction, and empirical verification, seems to leave us habitually nonplussed in face of the more subtle logic of story and iconography, of symbol and ritual. It is necessary to be about the business of building bridges of empathy into the wider world of this kind of language and to build them out of our own freely acknowledged deeper levels of experience. I believe that it is the contemplative habit in our own present circumstances that makes it possible to enter into the human questions and longings behind the stories. And this is essential to the task of a Christian theology, for historically we move to systematic explanations from these stories and images and rituals. These latter hold the clues to the deeper reasons for the systematic formulations and debates, and, therefore, also the clues to overcoming the alienation of our theology from our life experience.

Besides forging this link with the past, empathy has another crucial role to play. The personal experience of the theologian is a very small, and all too often a very shrivelled, part of human experience. It is always important and at present also very urgent that we should enter into the human questions of those whose voices do not ordinarily reach us — the destitute, the vast masses of the starving, the despised, the forgotten, the vast masses of oppressed people, the whole populations of uprooted refugees, the races and classes who "do not count," who are written off by the human makers of public history as waste, future generations threatened with overwhelming ecological and nuclear disaster, the elderly and handicapped, and otherwise "useless" people of our society. Without entering by empathy into such dimensions of human experience, human suffering and human hope, we are simply not dealing with the reality of the human situation — the reality of creation, sin and redemption, the real issue of human freedom and accountability. Unless the experience we draw upon has this kind of breadth and depth by virtue of a costly compassion, the theology we do is nothing but a passing cerebral aberration.

Again, it may be well to notice a contemporary temptation. Those of us who are drawn this way by temperament may find it all too easy to reduce theology to the exposition of contemporary human suffering and expressions of indignation or even accusation. Or, if we do not stop there, we might be tempted to enter into economic, sociological, and political analyses of the causes and never emerge again from the jungle of the social sciences. It is necessary to search constantly for the correlation between the reality revealed in contemporary experience both of suffering and of hope, both of conflict and of peace, on the one hand, and the gospel of salvation with its doctrinal elaborations through history on the other. The link of empathy is supposed to move both ways, and in a Christian context what, in the final analysis, anchors the process is the person of Jesus Christ in his concrete identification with human freedom and unfreedom and with the inbreaking of the divine in the human dilemma.

These would seem to be the roles of contemplation and empathy in the task of theology. Of the role of reason less need be said, for our graduate schools, seminaries, and professional journals promote it in some measure, though they promote sophistication, name dropping, and elaborate footnotes with considerably more enthusiasm. Perhaps we should look to the example of Jesus as portrayed in so many of the dialogues in the Gospels, to realize that a central role of true reason in theological discourse is in discerning and eliminating all unnecessary technical vocabulary, evasive citation of authorities, and the smoke-screen of convoluted arguments, in order to come to the real human issues because it is these that open to the revelation of the divine.

It may be helpful to suggest a method in which this can be done in teaching Christian theology to undergraduates. It assumes that the professor has developed some degree of contemplation and of empathy in both dimensions as well as having a good grasp of the literature and development of the tradition. It may be safely assumed that the students have for the most part not been encouraged by their past education to develop either contemplation or empathy and that their notion of study is rather univocally that of memorization. Yet it may also safely be assumed that people, especially young people, are always capable of waking to a deeper awareness and a more reflective consciousness, and that, as this happens, it has a self-validating quality that keeps beckoning further.

A method that I have found very fruitful is the following. First I reflect on some central Christian doctrine, identifying the stories, images, rituals, and other symbols from which the dogmatic formulations and systematic explanations seem to arise. Then I try to build my own bridges of empathy into that story or other representation, bearing in mind that whatever the redaction history may be, a story does not survive in a particular form unless it makes sense in that form — unless that form discloses the inner logic to the tellers and the listeners. In other words, I accept the story on its own terms first, jumping right into it and living in it according to its own rules. If the story has a ladder from earth to heaven, then I know that for the time being heaven is up there, and I do not try to displace it.

Having done this myself, I approach the students with the story. Perhaps I retell the story or perhaps I ask them to read it in the Bible and to discuss what it means to them, trying to draw them into the story and into deeper awareness of their own experience and its correlation with the questions probed by the story. I do this in the manner I learned from reading Jewish midrashic literature. Together, in the discussion, we try to clarify the human issue. Sometimes it is necessary to trace a sequence of stories through the Hebrew Scriptures and the New Testament, and occasionally we follow them still as stories in the further development of the Christian tradition.

From this level of symbolic expression of what is, of course, in itself ineffable, we move to an historical unfolding of the way those more spontaneous expressions became formulated in doctrines. We look appreciatively and critically at historical efforts to drop the metaphors and "tell it as it really is." We evaluate what presents itself as abstract and technical language with a claim to precision, and rediscover the concrete and metaphorical referents hidden in the etymology of the vocabulary used in theological formulations. That rediscovery makes lumin-ously clear that theology is not an escape from mystery. Meanwhile, I fill in for the students as best I can, the historical, cultural context in which people were phrasing the questions and the answers in this way. We do not stop there. I take them through some reflection on the historical loss and recovery of meaning in the development of doctrine and Christian theology, giving some sense of the ups and downs, periods of vigor and periods of stagnation. Finally, we return full circle and discuss the contemporary questions, experiences, and insights that relate to the doctrine we have traced. Needless to say, this final discussion usually reveals to the students themselves how much their eyes have been opened and their awareness increased.

This is one theologian's approach to the fine art of theology. The three elements of contemplation, empathy, and reason are, I think, essential. The ways of employing them must be many. The harvest is plentiful, and the hungry are waiting. May there be laborers aplenty for the task.

II

CLASSICS REVISITED

VARIATIONS ON A DUALIST THEME:
AUGUSTINE ON THE BODY AND THE SOUL

J. Patout Burns

Our attention in this volume focuses on tradition and its interpretation. I should like to take one of our oldest and most troubling themes, sketch different traditional ways of understanding it, and then show how one theologian attempted to interpret the traditions to which he was heir. Our theme is the dualism of body and soul; our theologian is Augustine. He is usually thought to have gotten things all wrong in this matter and to have established a tradition which made the whole of western Christendom get things all wrong. I intend to challenge that received interpretation of Augustine.

My method will be to concentrate on Augustine's early writings, especially those dating from the period between his conversion and ordination. I will then sample later works for developments and variations.

Augustine was heir to at least three traditions on the nature and relationship of body and soul. The North African tradition of traducianism, of the generation of the entire person from human parents, involved a materialism of both body and soul. The soul was a drier, finer, warmer, and thus more energetic form of matter. While Augustine generally considered this view quite naive, he continued to toy with its explanation of the origin of individual souls from the souls of parents.[1] The true influence of this theory, which would be very difficult to trace and establish, may have been in Augustine's appreciation of the body and of the unity of the individual human person.

A second tradition held Augustine for almost a decade: Manicheism. This radical dualism understood soul and body as two originally opposed forms of material reality. Each is possessed of its own energy and operations which are opposed and inimical to the other. The aetiological myth of their mixing portrays the realm of Darkness attacking that of Light; in defending itself, some of the Light is submerged in the Darkness. The Light falls into an oblivion, a self-forgetfulness; it is subject to the indignity of bodily existence and held captive to the desires of the flesh. In this situation, the Light is passive to the power of the Darkness. It must be rescued by a process of cosmic separation. Much of Augustine's early writing is directed to the refutation of Manichean dualism and the development of alternate explanations of the experience of opposition of the flesh and impotence of the spirit which the theory was intended to interpret.

A third tradition, that of Christian Platonism, reached Augustine through the

Latin translation of Plotinus prepared by Marius Victorinus, the allegorical interpretation of scripture which Ambrose drew from Philo, and from other sources which are more difficult to specify. This tradition reaches back to Plato himself and finds a clear expression in his allegory of the chariot. Two horses represent the energy of emotion and bodily appetite which the driver, the mind, may govern and direct to its own purposes. The energies of soul and body are opposed to those of the mind. In this hierarchical view, however, the mind can subdue and direct the lower energies; it is not their passive victim. Still, this tradition assigns different origins to the energies in the human individual and makes their integration a project to be achieved. Christian writers drew heavily on this tradition and modified it substantially. Some explained that God created the various forms of being and energy and then mixed them in human nature for his own good, but generally unsearchable, reasons. Others follow one or another form of Origen's theory of the soul's fall into the body and the formation of the material world as a means of restoring the soul to its original state. Christian asceticism calls upon the mind to subdue the energies of the body, to withdraw from its projects, and to dedicate its attention and forces to knowing and loving God.[2] In the form Augustine might have known the aetiological myth of this tradition, through the preaching of Ambrose and his *On Paradise,* the mind was originally free from the passions and appetites associated with the body. The passions did not assault and capture the mind; rather by successive sins of pride and negligence, the paradisal mind gave itself over to the forces of the body.[3]

Augustine drew heavily on this tradition. The Platonist books brought him to the understanding of the immateriality of the mind and of its power over the flesh. Ambrose's Platonic exegesis provided the religious form of his conversion and integrated his new wisdom with his childhood faith. Augustine's dialogues in his retirement between conversion and baptism exude the enthusiasm and optimism of his new world view.[4] He took over much of the tradition of Christian Platonism. He used a hierarchical view of reality which places the human soul in a middle position between God above and the body below: to follow the one and rule the other. He urged his readers to turn away from the desires of the flesh and to dedicate their energies to the pursuit of unchanging truth. He claimed that the mind can attain happiness apart from the satisfaction of bodily appetite.[5]

These early dialogues indicate Augustine's appropriation of an ontological foundation for the distinction of body and soul. The mind's capacity for unchanging or eternal truth indicates its own stability in being; it is immortal and incorruptible. The mind is, however, changeable in its dispositions. By focusing on the unchanging objects, however, it can participate in their stability.[6] Material bodies, by contrast, are both changeable in disposition and corruptible in being. Matter cannot contain eternal truths and cannot share their stability.[7] The human body stands as the single exception to this rule because of its special relationship to the intellectual soul, as shall be seen later.

Augustine located human happiness in the enjoyment of immaterial goods, in the contemplation of eternal truth. Unlike material satisfactions, these goods are stable of themselves and will be lost only if a person loses the desire for them. They are acquired and retained by one's own efforts, independently of the flux of time and the concurrence of bodily agents. Objects of sensation, by contrast, are unstable in themselves and their availability cannot be secured by one's own efforts. Love of such objects will be frustrated regularly. The key to the happy life, therefore, is to love what one can secure for oneself and to contemn what is unstable and beyond one's control.[8]

Augustine could have been expected to follow along the way of Platonism. His own tendency to dualism and experience of Manicheism might have fueled a horror of the flesh, especially of sexuality. As heir to the African tradition of moral rigorism and ascetic extremism which is so evident in Tertullian, Augustine might indeed have developed the rigorous dualism with which he is so often credited. Instead, he took a different path. He rejected dualism. He asserted that all the energy in an individual human person derives from the mind's grasp of eternal truth and that the one intellectual soul carries out all operations and activities of the person. He did not use a two-source theory to explain the division of opposing desires which each person feels. He did not call upon the mind to govern and direct energies which are not originally its own. Instead, Augustine asserted that animation, sensation, and motion are all activities of the soul in the body; that sense judgments, memory, and desire are operations of the mind.[9] He insisted that conflict or dissonance in human activity must be traced to opposing loves and desires within the one soul or mind.[10]

I wish that I could demonstrate the causes of this Augustinian variation on the traditional dualism of body and soul. I can only correlate it with certain of his concerns and interests. The most obvious of these was his concern to avoid and to refute Manicheism. A more important one, I believe, was his understanding of the role of number.

In discussions with his pupils at Cassiciacum while awaiting baptism, Augustine was looking for ways to lead them beyond the sensory realm to a recognition of immaterial reality and thence to the contemplation of God. In *On Order* he hit upon number as a bridge between the sensible and the intelligible. Numbers can be noticed in sensible things, such as poetic meter, which draw their beauty from the ratios between their parts. Analysis shows that although the sounds are transient and temporary, the numbers which make them pleasing are unchanging and eternal. Through the reflection on these qualities of number, Augustine hoped to purify the mind of its peculiar preoccupation with sensible things and its custom of thinking only in terms of extended, material reality. The purified soul might thus be led from sensible things to the contemplation of God.[11]

Augustine seemed to have projected a series of dialogues dealing with the liberal arts. The only one completed and surviving is the treatise *On Music*. The first five books deal with rhythm and meter in detail, considering the combinations of long and short syllables which constitute the various metric feet and the combinations of feet which define the meters. After working through the five books, one begins to appreciate the intervention of divine providence which made this man a presbyter, then a bishop, and forced him to abandon the whole project. Still, something very important is developed in those five books which comes to fruition in the sixth when Augustine brought forward a theory of animation, motion, and sensation.

Taking long and short syllables as his building blocks, Augustine noticed that some of the feet which are theoretically possible are in fact not pleasing to the ear. In sounding other feet and meters, the speaker unconsciously divides a long syllable or adds a rest in the line. In each case, the analysis of the numerical ratio involved confirms the accuracy of the sense judgment. Augustine came to the conclusion that the numbers which exist incorporeally and rule the human mind are also operative in the activity of the senses and in the relationship of sense objects. Because of the presence of these numbers, the senses make aesthetic judgments about the way sounds should be arranged in time and objects in space. These numbers guide sensible operations in producing harmonious sound and movement.[12]

In the sixth book of *On Music,* and in other contemporary works, Augustine built this insight into the role of incorporeal numbers in sense activity into a theory of the unity of all operations in the human subject. Because of the constraints of time and interest, as well as certain gaps in either Augustine's exposition or my comprehension of it, this will be given in summary form.[13]

The human mind has three types of activities. The highest of these is the knowledge of incorporeal truth. This operation takes place apart from the body. In the divine light which is above the mind, the person grasps perfect unity, equality, symmetry, proportion, and other such intelligibles; it understands the relations of points, lines, and planes. These objects and the divine light are always present to the mind and it never loses all contact with these intelligible principles. The soul is strongest when its attention focuses on these truths and guides its action by that clear knowledge.[14] At the opposite extreme are the soul's operations in the body: animation, sensation, and motion. In animation, the soul impresses the numbers of health upon the body. Through nourishment, elimination, and other processes, the mind establishes the proper proportion of the elements in each of the organs. The mind gives unity to the body and coordinates the interaction of its members. If the mind maintains a clear perception of unchanging principles, it has the strength to keep the body healthy and free of corruption. A body ruled by such a soul will be in harmony with God's ruling of the material world according to the same unchanging numbers.

In its original condition, the human mind preserved its body immortal and incorruptible.[15]

The soul's animating function establishes certain organs which are especially fluid. The soul maintains these in an equilibrium which it experiences as quiet. When the sense organ is disturbed by contact with another body, the soul's operation in the excited medium changes to restore the balance. The soul is aware of this change in its operation and thus senses the external object. Augustine explained that sensation is a reactive function of the soul; he insists that a material body cannot impress an image on the spiritual soul.[16]

The soul causes motion in the body by an impulse in the sinews which connect the members. The direction of the action comes from the numbers in the mind. The impulse of a determined mind can supplement the weight of the limbs to make its action effective.[17] Augustine's analysis also identified a sense judgment through which the soul coordinates the various functions in the body and a memory in which the mind retains images of sensible objects and operations, recalls these images in the absence of the object, and even constructs new images by combining those it stores. The intelligible universals are always present to the attentive mind but sensible particulars must be retained in memory.[18]

Through these operations in the body, the mind also carries out other activities in the material world. The mind can use bodily actions as signs or symbols to communicate with other minds through the material medium. Only God communicates knowledge directly to the mind. One human mind uses languages to direct another's attention to some universal truth known in the mind or some sensible particular either perceived in the senses or recalled in memory.[19]

Augustine's anthropology focused on the unity of mind and body and the active power of the intellectual soul. A single soul carries out the variety of human operations. Energy and guidance come from the eternal truth which the divine light provides to the mind. This mental energy organizes, maintains, and works through the body and its organs. In its original condition, the mind easily provided direction to all the operations of the soul. Because of the unity of the soul and the guidance of its animating activity by the eternal principle in the mind, the human body enjoyed the singular privilege of immortality and incorruptibility. No other body is guided by such a soul and enjoys such coherence and unity as the paradisal soul achieved in its body. Similarly, the mind exercised bodily motion and sensation with the greatest facility and accuracy. All its judgments and impulses were according to the eternal numbers. The mind expressed itself perfectly in its material medium: the whole body was then what only the face and eyes remain. Thus, the body served well as a medium of communication between rational souls.[20]

What Augustine described as a unity between soul and body was, by his explanation, a perfect unity within the soul itself. Each of the soul's operations was perfectly coordinated with the others because all are guided by the unchanging numbers. The soul carried on multiple activities at once while focusing on one or another of them. In its paradisal condition, attention was directed to the eternal principles of the mind; animation, sensation, and motion were carried out without attention or distraction. The mind's attention to the principles by which God orders the whole of creation also guaranteed the individual's harmonious interaction with the world.[21]

This perfect unity within the soul was damaged by the original sin. As might be expected, Augustine explained that the sin was occasioned by a temptation which was introduced by the devil. Somewhat contrary to his predecessors and his interpreters, Augustine described that sin as one of pride rather than sensuality. The devil had himself already turned from love of God to love of self. By this he had fallen into want and had become envious of humanity's happy condition. He caused a movement in the human body which was experienced as pleasure. Instead of simply adjusting to the change and restoring the state of balance and quiet in the bodily organs, the mind took this occasion to turn from its subjection to God. Instead of following the direction of the eternal laws, the mind claimed autonomy from God's rule and loved its dominion and power over the body as though it were its own. Turning from the light of truth within the mind, people focused attention on their own power in the body. Humanity sinned by desiring to rule the material world as its god, without the governance of a higher being.[22]

By the sin of self-love and love of dominion, the mind's orientation was shifted from God above to the body below. The person did not, of course, lose all knowledge of the eternal truths; that would have resulted in disintegration into chaos. The guiding principles are retained in a subliminal or unconscious state. As a consequence, the mind is weaker and a certain disunity and disharmony result in bodily operations.[23]

The most obvious consequence of the sin in the mind was mortality in the body. The weakened soul could not maintain perfect and stable harmony and the human body began to corrupt like other material realities. The body is no longer maintained in full harmony with the principles by which God governs the material universe. The action of other bodies in the environment either fosters or impedes the animating activity of the soul; the one is experienced as pleasure, the other as pain. In a fragile and mortal body, the soul is drawn to guide its operations according to these experiences of interaction with the material environment. Instead of seeking the peace of health, the person cultivates the ease of pleasure and avoids the labor of pain. The mind should neglect these outside forces and resort to its own source of strength, the unchanging truth, to restore harmony within the body and with the world.[24]

The mind has turned from its firm and clear grasp of unchanging truth which had guided all its activities and operations in the body. Ease and facility in bodily action are then achieved only by establishing a substitute in the sensible memory. Customs are sets of images which by repetition are firmly set in the memory. Once these patterns are fixed in memory, the activities they represent are easily carried out. The weakened mind must use these customs to perform complex bodily operations, such as surgery, with speed and accuracy. In the same way, customs facilitate evaluation and action in response to knowledge acquired in the senses. When the mind builds customs of evaluation and action which correspond to the unchanging principles of truth, these provide a certain stability in goodness and virtue. Unfortunately, the repetition of disordered actions and decisions also evolves into customs which lock the mind into its disorientation and distraction. Customs, like other images stored in the memory, will gradually fade and lose their power only if the person ignores them and refuses to repeat the actions through which they are built.[25]

These forms of custom establish a person in certain relationships to the environment. When the mind focuses on the eternal truths which are always present, the person has no need of such customs to act with facility in the body. When it is oriented toward the body, the mind must store sense images in the memory which will guide and stabilize its activity. In his early works, Augustine relied on the notion of custom to understand both virtues and vices. The fleshly will of the Manichees, the bodily appetites and emotions of the Christian Platonists, the flesh of St. Paul, all are understood as customs the mind builds in its sense memory.[26]

Another, more insidious, form of custom also results from the mind's orientation to the domination of the material world. The mind's attention is focused on its operations in and through the body; the knowledge of the eternal, incorporeal principles is unconscious; the mind accommodates itself to operation in the senses. The mind loses awareness of its own spiritual nature and begins to think of all reality, including itself, as extended and material. The person becomes incapable of thinking of an immaterial God and of understanding God's relationship to the world.[27] The problem of evil becomes insoluble without recourse to Manichean dualism. People become fully identified with their bodies and judge that they are subject to its fate of death and dissolution. They fear death as the end; they bend all efforts to secure the unstable goods which maintain bodily life or at least give joy to the brief time of existence. Human society is then organized to secure these bodily goods, and human society is destroyed by greed for them.[28]

According to Augustine's unitary anthropology, the mind's turning from God to self resulted in a weakening of its power to coordinate all its operations and to maintain the body in perfect unity. The resulting mortality of the body and the mind's dependence on custom in its sensible operations place the person in danger of being bound to the material world. This orientation would further distract attention from the incorporeal principles of action and disperse the soul's energies.

Even in its weakened condition which is characterized by the mortality of the body and accommodation of the spirit to the body through carnal customs, the mind is not without resources for regaining its original grasp of eternal truth and restoring unity and order to all its operations. The mind has not lost all awareness of eternal truth but has focused attention on its works in the body.[29] To redirect its energies so that its attention and operation are in harmony with the soul's nature, the mind must be purified from the customs which bind it to the senses. The person must withdraw from the love of bodily goods. These may, of course, be used; they must not be loved. The customs which orient the mind to sensible satisfactions and carnal delights must be allowed to weaken and fade by refusing to respond to the sense images which engage them. A program of abstinence gradually reduces their power in the person. Good customs of healthy living according to the law of God, the eternal truth, must be established in the sense memory. These good habits will stabilize the person in health and good living. The mind's energy will then be freed for the cultivation of eternal truth.[30]

The mind must also be freed from its other form of custom: thinking in sensible forms. Simply to restrain the bodily desires and not cultivate the mind will not restore a person to the true condition of humanity. The study of the liberal arts and the analysis of the function of numbers in particular will lead the mind to the recognition of incorporeal truth as the basis for order in the material world, the source of all goodness and beauty. Through this knowledge of unchanging truth which it achieves apart from the flesh, the mind will recognize its own incorporeality and immortality. Tasting the joy proper to its spiritual nature and conscious once again of the eternal truths which should guide all its operations, the mind will undertake its own purification from bodily desires with renewed vigor and guide its operations in the body by the principles of unity and justice.[31]

The purified mind will seek the contemplation of God who presides above the soul as its source of truth and joy. The person's corporeal operations will be directed to the health of the body and to aiding others in the search for wisdom. The person will live in tranquility and peace, will use the goods of the body but not love them. In exercising public authority, the person will seek to serve others rather than to dominate them. The person will look forward to death as a means of restoration and a return to original perfection of humanity.[32]

In these twelve early treatises, Augustine carefully constructed an alternative to the various forms of dualism of body and spirit which he had inherited. He asserted that the mind is the sole source of energy and operation within the person; he rejected an independent bodily energy which could oppose the mind and seduce it away from its proper joy. He explained that the divison and conflict which human beings experience, the perceived polarity of body and mind, is neither natural nor original. A sin of pride caused weakness in the mind and resulted in the mortality of the body. The carnal desires which bind the mind to the senses and oppose its return to the spiritual pursuit of eternal truths are customs which it has nourished against itself in a body made mortal by its own pride. Augustine insisted that the experienced dualism is an effect, not a cause, of the mind's sin of pride in refusing subjection to God and claiming autonomous rule over the material world.

Augustine's explanation of the origin of opposition between the body and mind within humanity applies fully to the first human beings who were, he supposed, created and established in a condition of unity and harmony. In dealing with Adam and Eve, he explained that although their souls may have preexisted the formation of their bodies, their sin and fall occurred in their bodily state. The human soul did not enter the body because of a prior fall, like that of Satan; nor did human beings sin because of their bodily condition. God placed the human soul in the body to animate it as a part of his ordering of the whole universe in goodness, not to punish for prior sins or to try humans so that he could then reward them for achievement under adverse conditions. Augustine considered such alternate explanations compatible with divine justice and goodness but he refused to endorse any of them.[33] He insisted that the mortality and difficulty which characterize the fallen human condition are a result, not a cause, of the soul's sin.

Augustine's explanation of the human condition can be fully applied only to Adam and Eve. He experienced great difficulty in adjusting it to their offspring. He was heir to a religious tradition which asserted that mortality is a punishment for the sin of Adam and that this mortality is inherited through generation from him. He had to admit that the children of Adam do not individually repeat his sin of pride after having been born in a state of wisdom and unity.[34] Yet he asserted that mortality results from the weakness of the soul and that this weakness is the consequence of the soul's sin. Because the condition of fallen humanity is a voluntary defect of the soul, it could not be transmitted through the body. In the works which followed his ordination, Augustine struggled with this problem which threatened to undo his rejection of dualism.[35]

The dilemma had two components. Augustine wanted to assert that the individual human soul is responsible for the experienced opposition and division in its operations. He also wanted to assert that the bodily mortality and the carnal desires which are the experienced focus of opposition to the soul's desire for God are the result of a weakness and lack of unity in the soul itself.

One of Augustine's attempted solutions was to minimize the role of inherited mortality and emphasize the role of freely established customs as the source of opposition to the mind. Infants have the freedom of Adam before they sin and lose it only by building evil customs through repeated choices. Mortality itself causes only a slight pleasure or pain which is easily disregarded. The real power of carnal attraction and revulsion comes from giving in to the suggestions of the flesh.[36]

Another solution involved the individual creation of the souls of the children of Adam in that weakened condition to which he fell by the sin of pride. The mortality of the flesh and the susceptibility of the spirit to carnal custom would be consequences of the weakness of the spirit. This weakness of spirit would be a penal condition imposed because of the sin of Adam. The individual would not be responsible for weakness and mortality. The individual would, however, bear responsibility for a refusal or failure to respond to divine assistance and to progress beyond that original condition. In particular, the offspring of Adam would be personally responsible for the carnal customs established by their own choices. In such a system, the children of Adam might triumph over obstacles and win a glorious crown.[37]

Augustine suggests only once the explanation which best fits the requirements of his problem. God might have created all human souls in the soul of Adam. His children would have lived and enjoyed the paradisal condition in him. In him they would have sinned by pride and fallen into a weakened state. They would then have been drawn from him by carnal generation and mortal succession rather than by the spiritual process God had originally established.[38] The children of Adam would then be responsible for the fallen state of their minds, the resultant mortality of their bodies, and the carnal customs they build in opposition to the natural orientation of their minds toward God. Adam's children would be collectively responsible in him for the sin of pride in which all turned from God to the love of self and the domination of the material world. They would be individually responsible for the sins of pride they commit in their restless love of action and in their attempts to extend their dominion over not only the material world but the rational souls of their fellows. They would be responsible for the sins of curiosity they commit when they inquire into sensible reality and seek vain knowledge. They would be responsible for consenting to and cultivating the movements of pleasure in the body which they have made mortal. They would be responsible for the customs which bind their hearts to mortal satisfactions and blind their minds to incorporeal truth.[39]

Augustine failed to adopt any of these explanations of the origin of the weakness in the souls of the children of Adam. He simply proposed these along with others which contradict his explanation of the fall of humanity by a sin of pride in ruling the material world. In fact, he began to ignore the insoluble problem of the origin of the individual soul and simply to assert that each of Adam's children is born heir to that condition into which his original sin of pride brought him.

The mortality of the body makes its needs and desires more insistent and demanding of the mind's attention. The foundational knowledge of God and the unchanging principles of action function only unconsciously in animation of the body and coordination of the senses. The mind ignores them as a guide to deliberate choice.[40] From this initial condition of need and ignorance, the children of Adam inevitably decline into an orientation toward the body which establishes carnal customs within the mind.[41] Although he traced sensuality to a prior weakness within human nature, Augustine seems to have considered pride and the desire for domination a general sin which requires only the appropriate occasion to spring from the human will.[42] The inherited mortality and ignorance result in universal personal sin, in the accommodation of the mind to sensual desires, and in its bondage to carnal satisfactions.[43]

Augustine interpreted the Pauline conflict between spirit and flesh as a struggle within the will between the old orientation which has been established by building customs on the foundation of mortality and the new orientation which responds to the revelation of the true principles of living through the divine law. This division is not, he explained, between mind and body. The will which commands the body without difficulty finds itself divided and unable to direct its own energies in one direction or the other. The established customs will eventually win out, unless fear holds the person back or the gift of God's love strengthens his or her desire for good. Charity makes the will's desire for God prevail and hold back the choices and actions which the same will desires according to its carnal customs. Gradually, the customs die, although the good will continues to suffer the desires which are grounded in mortality.[44]

Those whom God helps are gradually restored to a unity in which God is loved above all else and every other love is directed toward him. Augustine's analysis of the power of dreams to move him to action in sleep provides an example of the depth of integration which he sought but had not yet attained. The soul should cease to rebel against itself and by continence be unified in submission to God.[45]

In the Pauline *Commentaries* and the *Confessions*, Augustine made a significant addition to his understanding of the unity of the human person.[46] His coordination of all the soul's operations is not only directed by the divine truth; it is inspired by divine love. The Spirit's gift of charity is called upon to accomplish the reintegration of the soul which has been weakened by pride and scattered by sensuality. Augustine still hoped that his mind would be turned from pursuits in the material world to the contemplation of eternal truth. He no longer relied on asceticism and the liberal arts to lead him there.[47]

We have examined Augustine's appropriation of the dualistic anthropologies to which he was heir and his development of a new unitary view of human nature. He understood the intellectual soul as the principle of all human activity. Through its grasp of incorporeal principles, the mind acts in and through the material body. When the mind focuses its attention on the Divine Truth, it unifies the soul and harmonizes all its operations. When the mind turns to itself and to the domination of the material world, the soul loses its integrity;

its desires are dissonant, and it fails to maintain the body incorruptible. Augustine's explanation of the sin of the first humans charts their fall from unity into diversity. He asserted that their offspring are heirs to ignorance, conflict, and mortality. Yet he failed to develop a coherent explanation of the transmission of this weakened condition. In his commentaries on the Pauline Epistles, he asserted that in this weakened state, the children of Adam inevitably prefer lower goods and bind their minds to material satisfactions. The sin of Adam leads to personal sin.

In his later writings, especially the *Literal Commentary on Genesis, The City of God,* and the treatises against Julian of Eclanum, Augustine shifted his focus from mortality and evil customs to an inherited concupiscence. This desire of the mind and will for carnal satisfactions divides the soul so that the mind cannot control the bodily functions and cannot itself be fully integrated in love of God. This disorientation of the mind brings with it the guilt of the original sins of pride and sensuality. In these same works, Augustine insisted that bodily appetite and emotion are naturally good operations of the intellectual soul which should be inspired and guided by the love of God. He rejected an asceticism which attempts to sever the emotional bonds which link the person to the environment. Finally, he labored without success for an explanation of the origin of the human person which would account for its divided and sinful condition.[48]

Augustine did indeed move beyond the traditional dualism which was defined by the polarities of body and soul, matter and spirit. His attempt to locate the conflict and division within the soul or spirit failed to take hold and replace its predecessors. I suggest two reasons for this failure.

Augustine was unable to develop an explanation of the origin of the soul which would adequately account for the transmission of the weakness, disorientation, and guilt which were attributed to Adam's sin. His understanding of the condition of Adam became ever more clear and coherent; his explanation of the situation of his offspring became ever more confusing and unsatisfactory.

Another reason for the failure of Augustine's unitary anthropology may have been the dualism of sin and grace which gradually evolved from it. By insisting that all weakness within the human person originates in a division within the mind or spirit, Augustine introduced a moral dualism of inevitable sin and irresistible grace which restricts human freedom more than the physical dualism of mind and body ever had. By the sin of Adam, all humanity is dragged into guilt, mortality, sensuality, and absolute moral impotence. By the grace of Christ, the elect are called, forgiven, liberated, empowered, preserved, and finally glorified.

Augustine's anthropological innovation began as a reaction against the passivity and impotence of the Manichean Light trapped in Darkness. He rejected the limitations of Platonic political control over appetite and emotion. Yet he finished with a human who fell in the sin of the old Adam and can be raised only by the grace of the new Adam. Paul had certainly displaced Plotinus.

NOTES

1. *De lib. arb.* 3.20.56; *de Gen. ad litt.* 10.11.

2. See, for example, Gregory of Nyssa's *On the Making of Man.*

3. See, for example, Augustine's account of the anthropology he set forth in *de pulchro et apto* in *Conf.* 4.15.24-25. Ambrose seems to have followed Philo in his interpretation of the fall of humanity.

4. *Contra Academicos* (Corpus Cristianorum, series latina, 29), *de beata vita* (CCsl 29), *de ordine* (CCsl 29), *Soliloquorum* (Bibliotheque Augustineienne, 5), *de immortaliate animae* (BA 5).

5. *C.Acad.* 1.2.5; 1.3.9; 1.4.11; *de beata vita* 4.25,33; Solil. 1.1.3,5; 1.6.12; 2.18.32-19.33; *de immor. an.* 2.2; 10.17. This perspective is even more evident in the treatises which follow his baptism.

6. *De ord.* 2.19.50; *Solil.* 1.14.24; 1.15.29; 2.15.27-19.33; *de immor. an.* 2.2; 4.5-6; 5.9.

7. *Solil.* 1.1.4; 1.15.29; *de immor. an.* 2.2; *de quan. an.* 33.73; *de lib. arb.* 2.8.21-23; 2.11.30-32.

8. *C. Acad.* 4.11; *de beata vita* 2.11; *de ord.* 1.1.3; *Solil.* 1.1.5; 1.14.24; this is more fully developed in *de lib. arb.* 1.5.10; 1.13.27-29; 1.15.31-16.35.

9. *De quan. an.* 14.23; 22.38-39; 33.70-72; *de mus.* 6.4.7-5.15.

10. *De lib. arb.* 1.5.10; 1.15-31; 1.16.34; *de mus* 6.11.33.

11. *De ord.* 14.41-19.50.

12. *De lib. arb.* 2.16.41; *de mus.* 2.13.25; 4.16.34; 6.4.5; 6.8.20; 6.9.23; *de vera relig.* 30.54-56; 31.57-58; 52.101.

13. These works were composed between his baptism in Milan and his ordination in Hippo: *de moribus ecclesiae catholicae et de moribus Manichaeorum,* (BA 1), *de quantitate animae* (BA 5), *de libero arbitrio* (CCsl 29), *de Genesi contra Manichaeos* (Patrologia Latina 34), *de musica* (BA 7), *de vera religione* (CCsl 32), *de diversis quaestionibus* (CCsl 44A).

14. *De mus.* 6.4.7; 6.5.13; 6.12.34-13.38. The soul never loses all contact with these principles: *de ord.* 2.2.6; *Solil.* 2.18. 32-19.33; *de quan. an.* 33.70, 71.

15. *De mus.* 6.5.9.13; 6.11.33. See also: *de Gen. c. Man.* 2.7.9; *de vera relig.* 12.25; 15.29.

16. *De mus.* 6.5.8-11; *de quan. an.* 23.43.

17. De mus. 6.8.20; *de quan.an.* 22.38-39.

18. *De mus.* 6.8.21; 6.9.23; 6.10.25-28; 6.12.34-35; *de quan. an.* 33.71; *de mag.* 12. 39,40.

19. *De Gen. c. Man.* 2.4.5; *de mus.* 6.13.41; *de mag.* 11.36, 38; 12.39,40; 14.46.

20. *De Gen. c. Man.* 1.20,31; 2.4.5.7.9; 2.12.16; 2.21.31; *de mus,* 6.5.13; *de vera relig.* 12.25

21. *De quan. an.* 35.79; *de mus.* 6.5.14,15.

22. *De mor.* 1.12.20; *de mus.* 6.4.7; 6.13.39-41; 6.16.53; *de vera relig.* 11.21; 13.26; 20.38; 37.68; 45.84; *de Gen. c. Man.* 2.14.20-15.23; 2.17.25. The Manichees interpreted the fall as a sexual sin: *de mor.* 2.19.73.

23. *Solil.* 2.18.32-19.33; *de ord.* 2.2.6; *de quan. an.* 33.70, 71; *de mus.* 6.5.13. The truths can be noticed in the bodily operations of the soul; *de lib. arb.* 2.8.21-23; 2.11.30-13.37; *Conf.* 10.34.53.

24. *De mus.* 6.5.9,13,14; *de mor.* 1.7.12; *de Gen. c. Man.* 2.19.29; *de vera relig.* 12.23.

25. *De mus.* 1.4.9; 1.5.10; 6.5.14; 6.11.33; *de Gen c. Man.* 2.19.29; 2.21.31; *de quan. an.* 28.54; *de lib. arb.* 1.10.19.

26. *De mus.* 6.4.7.

27. *De mor.* 1.21.38; *de quan. an.* 3.4; 4.6; 14.24; *de vera relig.* 3.3; 20.40; *Conf.* 7.1.1.

28. *De quan. an* 33.73; *de lib. arb.* 1.5.10; 1.15. 31-33.

29. *Solil.* 2.18.32-19.33; *de ord.* 2.2.6; *de mus.* 6.5.13; *de quan. an.* 33.70,71; 35.79.

30. *De beata vita* 4.25.33; de lib. arb. 1.15.33; *de quan. an.* 33.71,73; *de Gen. c. Man.* 1.25.43; 1.35.77; 2.19.29; 2.21.31; *de mus.* 6.5.14; 6.8.21; 6.11.33; 6.14.45; *de vera relig.* 12.24.

31. *De ord.* 2.14.41-16.44; *de lib. arb.* 2.8.21-13.37; 2.16.41; *de quan. an.* 15.25; 28.54; 33.73,74; *de mus.* 6.12.34-36; *de vera relig.* 31.57-58.

32. *De ord.* 2.7.25; *de lib. arb.* 1.15.33; *de Gen. c. Man* 1.25.43; *de mus. 6.5.13.15;* 6.14.45.

33. *De quan. an.* 36.81; *de Gen. c. Man.* 2.8.10. See also: *de lib. arb.* 3.20.57,58.

34. *De lib. arb.* 1.11.23-12.24; In *de mus.* 6.13.39-41, he speaks as though each of Adam's children falls in the way he did.

35. *De duabus animabus, de libero arbitrio* (2.16.44ff), *Contra Fortunatum, de fide et symbolo, de sermone domini in monte.*

36. *C. Fort.* 22; *de serm. dom.* 1.12.34-36.

37. *De lib. arb.* 3.20.56; 3.22.64.

38. *De lib. arb.* 3.20.56. He occasionally uses language which has all fall in Adam: *de div. quaest.* 66.3; 68.3; 70.

39. *De mus.* 6.13.39-41.

40. *Solil.* 2.18.32-19.33; *de ord.* 2.2.6; *de mus.* 6.5.13; *de quan. an.* 33.70.71; *Conf.* 10. 34.53.

41. *Ad Simp.* 1.2.16,19,20: *de div. quaest.* 68.3,4.

42. *De mus.* 6.13.40-41; *de div. quaest.* 66.5; *Conf.* 2.4.9-8.16.

43. *De div. quaest.* 68.3,4; *Ad Simp.* 1.2.16,19, 20.

44. De div. quaest. 66.3-6; *Propp, exep. ad Rom.* 12.8; 38.3,7; 42.2; *Exp. ep. ad Gal.* 46.6-7; 47.1; 48.4-5; 54.2; *Ad Simp.* 1.1.10, 13; *Conf.* 8.5.10-12; 8.8.19-10.24.

45. *Conf.* 10.29.40-30.42.

46. *De diversis quaestionibus* (66-70), *Expositio propositionum ex epistula ad Romanos* (Corpus Scriptorum Ecclesiasticorum Latinorum 84), *Expositio epistulae ad Galatas* (CSEL 84), *Ad Simplicianum* (CCsl 44), *Confessiones* (BA 13, 14).

47. *De Div. Quaest.* 66.3.

48. *De Gen ad litt.* 10.11-13. In general see: *de Gen. ad litt.* 6; 7; 10; and *de civ. dei* 12-14.

THE THEOLOGICAL FATE OF BERENGAR'S OATH OF 1059: INTERPRETING A BLUNDER BECOME TRADITION

Gary Macy

One of the more interesting problems which a theologian can confront when attempting to preserve and interpret his or her own tradition remains that engendered by received, approved, and preserved teachings which are theologically incorrect. I am not referring here to ecclesial statements that now seem inadequate, but which when placed within their social, historical, and cultural setting provide a consistent presentation of the Christian message. What I intend to address in this paper is a different problem, that of true blunders. By this, I mean statements of the official church that embarrassed theologians when they were written and have haunted their successors down through the centuries. It seems somewhat naive historically to presume that such statements do not exist. A quick review of Denzinger should surely disabuse even a cursory reader of any such notions. It seems equally naive theologically to presume that the Holy Spirit could not allow such statements to be made. If the serious foundational problems entailed in such an assumption were not enough, there would remain the strange picture of an irresponsible church that believes it can say anything on the grounds that the Holy Spirit will miraculously intervene to close ecclesial mouths before officious feet are placed therein. One might then argue that only those statements which are theologically ept make up the tradition, but this would require a major rewriting of history for our own dogmatic purposes. Besides, one is then faced with the thorny question of who will determine which statements will be the tradition.

The simplest and most straightforward means of handling the problem might be to simply admit that the Church, in certain instances, taught the wrong thing, and be done with it. Problems arise here too, however. Surely no one would object if the synodal proceedings of the fourth century council of Elvira were not required for belief, but what about the proceedings of Lateran IV, or the teachings of Paul, or even Jesus? Surely cases have been made that these sources too lack theological clarity.[1] Again the problem seems to be one of choosing, rather than uncovering our tradition.

Fortunately, this is not a new problem. Theologians in the past have also faced such dilemmas, and found methods to minimize the damage done by episcopal or papal gaucherie. This paper will present the history of one such misstep. In many ways, the solemn oath taken by Berengar of Tours at the

Council of Rome in 1059 is a classic case of the kind of problem outlined thus far. Adopted in solemn assembly at a valid synod called by a legitimate pope, the oath of Berengar was subsequently included in several canon law collections of the early twelfth century, thus finding its way into Gratian's *Decretum* in the mid-twelfth century.[2] Gratian's work, although unofficial made up a great part of canon law until a new code was issued in 1917. As might be expected, the ever zealous Denzinger included Berengar's oath in his collection of church teachings.[3] Nor would the oath simply slip into the natural, dusty death of obscurity. Starting with the Cathars in the twelfth century, the oath has been used right up to the present time to demonstrate that the Roman Church ascribes to some strange sort of cannibalism in the celebration of the Eucharist.[4] Theologians again and again had to address themselves to the difficult task of making some sense of the oath in the face of cogent oppostion.

The source of this long discussion is short, and very blunt:

> I agree with the holy Roman Church and the Apostolic See, and I profess with mouth and heart to hold as the faith concerning the sacrament of the Lord's supper what the lord and venerable Pope Nicholas and this holy synod by the autthority of the gospels and the apostles have given to be held and have ratified to me: Namely, that the bread and wine which are placed on the altar after the consecration are not only signs *(non solum sacramentum)*, but also the true body and blood of our Lord Jesus Christ, and that sensually, not only in sign, but in truth *(non solum sacramento, sed in veritate)* they are handled and broken by the hands of the priest and crushed by the teeth of the faithful, swearing by the holy and one-in-substance Trinity and by the most holy gospel of Christ.[5]

From where did this strange statement come, and why was it written? For some ten years before the synod met, Berengar, a teacher at the cathedral school at Tours, had been waging a literary war with his fellow theologians, especially those in Normandy, over the proper understanding of the presence of the Lord in the Eucharist. Berengar had, albeit somewhat clumsily, revived an Augustinian understanding of this presence which insisted on its spiritual nature. The theologians of Normandy, were, like most theologians of this time, heavily influenced by Paschasius Radbertus' teaching on the presence of the Lord in the Eucharist. This ninth century monk, basing himself on passages from Hilary of Poitiers, insisted that only a natural union between the body of the risen Lord and the body of the Christian believer could effect salvation. Further, this natural union took place through the reception of the eucharistic species. The followers of Paschasius felt that Berengar's insistence on a spiritual rather than a physical or natural presence of the Lord in the sacrament undermined the very possibility of our salvation.[6]

After much discussion, and several condemnations, Berengar was called to Rome by Pope Nicholas II to defend his position. Unfortunately for Berengar, the papal legate, Humbert, cardinal bishop of Silva-Candida, was chosen to draw up an oath for Berengar to sign. Humbert was in no mood for compromise or even understanding. Five years before, he had laid a writ of excommunication on the high altar of Hagia Sophia in Constantinople, thus initiating what would become a permanent schism between the Christians of the East and those of the West. One of the areas in which Humbert judged the Greeks to be heretical was in their teaching on the Eucharist. Humbert felt that the Greeks, in some obscure way, denied a true presence of the Lord in the sacrament by their use of leavened bread in the Mass. Humbert, not known for his tact in any case, may well have felt that both the Greeks and Berengar could be countered once and for all by a clear, bold and strongly worded insistence on the real, physical presence of the risen Lord in the Eucharist.[7] In many ways, he succeeded. The oath of Berengar is clear, blunt, and forceful. It is also, theologically, a disaster.

By juxtaposing the real presence of the Lord in the Eucharist (*in veritate*) with the sacramental presence of the Lord (*in sacramento*) Humbert undermined any understanding of sacramental presence itself as a form of reality. Further, by insisting on a grossly sensual presence of the Lord in the sacrament, Humbert raised serious problems involving the impassibility and locality of the risen Lord. Theologians were not slow to realize the issues, especially since Berengar, having returned home and repudiated his oath, threw the logical conclusions of Humbert's statement in his opponent's faces. Are we to believe, Berengar smirked, that "little chunks" of Christ's body would be spread about on all the altars in Europe to be savaged by the faithful?[8] Does this mean a little more Jesus is made each day as thousands of Masses are being said?[9] Most blasphemous of all, would not such a presence of the body of Christ on earth entail the faithful in a kind of cannibalism, to say nothing of the indignity of digestion, or desecration by rot, fire, or animals?[10] How is such a teaching compatible with Christian belief that the risen Lord is now incorruptible and seated at the right hand of the Father?[11]

Berengar was brought to heel once again at the Council of Rome held in 1079. Here he signed yet another, and this time more sophisticated, oath.[12] By 1080, Berengar had retired from the theological scene, but his taunts reappeared in the teachings of the Cathars, that amorphous group of dualists who would come to control most of southern France and northern Italy by the end of the twelfth century.[13] For over a hundred and fifty years, European theologians would not be allowed to forget, or ignore, Humbert's debacle. Their responses make fascinating reading.

The earliest of the tracts directed against Berengar's teachings countered his claims merely by asserting the incorruptibility of the risen Christ, thus denying that any change could affect his body.[14] The first theologian to tackle Berengar's arguments in a more systematic way appears to have been Guitmund, a monk of Bec and student of Lanfranc, Berengar's most gifted foe. In his treatise, *De corporis et sanguinis Christi Veritate in eucharistia,* written between 1073 and 1075, Guitmund defended Humbert's wording in a fairly literal fashion.

First, Guitmund argued that the verb, *attero,* to crush, can mean just to touch, or to press, really hard. Since both Thomas and the holy women touched the risen Lord, albeit lightly, surely there is no indignity involved in Humbert's assertion that the body of Christ (in this reading) is touched very hard by the teeth of the faithful. Besides teeth are cleaner than hands. Just think, Guitmund mused, of all the filthy things you touch with your hands that you would not dare to put in your mouth. Even Guitmund must have sensed that this line of thought was becoming (literally and figuratively) a bit messy, so he then asserted that even if the body of Christ were divided by teeth or hands, no indignity would result. Appealing to the omnipotence of God, Guitmund argued that the body of the risen Lord remained impassible, inviolate, and entire in each portion of the species. Here Guitmund found himself on firmer ground, and he used the same principle to argue that even though Christ is present on a thousand different altars, there is only one Lord simultaneously present in many places.[15]

Responding to Berengar's argument that a substantial presence would involve sacrilege, Guitmund insisted that the true body and blood remain even when the bread and wine appear to rot or putrify. Just as our Lord took on the form of a gardener to teach Mary Magdalene and that of a pilgrim to teach the disciples at Emmaus, so He takes the form of putrified bread and wine to admonish us for improper care of the reserved species.[16] If an animal is seen to eat the species, this too is for our edification, nor should we be shocked to think of Christ as descending into the bowels of an animal. After all, Guitmund reminded his readers, Christ had been in worst places, like the tomb.[17] When asked what happens when the host is burned, Guitmund allowed that the "sensible qualities" remain behind, but the true body ascends back to heaven. He denied, however, that any part of the species can be digested, and that if certain of the Fathers lived on communion alone for many years, this was only by means of a miracle.[18] Few theologians would follow Guitmund in defending this more literal understanding of the Berengarian oath. Alger, canon of St. Lamberts in Liege, offered a similar theology in his *De sacramentis corporis et sanguinis domini* written in the second decade of the twelfth century. Going somewhat beyond Guitmund's position, Alger argued that the appearances of bread and wine were sheer illusion, and digestion or putrification of the species cannot naturally occur, since there is no substance left to undergo such a change.[19]

An interesting twist to this particular attempt to explain how the body of Christ can be "broken" occurred in the teaching of Gilbert of La Porree, the controversial and influential scripture scholar. Writing in the 1140's, Gilbert argued that the host only appears to be broken, just as a stick placed in water appears to bend, although the mind recognizes that this is not the case.[20] The anonymous work, the *Summa de sacramentis "Totus homo,"* a work associated with Gilbert's students, made this argument at length.[21] The body of Christ is not, and cannot be, broken here for each section of the species contains the entire presence of Christ. On the other hand, the substance of the bread and wine are gone, so they cannot be the subject of any change. Therefore, a real fraction does not take place, but only appears to take place.[22]

A number of works connected with the contentious but brilliant theologian Abelard both argued that the breaking of the bread is an illusion, and also followed Alger in teaching that abuse of the species is an illusion for our edification.[23] These writings added a new note to this teaching, however. They argued that the form of the bread and wine continue to exist after the consecration, and they miraculously subsist in the air.[24]

Slowly, but clearly, these theologians were moving away from the literal meaning of the oath. They still attempted to make some sense out of that part of the statement that claimed the body of the Lord was not broken in sign alone, by asserting that nothing was broken at all since all was an illusion. The larger claim that the body of the Lord was really and sensually broken by the hands of the priest and crushed by the teeth of the faithful was denied by these authors, despite the half-hearted attempts by Guitmund to make some sense of out of this strange statement. Far more of the theologians of this time, however, directly or indirectly, simply rejected the intention of the oath.

A set of commentaries on 1 Corinthians, dating from the end of the eleventh century, stated that although the true body of Christ is present under the species of bread, it is the species alone that is crushed, divided in parts, consumed or eaten by mice, while the body of Christ remains in truth incorruptible and indivisible.[25] This teaching was copied into a collection of *sententiae* used at the famous cathedral school of Laon; not too surprisingly, the teaching appeared in the writings of its graduates.[26] The clearest example of this influence is contained in the writing of Guibert, abbot of Nogent-sous-Coucy near Laon from 1104-1124. In a discussion of how sacrilege might affect the Lord present in the Eucharist, Guibert recorded the opinion of Guitmund. He concluded, "I do not know if these arguments (of Guitmund) would ever be satisfactory to myself or to many others. This, however, we know, that it is thought to be subject to these sort of so-called misfortunes from that part, which are the species . . ."[27] Guibert rejected not only the teaching contained in the oath, but even the milder interpretation given to it by Guitmund.

Hugh of St. Victor, the famous Parisian master, himself influenced by the teachings of Laon, preferred to gently remove any thoughts of sensual involvement by the Lord in the sacrament from the minds of his students. "Do not think, when you see the parts in the sacrament of the altar, that the body of Christ has, as it were, been divided or separated from itself or as if torn limb from limb. He Himself remains whole in himself; neither is He divided nor parted. Therefore, He shows you the external appearance (speciem), by which your sense is instructed, and He preserves the internal incorruption of His body, in which his unity is not divided."[28] Hugh's teaching completely contradicted the Berengarian oath, and his teaching on this matter appeared in the writings of several other twelfth century theologians.[29]

It was Peter Lombard, the Parisian master whose Sententiae, written between 1153 and 1155, would become the standard textbook of the scholastic period, who first directly repudiated the oath of 1059. He first treated the whole issue in his commentary on 1 Corinthians, and came to no conclusion on the matter.[30] In the Sententiae, however, Peter took a firm stand. After discussing the opinions of Guitmund, Gilbert, and the School of Abelard, he tackled the oath itself, from which he quoted. His commentary reads: "From this it is given to be understood that the breaking, and parts which here seem to be made, are being done in sign (in sacramento), that is in the visible species. And for this reason those words of Berengar that the body of Christ is said to be handled by the hands of the priest, truly broken and crushed by teeth, not sensually in the mode of a sign (non modo in sacramento), but in truth, are to be distinguished; something truly (is done), but in sign alone (in sacramentum tantum)."[31] Peter Lombard made sense of the Berengarian oath by completely reversing its meaning. Since the body of Christ is certainly now risen and immune to all division, the words of the oath, for the Lombard, must mean the opposite of what they appear to mean. The Lombard had thus simply explained the oath away, and, what is more, this understanding was to become the standard interpretation of the oath by the beginning of the thirteenth century.

Not that the opinion of the Lombard went unchallenged. Walter of St. Victor, the archconservative Parisian master writing c. 1178, accused Peter of being another Berengar, and demanded a return to the literal meaning of the oath.[32] A certain unidentified abbot Abbaudus, also writing in the twelfth century, railed against those who denied that the Lord's body was broken in the Eucharist, claiming that "whoever does not truly accept the body of Christ to have been broken, breaks the entire faith in such sacraments, in so far as it exists."[33] Writing about the time of the Lombard, Zachary, the scholasticus of Besançon, claimed, "The body of Christ is incorruptible, but on the other hand, the body of Christ is crushed by teeth and gulped down. Read," Zachary insisted, "the faith of Berengar, which the Church declared under Pope Nicholas, and you will find it to be so."[34] Zachary went on to lament, "There are not a few, perhaps rather I should say many, but they would be difficult to recognize, who feel the same as the damned Berengar, however they might damn him with the

Church. They damn him in this because, casting away the literal meaning of the words of the Church, the scandal is removed from the simplicity of the language."[35] Zachary was quite correct in his perceptions. Most theologians in the twelfth century did not accept the literal meaning of the oath of 1059. They either put forward teachings which implicitly denied the oath, or like Peter Lombard, re-interpreted the oath in such a way as to practically reverse its meaning. Yet Walter, Abbaudus, and Zachary were voices in the wilderness. There was to be no return to the simple, clear theological ineptitude of Humbert of Silva-Candida.

Theologians adopted the language of the School of Laon, or of Hugh of St. Victor, or of the Lombard. When the words of the oath were mentioned, theologians fell back on the interpretation of the Lombard.[36] One of the most complete discussions of the oath occurs in an anonymous commentary on 1 Corinthians written sometime before 1180. "It is customary to ask," the author began, "concerning the fraction, in what thing it might be, that is, what here is broken and what the parts of the fraction might signify. Some say that only the sign *(solum sacramentum)* is broken here, for the reason that the body of Christ is impassible and would accept no fraction, no divisions of parts. But how then will that confession of Berengar be true which at Rome before Pope Nicholas with thirteen bishops present was prepared and ratified? It is confessed 'that the bread and wine which are laid on the altar are after consecration not only a sacrament but also the true body and blood of Christ, and they are sensually taken up and broken in the hands of the priest and crushed by the teeth of the faithful, not only sacramentally, but in truth.' Clearly the oath says that the body of Christ in truth is broken, in truth crushed by the teeth of the faithful. For the same reason, in the same manner, in truth, it is seen not only with the eyes of the heart, but also those of the body. The error of Berengar was that after the consecration of the bread, bread remained and the sign alone of the body of Christ not His true body remained here. His confession of faith expressed the truth, saying he had believed the body of Christ in truth to be present, not just a sign of the breaking of what first was present. The body of Christ is in truth what is seen, what is broken, and what is crushed by the teeth of the faithful. But how, you ask, is the impassible broken, how is the undivided divided? I answer; how was God able to die if He was immortal, how is He is to be understood if He is incomprehensible? You say according to one in one way, another in another way, yet it is one and same. Thus one and same body is impassible and still broken, according to one in one way, another in another way and yet both in truth. What it is according to itself and in itself, is impassible; in sign it is divided, in sign seen and crushed by the teeth of the faithful. All of this is done in truth, however, and nothing in mere illusion."[37]

The anonymous author had a good sense of the theological problem involved here. He realized that the Berengarian oath was intended to affirm the real presence, and so he interpreted it. Yet he also realized that the oath as it was written asserted the impossible, that the body of the risen Lord was subject to change and suffering. Like all good academics, he distinguished. In truth, the body of the Lord is present, and is impassible. Equally in truth, the signs (sacramenta) are here handled, broken and crushed. Thus, this is how the oath must be understood.

William of Auxerre, Albert the Great, Thomas Aquinas, and Bonaventure all followed the twelfth century theologians in affirming the impassibility of the body of Christ, and in teaching that any changes that occur, occur in the species alone. Albert and Thomas both interpreted the oath of 1059 in the same manner as the Lombard and the commentator on 1 Corinthians. [38] Within one hundred years after the oath had been written, Peter Lombard had effectively reversed the literal meaning of the oath through re-interpretation. Within another hundred years, this re-interpretation had become the standard and accepted theological understanding of the oath. In sum, within two hundred years, theologians had effectively defused the potentially dangerous and certainly unfortunate language of an accepted, and clearly valid, magisterial pronouncement.

Further, throughout most of those two hundred years, theologians had simultaneously affirmed the condemnation of Berengar and rejected the language of the 1059 oath. In this Zachary of Besançon was quite correct. This, then, is how medieval theologians handled at least one instance of inept magisterial teaching. They just "distinguished" it away. Without confrontation, without refutation, they slowly changed the understanding of the offensive document.

What conclusions, then, can be drawn from this example? First, and probably most obviously, the Berengarian oath of 1059, by its very existence, refutes the claim that the Holy Spirit could not allow the magisterium to promulgate theological blunders, nor allow such blunders to become part of the received teaching of the Church. The oath indeed was such a blunder, and it was so received. The point made here may seem obvious or even trivial, since most practicing theologians would not seriously entertain such an understanding of the magisterium. This notion still does play a role, however, in the thought and practice of lamentably large numbers of both laity and clergy. The point bears repeating.

Once this said, it becomes more difficult to draw any definite conclusions. Perhaps what this example best provides for the modern theologian is an option, a possibility, a different perspective on the problems involved in recovering the Christian tradition. The medieval authors cited here, with few exceptions, knew quite well the meaning of the Berengarian oath, and, when they found it to be theologically unacceptable, they changed that meaning. They appear to do so deliberately, and without qualm. Reason was accepted as playing an important role in accepting, molding, and, in a real sense, creating the tradition through continous re-interpretation. The appropriation, modification, and even nullification, on reasonable grounds, of magisterial statements is then clearly one way in which theologians have dealt with official statements of Church teaching.

The problems of the Middle Ages are not our problems and their methods are not our methods, and yet their problems and their methods are part of our tradition. They can provide us with models and options from outside our immediate cultural and intellectual setting. In the words of Maurice Wiles, " . . . whether we recognize it or not the work of the Fathers is an important constitutive part of the background of our own thinking. To ignore them is to cut themselves off from our heritage; it is to refuse to see the issues of faith today in their proper historical perspective. The problems of contemporary theology are new in form, but they are not wholly new in substance. The Fathers cannot solve them for us. That task remains ours. But we limit unnecessarily the resources with which we attempt it if we believe that it can be done without reference to them."[39] It seems, at least to me, that the medieval authors' assumption that the statements of the magisterium must be reasonable to be true, and that the received tradition is subject to critical reformulation in order to make that tradition compatible with reason, is not only a resource worth recovering, it is an inescapable part of our tradition.

Perhaps, briefly, another point could be made here. None of the authors to which this paper refers (except of course Berengar) were condemned for their theology of the Eucharist — neither Guitmund for his crassness, nor Hugh of St. Victor for his deeply spiritual understanding, nor Peter the Lombard for his contradiction of the oath. All were respected scholars; two became bishops. The Church in which they lived allowed the freedom of thought, the pluralism, if you like, that fostered the kind of appropriation and interpretation of church teaching embodied in the present example. As Henry Adams once so eloquently put it: "A Church which embraced, with equal sympathy, and within a hundred years, the Virgin, Saint Bernard, William of Champeaux and the School of Saint-Victor, Peter the Venerable, Saint Francis of Assisi, Saint Dominic, Saint Thomas Aquinas, and St. Bonaventure, was more liberal than any modern State can afford to be. Radical contradictions the State may perhaps tolerate, though hardly, but never embrace or profess. Such elasticity long ago vanished from human thought."[40] Theologians in particular ought to be made more aware that this kind of pluralism *is* our tradition. Pluralism is not a twentieth century idea which somehow challenges a monolithic tradition, but rather the history of the church, and especially the history of the medieval church, *is* a history of pluralism. To appeal to tradition is to appeal to the history of the Church, and this history often reveals a pluralism and a respect for reason which make our modern efforts appear timid. Tucked away on the back shelves of Wisdom's great storehouse, many such treasures await discovery.

NOTES

1. The decisions of the Fourth Lateran Council are not accepted as valid, by, for example, the Orthodox Churches. The exact importance of the teaching of Paul has been debated at least since the time of Marcion, and occasioned lively debate in the Tübigen School of the nineteenth century. The discussion of which of the teachings of Jesus are genuine, and even which of these genuine teachings are necessary for belief, goes back at least as far as the second century gnostic Christians, and becomes central, for example, in the theology of Rudolf Bultmann.

2. Gratian, *Decretum, de con. dist.* 2, c. 42. A. Friedberg, *Corpus Iuris Canonici,* vol 1, cols. 1328-1329 (Leipzig, 1879). Friedberg gives references to earlier collections which included the oath.

3. *Enchiridion symbolorum,* ed. Henry Denzinger, rev. ed. by Adolf Shönmetzer, 33rd. ed. (Herder: Freiburg, 1965), n. 690.

4. On the use of Berengar's arguments by the Cathars and others in the twelfth century, see chapter three of the forthcoming book, Gary Macy, *Theologies of the Eucharist in the Early Scholastic Period,* to be published by Oxford University Press.

5. The text is recorded by Lanfranc, *Liber de corpore et sanguine domini,* c. 2. *Patrologiae cursus completus,* Series latina, ed. Jacques Paul Migne (Paris, 1878-1890), (hereafter referred to as *PL*) vol. 150, col. 410D.

6. See Macy, *Theologies,* chaper three.

7. See Joseph Geiselmann, *Die Abendmahlslehre an der Wender der christlichen Spätantike zum Frühmittelalter.* (Munich, 1933), pp. 73-85, 248-52.

8. *De sacra coena adversus Lanfrancum,* ed. W.H. Beekenkamp (The Hague, 1941), c. 9 (pp. 13-14), c. 30 (p. 66), and c. 35 (p. 94).

9. *Ibid.,* c. 20 (p. 41), c. 21 (pp. 44-45), c. 30 (pp. 67-68) and c. 37 (p. 109).

10. *Ibid.,* c. 39 (p. 123), c. 42 (p. 141), and c. 46 (pp. 159-160).

11. *Ibid.,* c. 6 (p. 7), c. 37 (p. 58), and c. 30 (p. 67).

12. Gregory VII, *Registrum,* ed. E. Caspar, 2 vols (Berlin, 1920-23), 6:17a (Caspar, 2:426-7). *Enchiridion,* n. 700.

13. See Macy, *Theologies,* chapter three.

14. Durand of Troarn, *De corpore et sanguine domini,* pars 3 (*PL* 149: 1382A-B); Hugh of Langres, *Tractatus de corpore et sanguine Christi* (*PL* 142: 1331B-C); Lanfranc of Bec, *Liber de corpore et sanguine Domini,* c. 18 (*PL* 150: 430B-C).

15. Guitmund of Aversa, *De corporis et sanguinis Christi veritate in eucharista,* 1. 1 (*PL* 149: 1432A-1436B).

16. *Ibid.,* 1. 2 (*Ibid.:* 1445C-1448C). Guitmund borrowed the idea that Christ took on different forms in speaking to Mary and the disciples from Lanfranc, *De corpore* (*PL* 150: 424C), although Lanfranc did not use the example for this purpose.

17. *De veritate,* 1. 2 (*PL* 149: 1448C-1449C).

18. *Ibid.,* 1.2. (*Ibid.:* 1450A-B, 1451-1453B).

19. *De sacramentis,* 1. 2, c. 1 (*PL* 180: 807B-814B).

20. Nicolaus Häring, "Die Sententie magistri gisleberti pictavensis episcopi," *Archives d'histoire et littéraire du moyen âge* 46 (1979): 64, *sententia* no. 25. For a discussion of other masters who followed Gilbert in this teaching, see Häring, *ibid.,* 45 (1978), 91, and

P.C. Boeren, "Un traite ine⁄dit du XII sie⁄cle, *Convenientibus vobis in unum* (1 Cor. 11.20), *"Archives d'historie doctrinale et litteraire du moyen age* 45 (1978), 191 and p. 201, n. 1.

21. The authorship of this work is disputed, although it is commonly included among the works associated with the school of Gilbert. See Artur Landgraf, *Introduction a l'histoire de la littérature theologique de la scolastique naissante* (Montreal and Paris, 1973), p. 118, n. 337.

22. *Summa de sacramentis "Totus homo",* De eucharistia, c. 19, ed. Umberto Betti (Rome, 1955, pp. 51-53).

23. The teaching appears in three books of sentences; the *Sententie Florianenses,* the *Sententie Parisienses I,* and the *Sententie Hermanni.* On their relation to the School of Abelard, see David Luscombe, *The School of Peter Abelard* (Cambridge, 1969), pp. 153-168. for this teaching, see *Sententie Florianensis,* c. 69-71, ed. Heinrich Ostlender (Bonn, 1929), p. 31; *Sententie Parisiensis I,* ed. Artur Landgraf, *Écrit théologique de l'école d'Abélard* (Louvain, 1934), p. 42, and *Sententie Hermanni (Pl* 178: 174C-43A).

24. *Sententie Florianenses,* c. 70 (Ostlender, p. 31); *Sententie Parisiensis I* (Landgraf, p. 43), and *Sententie Hermanni (PL* 178: 1743D).

25. The passage is contained in two commentaries, one attributed to Bruno the Carthusian and the other to an unknown author. Gratiadei. On the complicated problems of dating and attribution associated with these glosses, see Anselm Stoelen, "Les commentaries scriptuaires attribués a⁄ Bruno le Chartreux," *Récherches de théologie ancienne et médiévale* 25 (1958), 177-247 and *idem.* "Bruno le Chartreux, Jean Gratiadei et la 'Lettre de S. Anselme' sur l'eucharistie," *Récherches de théologie ancienne et medievale* 34 (1967), 18-83. The passages referred to in the text have been edited by Stoelen, "Bruno le Chartreux," pp. 46-47.

26. "Nec remanere substantiam panis et uini, speciem enim tamen uidemus remanere de hoc quod prius fuerat, scilicet formam, colorem et saporem. Et secundum speciem remanentem quedam ibi fiunt que nullomodo secundum hoc quod est fieri possit, uidelicet guod conteritur, in uno loco concluditur, a mure roditur, in uentrum trahicitur. Ideo uero guod non est apparet, at quod est celatur, quia si quod est uideretur et separetur, homines sumere uererentur." *Sententie magistri A.* (Vatican City, Biblioteca Vaticana, Vaticana lat. MS. 4361, fol. 112vl-2). On the influence of this book of *sententie* on the school at Laon, see Nicolaus Ha⁄ring, *"The Sententiae Magistri A* (Vat. MS lat 4361) and the School of Laon," *Medieval Studies* 17 (1955), 1-45 and Heinrich Reinhardt, "Die Identita⁄t der Sententiae Magistri A. mit dem Compilationes Ailmeri und die Frage nach dem Autor dieser frühscholastischen Sentenzensammlung," *Theologie und Philosophie* 50 (1975), 381-403. Students who followed this teaching include William of Champeux in the sententia published by Odon Lottin, *Psychologie et morale aux XIIe et XIIIe siécles,* vol. 5 (Gembloux, 1959), p. 218, and William of St. Thierry, *De corpore et sanguine domini,* c.10 (*PL* 180: 358B).

27. *De pignoribus sanctorum,* 1.2, c. 4 (*PL* 156: 643B-C).

28. *De sacramentis Christianae fidei,* 1. 2, pars 8, c. 11 (*PL* 176: 469B).

29. Cf. *Summa sententiarum,* tract. 6, c. 8 (*PL* 176: 144C-145B); Robert Pullen, *Sententie,* 1. 8, c. 5 (*PL* 186: 966C-D). *Questiones super epistolam primam ad Corinthios (PL* 175: 531C-D); Adam of Dryburgh, *De tripartito tabernaculo,* pars 2, c. 10 (*PL* 198: 705A-C); Baldwin of Canterbury, *De sacramentis altaris,* ed. J. Morson, Vol. 1(Paris, 1963), 126; Gerald of Wales, *Gemma ecclesiastica,* 1. c. 11, ed. J.S. Brewer, *Giraldis Cambrensis opera,* vol. 2 (London, 1862), 30; Peter of Vienna, *Summa,* cc. 183-186, ed. Nicolaus Ha⁄ring, *Die Zwettler Summe,* (Munster, 1977), p. 174. See also note 36.

30. *Pl* 191: 1644C-1645B.

31. "Ex his datur intelligi guod fractio et partes quae ibi videntur fieri, in sacramento fiunt, id est, in specie visibili. Ideoque illa Berengarii verba ita distinguendo sunt, ut sensualiter non modo in sacramento, sed in veritate dicatur corpus Christi tractori manibus sacerdotum; frangi vero et atteri dentibus, vere quidem, sed in sacramento tantum" *Sententiae,* lib. 4, dist. 12 ed. J.P. Migne (Paris, 1841), col. 355.

32. *Contra quatuor labyrinthos* Franciae, 1. 3, c. 11, ed. P. Glorieux, "Le Contra quatuor labyrinthos Franciae de Gauthier de Saint-Victor. Édition critique," *Archives d'histoire et littéraire du moyen âge* 19 (1952), 261.

33. "Itaque qui vere frangi corpus Christi non concedit, totam fidem tanti sacramenti, quantum in se est, fregit." *De fractione corporis Christi* (PL 166: 1344C-D).

34. "Corpus Christi incorruptibile est; iterum, corpus Christi dentibus atteritur et tranglutitur. Lege fidem Berengarii, quam sibi firmavit Ecclesia sub Nicolao papa, et ita esse invenies." *In unum ex quatuor*, 1. 4, c. 156 (PL 186: 508A).

35. "Sunt nonnulli, imo forsan multi, sed vix notari possunt, qui cum damnato Berengario idem sentiunt, et tamen eumdem cum Ecclesia damnant. In hoc videlicet damnant eum, qui formum verborum Ecclesiae abjiciens, nuditate sermonis scandalum movebat." *Ibid.* (*Ibid.*: 508B).

36. Cf. Odo of Ourscamp, *Quaestiones*, q. 266, ed J-P. Pitra, *Analecta novissima Spicilegii Solesmensis*, vol 2 (Tusculum, 1888), 92-93; Peter of Capua, *Summa "Vestustissima veterum"* (Vatican City, Biblioteca Apostolica Vaticana, Vaticana lat. MS. 4296, fols. 69v2-70rl); Peter Comestor, *De sacramentis*, c. 23, ed. Raymond Martin in H. Weisweiler, *Maitre Simon et son groupe* (Louvain, 1937), pp. 54-55; Peter of Poitiers, *Sententie*, 1. 5 c. 12 (PL 211: 1250A); Magister Rolandus, *Sententie*, ed. Ambrose Gietl (Freiburg im Freisgau, 1891), p. 234; Magister Simon, *De sacramentis*, cc. 14, 26, 29, 30, ed. H. Weisweiler (Louvain, 1937), pp. 31, 38, 39-40. See especially Praepositinus of Cremona, *Summa:* "Item queritur in quo sit fractio que habet fieri an sit in corpore Christi vel tantum in specie. Quod sit in corpore videtur ex confessione Berengarii qui iurare compulsus est quod corpus Christ sensualiter frangitur et dentibus atterituri . . . Solutio. Magistri nostri dicunt quod fractio ipsa tantum est in specie et non in corpore. . . . Sed quod Berengarius dixit sic est intelligendum, sensualiter frangitur, idest species sub qua ipsum est. Non enim credebat sub illa specie esse corpus Christi. Quod dicit, dentibus atteritur, idest sub specie contrita dentibus sumitur." Ed. E. Pilarczyk (Rome, 1964), pp. 85-86. See also the references given in n. 29.

37. "De fractione illa etiam queri solet, cuius rei sit, id est, quid ibi frangatur et quid partes ille significent fractionis. Dicunt quidam solum sacramentum ibi frangi eo quod corpus christi inpassibile sit, et nullam recipiat fractionem, nullam partium diuisionem. Sed quomodo uera tunc erit illa confessio Berengarius que rome coram papa Nicholao presentibus cum xiii episcopis facta est et scripta? Confessus est enim panem et uinum que in altari ponuntur post consecrationem non solum sacramentum, sed etiam uerum corpus et sanguinem christi esse et sensualiter, non solum sacramentum, sed in ueritate manibus sacerdotum tractari et frangi et fidelium dentibus atteri. Ecce dicit quia corpus christi in ueritate frangitur, in ueritate fidelium dentibus atteritur. Eadem ratione ibidem in ueritate uidetur, non solum oculis cordis, sed corporis. Error Berengarii fuit quod post consecrationem panis, panis remanebat et solum sacramentum corporis christi non uerum corpus eius ibi erat. Sua ergo confessione fidei expressit ueritatem, dicens non solum sacramentum fractioni illi sub esse quod prius crediderat, sed corpus christi in ueritate. Corpus enim christi est in ueritate quod uidetur, quod frangitur, et fidelium dentibus atteribur. Sed quomodo inquis si inpassibile frangitur, quomodo si indiuisibile diuiditur? Responsio. Quomodo deus mori potuit si immortalis fuit; quomodo comprehendi si incomprehensibilis? Secundum aliud et aliud dices, et tamen unus et idem. Sic unum et idem corpus inpassible et tamen frangitur, sed secundum aliud et aliud utrumque tamen in ueritate. Quod secundum se et in se inpassible est; in sacramento diuiditur, in sacramento uidetur, et fidelium dentibus atteribur. Hec omnia tamen in ueritate et in fantasmate nichil." (Vatican City, Biblioteca Apostolica Vaticana, Ottoboniana lat. MS. 445, fol. 117rl-vl).

38. William of Auxerre, *Summa aurea*, 1.4 (ed. anonymously Paris, 1500 [?], fols 259v2-260rl); Albert the Great, *De sacramentis*, tract. 5, pars 2, q. 3, art. 4, ed. Albert Ohlmeyer, *Opera omnia*, vol. 26 (Aschendorff, 1958), 68; Thomas Aquinas *Summa theologiae*, pars 3, q. 77, art. 7, ed. the Order of Preachers, *Opera omnia*, vol. 12 (Rome 1906), 202-203; Bonventure, *Breviloquium*, pars 6, c. 9, ed. A Sepinski, *Opera theologica selecta*, vol. 5 (Florence, 1964), 142-143.

39. Maurice Wiles, *The Christian Fathers* (New York: Oxford University Press, 1982), p. 180.

40. Henry Adams, *Mon-Saint-Michel and Chartres* (Boston and New York: Houghton Mifflin Company, 1933), p. 356.

MYTH AND COUNTER-MYTH:
IRENAEUS' STORY OF SALVATION

William P. Loewe

The historicity of both theology and the history of theology is commonly acknowledged today. Once theology recognizes its task to be one of mediating between the Christian religion and the world of human culture, the open-ended character of the theological enterprise becomes patent. Every shift in the culture theology would address poses the challenge of change, while every genuine cultural advance offers new resources to be appropriated. Furthermore, not only must theology advance in the present, but each enrichment of the theologian's self-understanding sheds light backwards as well, affording a clearer, more adequately differentiated grasp of the significance of those who forged the tradition in which the theologian stands. Hence the history of theology remains an unfinished tale, needing constantly to be recast.

Irenaeus of Lyons, often honored as the father of Christian theology, may serve as a case in point. A standard manual of patrology finds him important because he was the first to have offered a comprehensive presentation of the doctrines of Christianity.[1] Somewhat more recently, however, Irenaeus has been lauded as the first theologian of salvation history.[2] In both instances he is accorded prominent status, but for different reasons. The difference stems, of course, not from the works of Irenaeus but from the theological present of the respective historians. The shift in focus from doctrines to salvation history corresponds to a development in the recent, not the remote, past.

The significance of a categorical shift like this in interpreting the past is more than merely verbal. Such shifts may signal genuine progress in understanding the material to which the categories are applied. To view Irenaeus primarily through the lens of doctrine now seems anachronistic, neglecting as it does the vast difference in form and content between his writings and any medieval *summa* or post-Reformation manual of theses. While Irenaeus' works bear enormous significance for the history of doctrine, an approach which concentrates entirely on the doctrinal perspective entails the risk of reducing those works to a source of proof-texts for the kind of dogmatic theology dominant until recently but whose deficiencies are now widely recognized.

By drawing attention to the prior narrative matrix from which doctrines arise, the shift to salvation history proved an advance; with regard to Irenaeus, it took fuller account of the actual data yielded by his works. Yet the salvation history approach also had its limits. Enthusiasm for the recital of God's mighty deeds obfuscated the critical questions evoked by such discourse, but without the acknowledgement of those questions the salvation history approach lent itself to a theological positivism content to superimpose a string of divine "facts" upon or alongside the events of ordinary human history.

Hence, because of insufficient critical reflection on its central category, the theology of salvation history proved transitional, while the questions it evoked have generated a new conceptuality or set of categories. Critical reflection on the performance of assembling, reciting, and writing salvation history has brought to light the operation within that performance of the religious imagination expressing itself in the mode of symbolic discourse. From this perspective salvation history, as a narrative expansion of religious symbolic discourse, constitutes a myth.[3]

Accordingly this paper suggests a quite modest revision in our assessment of Irenaeus and our understanding of the nature of his achievement. The paper suggests that Irenaeus responded to the challenge of Gnosticism by forging diverse elements of the Christian tradition into a myth the comprehensiveness of which matched that of the Gnostics, and that the structure of this myth, governed by the notions of dispensation, recapitulation, and the Pauline Christ-Adam typology, expresses Irenaeus' own creative originality. In a word, Irenaeus met the Gnostic myth with a Christian counter-myth, a narrative expression of the significance of Jesus in the story of God and God's redemptive dealings with humanity. To show that Irenaeus is telling a story of salvation, however, it will be necessary to ascertain what his story is.

Myth and Counter-myth

The year 177 A.D. saw a wave of persecution break over the Christian churches at Vienne and Lyons in southeastern France. Much of a contemporary letter describing the trials of these communities to their sister-churches in Asia Minor has been preserved for us by the fourth century historian, Eusebius of Caesarea.[4] The letter depicts in vivid detail the mob fury, imprisonment, torture, and execution which fell upon Christians old and young, women and men alike. Among those to perish was the ninety-year-old bishop of Lyons, Pothinus.

One member of the community who escaped martyrdom was a presbyter named Irenaeus. He came originally from Smyrna, where as a boy he had encountered Polycarp, known as a disciple of John. While the Christians of Lyons were being savaged, Irenaeus found himself at Rome, sent with a letter to Pope Eleutherius concerning Montanism. Upon his return home he was elected to succeed Pothinus, and he remained bishop of Lyons until his death approximately twenty-five years later. During his episcopate Irenaeus emerged as the most important theologian of his time, so that, as we have noted, some historians regard him as the father of Christian theology.

The experience of persecution marked Irenaeus deeply. Still, unlike the apologists before him, he did not devote his energies to trying to win tolerance for Christians from the civil authorities. Instead he took up his pen to oppose the other major threat to the church of his day, Gnosticism. This widespread movement appeared in many forms.[5] There were Jewish Gnostics, and Plotinus would find the movement subverting Platonism as well.

In a Christian setting Gnostics of course honored the name of Christ and appealed to the apostolic traditions which related his deeds and sayings. They interpreted these, however, to fit their own comprehensive myth of God, the universe, and the redemption of humanity. Gnostics worshipped a hitherto unknown deity far and completely removed from this world. They recounted how there had emanated from this deity a complex series of aeons to the number of thirty. These completed the *pleroma,* or realm of the divine; it counted among its inhabitants figures bearing such names as Only-Begotten, Word, Holy Spirit, Church, Christ, and Savior. The youngest aeon was Wisdom, and in one version of their story, Gnostics related how, having been overcome by a passion to know the ineffable deity, she had nearly perished, and how her passion provided the original principle from which all matter was derived.

The Gnostic myth reduced the creator God of the Old Testament to a Demiurge who came after and beneath the divine *pleroma.* He was regarded as imperfect, ignorant, and deluded, tainted by the matter which it was his business to order. Gnostics looked upon matter itself, including the human body, as evil. The true destiny of human beings, or at least of that class of them who were born spiritual rather than animal or material, lay in ascending to the divine realm of pure spirit. Redemption for them consisted in *gnosis,* knowledge of one's spiritual nature and destiny. Christ descended from the *pleroma* to communicate this saving knowledge, but even on earth he in no way degraded himself by real involvement with a human body. Gnostic christology took dualistic forms. The heavenly Christ inhabited Jesus only temporarily, departing before the passion. For some Gnostics even Jesus, though distinct from the heavenly Christ, only appeared to be material. At the transfiguration, they explained, the non-physical character of his substance became evident. Like his body, his sufferings were only apparent, so that of itself his death possessed no saving efficacy.

Irenaeus entitled his major work *On the Detection and Overthrow of Knowledge (Gnosis) Falsely So-Called;* it is more commonly referred to as *Against Heresies.*[6] One other of his writings survives in its entirety, the *Proof of the Apostolic Preaching,*[7] rediscovered only in 1904. The first two of the five books into which Irenaeus divided the *Against Heresies* contain the fullest exposition of Gnosticism, its variants, and other early heresies to be found in patristic literature.

If Irenaeus recounts Gnostic beliefs in great detail, tedious apparently even to his contemporaries (I, 31/4) as well as to the modern reader, his goal is to refute them, and he considers their mere exposure to public scrutiny a major step to that end (I, 31/3). He also draws upon the broad repertoire of polemical devices standardized in the rhetorical manuals of the age.[8] Thus he underscores the novelty of Gnostic teaching, lays bare the internal contradictions of its literal sense, and shows it to differ from teacher to teacher. The teachers themselves, he charges, are greedy and immoral persons who prey especially on credulous women.

Since each teacher assigns names of his own devising to the emanations which make up the divine *pleroma,* Irenaeus is emboldened at one point to follow suit. Having expounded the doctrines of Valentinus, Secundus, and another, unnamed Gnostic teacher, Irenaeus proposes a system of his own. He begins plausibly enough:

> There is a certain Proarche, royal, surpassing all thought, a power existing beside every substance, and extended into space in every direction (I, 11/4).

He then continues:

> But along with it there exists a power which I term a *Gourd;* and along with this Gourd there exists a power which again I term *Utter-Emptiness.* This Gourd and Emptiness, since they are one, produced (and yet did not simply produce, so as to be apart from themselves) a fruit, everywhere visible, eatable, and delicious, which fruit-language calls a *Cucumber.* Along with this Cucumber exists a power of the same essence, which again I call a *Melon.* These powers, the Gourd, Utter-Emptiness, the Cucumber, and the Melon, brought forth the remaining multitude of the delirious melons of Valentinus.

Irenaeus can parody the Gnostic myth in its literal sense as arbitrary, fanciful, and in the end ludicrous — "I well know, my friend, that when thou hast read through all this, thou wilt engage in a hearty laugh over this their inflated wise folly" (I, 16/3) — but his basic objection lies deeper. Quite simply, Gnosticism is false. Setting up an unreal deity, it heaps scorn on the only true God and draws men and women away from him. Gnostic falsehood becomes insidious because of the plausibility it wins when it uses the common language of Christianity, while its claim to represent the secret, higher meaning of Christianity endows Gnosticism with the appeal of an esoteric doctrine reserved for select initiates.

What is at stake between Gnosticism and Christianity is the true story about God and humanity. For this reason Irenaeus does not rest content with internal arguments and rhetorical devices. Against the Gnostic corruption of Christianity, he is eager to set the record straight with a positive exposition of the truth of Christian faith.

Where is that truth to be found? Irenaeus invokes a range of authoritative sources.[9] He can appeal to the rule of faith received at baptism, or to the tradition of the church, especially the teaching of the succession of bishops. He has recourse to the apostolic preaching and cites the four gospels and other apostolic writings as well as the law and the prophets. All these, he asserts, witness to the single, self-same Christian faith.

The fact remains, however, that none of these authorities by itself matches the comprehensive sweep of the Gnostic myth. Under the pressure of Gnosticism a need was emerging to weave from the diverse sources available a single narrative statement of the truth about God and humanity.[10] Irenaeus' originality lies precisely here, that he rose to the challenge of meeting the Gnostic myth with an equally comprehensive counter-myth. For this purpose his authorities provided an abundance of material, but Irenaeus was no mere compiler; a comprehensive narrative of the saving truth of Christianity remains his own achievement.[11]

This is not to deny that the form of Irenaeus' works is dictated by the apologetic and catechetical purposes which occasioned them, nor that he was interested as well in the intelligibility of the narrative he was forging; the list of some fourteen questions which he proposes in I, 10/3 indicates that he was aware of having an original contribution to make on this latter score as well. But if Irenaeus does not simply recite his narrative as a well-ordered story with beginning, middle, and end, the elements and distinctive shape of his story do emerge from his response to Gnosticism and his elaboration of the truths of Christianity contested by it.

Irenaeus' project rests on the bedrock of Christian belief in God, one and triune, creator of all *ex nihilo*.[12] Against the Gnostic tale of a *pleroma* with its multiplicity of aeons Irenaeus cites the "rule of truth" received at baptism, which affirms the existence of " . . .one God, the Father Almighty, Maker of heaven and earth. . . " (I, 10/1). According to this rule the Father " . . .made all things by His Word, and fashioned and formed out of that which had no existence, all things that exist." It " . . .is He who, by His Word and Spirit, makes, and disposes, and governs all things, and commands all things into existence. . . " (I, 22/1). Irenaeus reads Gen 1:16 as a witness to the triune character of God:

> For with Him were always present the Word and Wisdom, the Son and Spirit, by whom and in whom, freely and spontaneously, He

made all things, saying, "Let Us make man after Our image and likeness" . . . (III, 20/1).

Against the Gnostics Irenaeus insists that the story can properly begin only with creation, not before. God exists eternally as Father, Son, and Spirit, but to inquire back before existence is, for Irenaeus, a vain endeavor. "If, for example, anyone asks, 'What was God doing before He made the world?' we reply that the answer to such a question lies with God Himself" (II, 28/31). Irenaeus was less successful in scotching another question of this sort:

> If anyone, therefore, say to us, 'How then was the Son produced by the Father?' we reply to him that no man understands the production, or generation, or calling, or revelation, or by whatever other name one may describe His generation, which is in fact altogether indescribable (II, 28/6).

Clearly Arianism had not yet set the church on its way to Nicea, and to Athanasius' eventual clarification of the eternal begetting of the Son. In the end, though, that clarification would only reinforce the limit Irenaeus posted to what we can properly imagine about the inner life of God.

The Dispensation

Two terms play an especially prominent role in shaping Irenaeus' narrative of God and humanity and in binding together its various elements. First, he frequently remarks that what his opponents have failed to grasp, or what they are distorting, is the dispensation *(dispensatio, oikonomia)* of God. Or, he can make the same point using the term in the plural. Marcion, for example, is among those who mutilate Scripture in order that "they may set the dispensations of God aside" (II, 11/9). Similarly, in a positive vein, Irenaeus affirms that " . . .the Son of God accomplished the whole dispensation" (IV, Pref/4), but he also makes reference to a plurality of dispensations. To give but a sampling, he mentions "the new dispensation of liberty" (III, 10/4), "the dispensation of the law" (III, 11/7), "the dispensation of the advent of this Person" (III, 16/3), "the dispensation of suffering" (III, 18/5), "the marvellous dispensation" of the virginal conception (III, 21/4), "the future dispensation of the human race" (III, 22/3), and "the dispensation of the tree" (V, 17/4).

Irenaeus employs the notion of dispensation to link God with creation and to express the character of the relationship between them. The term sets forth God's active care and concern for his handiwork, in contrast to the remote indifference of the Gnostics' ultimate deity. And unlike the Gnostic Demiurge, the true God creates freely and purposively; creation exhibits an order and harmony which reflect the power, wisdom, and goodness of the Creator (IV, 38/3). Since, furthermore, creation is precisely that, created and not divine, it is the proper realm of becoming. This means that the order of creation takes on a dynamic character. The purpose for which God created reaches fulfillment through an orderly succession of events, each suited to its particular time. For this reason Irenaeus can speak of both the one dispensation through which God intends to fulfill his purpose in creating and also, because of the finite and temporal nature of creation, he can speak as well of the plurality of particular dispensations through which the one dispensation is realized.

What is that divine purpose, the goal to be achieved through the multi-faceted dispensation of God? For Irenaeus there can be no thought of any neediness on God's part, of a lack which creation would supply. When God creates, God does so out of a sheer abundance of goodness. "In the beginning, therefore, did God form Adam, not as if He stood in need of man, but that He might have some one upon whom to confer His benefits" (IV, 14/1). God's goodness establishes humanity as its primary recipient, and Irenaeus displays humanity as the centerpiece of creation, ". . .for man was not made for its sake, but creation for the sake of man" (V, 29/1). All else God created by the voice of his command. With Adam, however, he took special care. Adam is the work of God's hands, his body formed with divine skill from the choicest dust of the earth *(Proof, 11)*, joined to a soul and enlivened with the breath of life.

Of all creatures only humanity is created in God's own image and likeness. Irenaeus gives an interpretation of his own to this scriptural datum.[13] Adam, and all human beings, bear the image of God in their very bodies. Human corporeality is formed in the image of the Son who will himself become incarnate.[14] The likeness of God, on the other hand, is referred in a special way to the Spirit. It consists above all in the incorruptibility to be conferred on the just when they are raised, body and soul, at the final judgment. As such the likeness of God does not belong to humanity by nature. Originally conferred on Adam, it could be and was lost, and its restoration remains an act of pure gratuity on God's part, totally beyond the power of any human beings to effect for themselves.

The goal of creation lies with humanity, but since human beings have an open, unfinished, temporal nature, that goal is not achieved by the act of creation alone. Creation is but the starting point for the dispensation whose aim consists in "promotion into God" (III, 19/1). In Irenaeus' famous phrase, "the glory of God is a living man" (IV, 20/7), and the life Irenaeus has in mind is the life of human beings as perfected, the immortal, incorruptible life to be conferred at the final resurrection.

Corresponding to his view of creation as temporal and of humanity as incomplete at the outset, Irenaeus constructs the divine dispensation as a pedagogical process. Adam and Eve may have been created in the image and likeness of God, but, as Irenaeus tells the story, they also found themselves in a childish state, both innocent and ignorant. Their lack of experience made them easy dupes of Satan, to whom Irenaeus takes care to assign by far the greater part of responsibility for the fall (III, 23/5-7). Even without the fall the unformed youthfulness of the first couple would have required a gradual preparation and growth into maturity before they could bear the dazzling glory of the destiny prepared for them: " . . .it was possible for God Himself to have made man perfect from the first, but man could not receive this perfection, being as yet an infant" (IV, 38/1). Since Adam and Eve did in fact fall, Irenaeus is quick to emphasize the pedagogical value of the consequences: the fall offered human beings a first-hand taste of the misery of evil and of their own powerlessness, preparing them to appreciate all the more gratefully the rescuing hand of God who alone can confer life and immortality (IV, 39/1).

This divine pedagogy demanded long-suffering on the part of God:

> For God has displayed long-suffering in the case of man's apostasy: while man has been instructed by means of it, as also the prophet says, "Thine own apostasy shall heal thee" (Jer 2:19); God thus determining all things beforehand for the bringing of man to perfection, for his edification, and for the revelation of His dispensations, that goodness might both be made apparent, and righteousness perfected, and that the Church may be fashioned after the image of His Son, and that man may finally be brought to maturity at some future time, becoming ripe through such privileges to see and comprehend God (IV, 37/7).

Irenaeus finds the same pedagogical dynamic running through the history of Israel. Once the knowledge of the Decalogue which is natural to all people had been dimmed by sin, God revealed the commandments to Moses and, in order to subdue an unruly nation, imposed additional precepts as well (IV, 15/2). Besides this disciplinary function, the divine pedagogy has positive aspects as well; Israel's law abounds in types of the covenant of liberty which will succeed it, and in both patriarchs and prophets humanity gradually becomes accustomed to receiving the Spirit and following the Word.

Recapitulation

The notion of dispensation, constructed as a process of divine pedagogy, serves to integrate both the fall and the history of Israel into Irenaeus' story of God and creation. Another motif which plays an important role in further shaping Irenaeus' narrative appears in a rich passage directed against the Ebionites:

. . .as, at the beginning of our formation in Adam, that breath of life which proceeded from God, having been united to what had been fashioned, animated the man, and manifested him as being endowed with reason; so also, in the times of the end, the Word of the Father and the Spirit of God, having become united with the ancient substance of Adam's formation, rendered man living and perfect, receptive of the perfect Father, in order that as in the natural Adam all were dead, so in the spiritual we may all be alive (V, 1/3).

The motif "as at the beginning, so in the end" recurs throughout Irenaeus' work. It proves to be decisive in plotting the course through which he unfolds his account of the divine dispensation, and it establishes the space for a second major image, Irenaeus' well-known "recapitulation." With this consideration we are brought directly to the heart of the matter, Irenaeus' thought on Christ.

"The Son of God," writes Irenaeus, "accomplished the whole dispensation. . ." (IV, Pref/4). If Irenaeus binds God to his handiwork through the notion of dispensation, he concretizes that notion in the constant presence and activity of the Word. The story of salvation culminates with Christ's coming in the flesh, but it also begins with him and centers on him at each stage of its unfolding: ". . .there is one and the same God the Father, and His Word, who has been always present to the human race, by means indeed of the various dispensations . . ." (IV, 28/1). Christ stands at the heart of both the single, comprehensive dispensation and of each of the particular dispensations through which God's purpose seeks its goal.

At the creation of humanity, we have seen, Irenaeus assigns the Word a dual role. He is one of the "hands" with which God formed Adam from the dust of the earth, the Spirit being the the other, and it is also in the image of the Word's future incarnate state that Adam is fashioned in his corporeality. From this beginning Irenaeus goes on to present a thoroughly christological reading of the Old Testament. It was the Word who walked and conversed with Adam and Eve in paradise (*Proof*, 12). In the days of Noah he flooded the earth in judgment (IV, 36/3). He spoke with the patriarchs, promising them his future coming. Abraham saw him in human form at the oak of Mambre. He rained fire and brimstone over Sodom and Gomorrah (III, 6/1). The writings of Moses are his words (IV, 2/3), and to each of the prophets he accorded a vision of some particular aspect of his future life as man, so that taken together the prophets witness in detail to the whole dispensation of his coming in the flesh (IV, 20/11).

When Christ finally did come visibly, he brought to a head the activity through which he had been present to humanity at creation and ever since. By his incarnation he summed up all that preceded it, " . . . making recapitulation of so comprehensive a dispensation . . . " (III, 23/1). Irenaeus can even refer to the particular dispensations as "dispensations of his recapitulation" (IV, 20/8). Irenaeus uses the image of recapitulation to bring his story of the divine dispensation to its clear focus in Christ. It allows him to express in concrete terms Christ's universal significance. Luke's genealogy, for example,

> . . . which traces the generation of our Lord back to Adam contains seventy-two generations, connecting the end with the beginning, and implying that it is He who has summed up in Himself all nations dispersed from Adam downwards, and all languages and generations of men, together with Adam himself (III, 22/3).

Similarly, besides all nations, languages, and generations, Christ recapitulates the individual human life cycle and each of its stages. Having asserted that Christ sanctified infants, children, and youths by passing through those stages of life, Irenaeus concludes consistently enough that " . . . likewise He was an old man for old men . . . " (II, 22/4). On this basis Irenaeus argues that Christ experienced the aging process which, in Irenaeus' view, sets in at forty, and that Christ was over fifty years of age when he died (II, 22/6).

In every respect, then, Christ " . . . summed up in Himself the ancient formation of Adam" (V, 5/2). With his image of the recapitulation of the human race in Christ, Irenaeus is developing a more fundamental idea, namely, that the Lord became " . . . what we are, that He might bring us to be even what He is Himself" (V, Pref). For this reason Irenaeus singles out the reality of the incarnation as the common point on whose denial all heresies converge and shatter, for " . . . according to the opinion of no one of the heretics was the Word made flesh" (III, 11/3). Within this context Irenaeus affirms that " . . the Lord has restored us into friendship through His incarnation" (V, 17/1).

Does this mean that we have already arrived at Irenaeus' soteriology? Is he proposing a so-called Greek theory of redemption, an incarnational soteriology centered on the union of divine and human natures in Christ? At least three lines of reflection render this conclusion unlikely. First, given the narrative mode in which Irenaeus conducts his theology, it is doubtful whether "theory" is itself a relevant category with which to typify his work. Second, if Greek soteriology is often constructed by historians as a "physical" theory whereby redemption occurs in some quasi-automatic fashion at the level of nature, such an idea is positively excluded in Irenaeus' polemic against the Gnostics. If, as the Gnostics have it, redemption is a matter of nature, " . . . then it follows that faith is altogether superfluous, as was also the descent of the Saviour to this world" (II, 29/1). Salvation, Irenaeus argues, is a matter of faith and righteousness, not nature and substance.

Third, Irenaeus does not regard the incarnation as a discrete point or single event; rather, it is for him the decisive dispensation through which the divine plan is fulfilled. As such the incarnation designates not simply the virginal conception and birth of Christ, but Christ's whole earthly career.[15] The uses to which we have seen Irenaeus put the image of recapitulation dramatize the reality of Christ's humanity and its solidarity with Adam's. But Christ's assumption of humanity does not, of itself, achieve redemption. Rather it establishes Christ as mediator between God and the race of Adam, and that mediation works itself out through the whole of Christ's earthly career and especially at its end.

Christ and Adam

One further development of Irenaeus' master-image remains to be mentioned. He tells the story of God and humanity as one of immaturity, growth, and divinely guided progress toward perfection, but the story includes the fall and sin as well. We have also seen that Irenaeus plots the story according to the dictum, "as at the beginning, so also in the end." These factors require that Christ, in accomplishing the divine dispensation, recapitulate — that is, reenact and reverse — the role played by Adam at the beginning. Christ acts as mediator to bring the human race to maturity, enabling human beings to receive at last the likeness of God, but in order to do this he must also reverse Adam's fall and overcome its consequences. The dynamics of recapitulation thus converge on Paul's Christ-Adam typology which, once set within the context of Irenaeus' narrative, undergoes considerable development and expansion.

From virgin soil. A first line of expansion is found in III, 21/10, where Irenaeus links Christ's birth from a virgin with the manner of Adam's formation. God formed Adam from the dust of the earth. Irenaeus cites Gen 2:15 to glean the further details that ". . . God had not yet sent rain, and man had not tilled the ground." With this citation at hand Irenaeus can assert that "Adam had his substance from untilled and yet virgin soil . . .," and thus the correspondence which he wants to establish is secured: ". . . so did He who is the Word, recapitulating Adam in Himself, rightly receive a birth . . . from Mary, who was yet a virgin."

In the same passage Irenaeus faces an obvious objection. The correspondence is imperfect. "Why, then, did not God again take dust?" His answer follows:

> It was that there might not be another formation called into being, nor any other which should require to be saved, but that the very same formation should be summed up in Christ as had existed in Adam, the analogy being preserved.

Thus Irenaeus' point in developing the virgin-image under the rubric of recapitulation is to underscore the solidarity of Christ's humanity with Adam's. A human being was required to rescue humanity from its plight, and yet ". . .it was not possible for the man who had once for all been conquered, and who had been destroyed by disobedience, to reform himself, and obtain the prize of victory . . ." (III, 18/2). Satan had proven more powerful than those human beings whom he had conquered and enslaved, and so one stronger yet was needed. "But who else is superior to, and more eminent than, that man who was formed after the likeness of God, except the Son of God, after whose image man was created" (IV, 33/4)? Still, even if only the incarnate Son of God could meet the need of humankind, it is precisely in his humanity that the Son wins through for us:[16]

> And therefore does the Lord profess Himself to be the Son of Man . . . in order that, as our species went down to death through a vanquished man, so we may ascend to life again through a victorious one; and as through a man death received the palm of victory against us, so again by a man we may receive the palm against death (V, 21/1).

In sum, the correspondence between the Virgin Mary and the "virgin soil" from which God formed Adam at the beginning expresses the primary significance which Irenaeus attributes to Mary in his development of the Christ-Adam typology. Satan is to be overcome by one of Adam's race. But according to certain Gnostics, Jesus passed throgh Mary like water through a tube, taking nothing from her and remaining remote from our humanity. For Irenaeus, on the contrary, Jesus' humanity is no isolated new creation. Mary's virginal motherhood ensures Jesus' solidarity with the race of Adam, and this is her primary function, to provide the link between the humanity of the Savior and those he is to save.

This does not mean that Irenaeus fails to perceive a further correspondence which grants Mary a more active role. Shifting his attention from the virgin soil to Eve who ". . . did not obey while yet she was a virgin," he notes that ". . . the knot of Eve's disobedience was loosed by the obedience of Mary. For what the virgin Eve had bound fast through unbelief, this did the Virgin Mary set free through faith" (III, 22/4).

Born to be tempted. When Adam was tempted, he succumbed to Satan's lies and fell into disobedience. Irenaeus follows Paul closely on the consequences: "For as by one man's disobedience sin entered, and death obtained a place through sin; so also by the obedience of one man, righteousness, having been introduced, shall cause life to fructify in those who in times past were dead" (III, 21/10). Obedience, however, requires an occasion, and hence Irenaeus can also say of Christ that ". . . He became man in order to undergo temptation" (III, 19/3).

As with the virgin birth, the Christ-Adam typology likewise dominates Irenaeus' perspective on Christ's temptation in the desert. He introduces his account of the scene by relating it explicitly to the text of Gen 2:16:

> He has, therefore, in His work of recapitulation, summed up all
> things, both waging war against our enemy, and crushing him who
> had at the beginning led us away captives in Adam, and trampled
> upon his head as thou canst perceive in Genesis that God said to
> the serpent, "And I will put enmity between thee and the woman,
> and between thy seed and her seed; He shall be on the watch for
> your head, and thou on the watch for His heel" (V, 21/1).

Modern exegetes may relate the individual temptations to Israel's fortunes,
but Irenaeus draws a line from each straight back to the scene in paradise.
Christ's fasting, for example, suggests his comment on the first temptation:

> For as at the beginning it was through food that the Adversary
> seduced man, even though he did not suffer hunger, into trans-
> gressing God's command, so in the end he could not dissuade the
> Man who was hungry from holding out for the food which comes
> from God (V, 21/2), translation emended).

In like manner Irenaeus concludes his account of the second temptation with a
contrast between Christ's humility and the serpent's pride. His presentation of
the entire incident ends on a similar note:

> . . . there was done away with that infringement of God's command-
> ment which had occurred in Adam by means of the precept of the
> law, which the Son of Man observed, who did not transgress the
> commandment of God (V, 21/2).

The dispensation of the tree. Irenaeus presents the temptation in the desert
as the occasion of Christ's victory over Satan whereby the disobedience of
Adam is cancelled, Satan bound, and the race of Adam liberated (V, 21/3).
Yet the story continues; Christ's obedience is unto death, and so Irenaeus
attributes the same effects to the passion as to the temptation, and again he
traces the lines of correspondence which run back to the situation of Adam
"at the beginning."

Thus, in an argument similar to the one with which he ascertained the age at
which Christ died, Irenaeus appeals to his image of recapitulation to determine
as well the day of Christ's death. He states the general principle, that Christ,
" . . . by summing up in Himself the whole human race from the beginning,
He has also summed up its death," from which it follows that Christ, dying in
obedience, died on the same day on which Adam disobeyed and died, namely,

the sixth day of creation, the day before the Sabbath (V, 23/2).

Christ's passion recapitulates not only the day of Adam's fall but also its manner. If Adam sinned by eating of the fruit of a certain tree, ". . . the sin that was wrought through the tree was undone by the obedience of the tree, obedience to God whereby the Son of Man was nailed to the tree. . ." (*Proof,* 34). Adam and Eve had enjoyed familiar access to the Word before the fall, but not until the passion was this restored:

> This word, then, which was hidden from us, did the dispensation of the tree make manifest . . . . For as we lost it by means of a tree, by means of a tree again was it made manifest to all . . . (V, 17/3).

Foreseen by Abraham (IV, 15/5), prefigured by the scarlet thread bound to the wrist of the infant Zerah (IV, 25/2), see Gen 38:27-30), predicted in detail by the prophets (IV, 33/12), and anticipated by the magi's gift of myrrh (III, 9/3), the dispensation of the tree is finally the key to scripture which,

> . . . when it is read by the Christians, it is a treasure, hid indeed in a field, but brought to light by the cross of Christ, and explained, both enriching the understanding of men and showing forth the wisdom of God, and declaring his dispensation with regard to man . . . (IV, 26/1).

For Irenaeus the cross of Christ provides the key which unlocks the treasure hidden in scripture. What might that treasure be? In light of the Lord's pasch the unity of scripture comes into view for Irenaeus as the story of the single divine dispensation which, unfolding in good order through a series of particular dispensations, has been guiding creation to its goal. It becomes evident to Irenaeus that since the beginning the Word of God has been actively preparing humanity for his advent in the flesh. Becoming incarnate, Christ recapitulated every aspect of humanity in himself and thus entered into total solidarity with the race of Adam. His life of perfect obedience led through the victory over temptation in the desert to culminate in the dispensation of the tree. Born of a virgin, tempted, and persevering in obedience unto death, Christ reenacted and reversed the fall of Adam and brought the human race to maturity, overcoming Satan and enabling humankind to receive the likeness of God for which it had been destined.

Such, in broad outline, is the story of salvation which Irenaeus counterposes to Gnosticism as the true story of God and humanity. Wholly traditional, it is also, as Irenaeus shapes and structures it though his development of the notions of dispensation, recapitulation, and the Christ-Adam typology, wholly his own. Traditions live only in the consciousness of those whose world they form; for the most part the latter rest content with received articulations of the tradition, contributing to its vitality primarily by animating the tradition and expressing it on the level of praxis. In Irenaeus, however, we may observe the final identity of living tradition with the act of creative interpretation. The contest with Gnosticism arose not over particular texts or doctrines but from a clash of worlds. Irenaeus' significance, we would suggest, lies first of all in the imaginative power which allowed him to meet the Gnostic crisis by forging traditional sources into a comprehensive narrative, an aesthetic unity, capable of evoking in its fullness the world of Christian faith.

NOTES

1. Johannes Quasten, *Patrology*, Vol. 1 (Utrecht: Spectrum, 1950), 294.

2. Alfred Bengsch gathers citations to this effect in *Heilsgeschichte und Heilswissen* (Leipzig: St. Benno Verlag, 1957), pp. XIII-XIV.

3. For a fuller statement developing the terms religious imagination, symbol, and myth as general theological categories, see W. Loewe, "Toward a Responsible Contemporary Soteriology," in M. Lamb, ed., *Creativity and Method: Essays in Honor of Bernard Lonergan, S.J.* (Milwaukee: Marquette University Press, 1981), especially pp. 220-221.

4. Eusebius of Caesarea, *Ecclesiastical History*, Book V, 1-3.

5. James M. Robinson, ed., *The Nag Hammadi Library* (San Francisco: Harper and Row, 1981), pp. 1-10.

6. Unless otherwise indicated, citations will be taken from the English translation in volume I of A. Roberts and J. Donaldson, eds., *The Ante-Nicene Fathers* (Grand Rapids: Eerdmans, 1979).

7. Citations will be taken from the English translation by Joseph P. Smith in No. 16 of the *Ancient Christian Writers* (New York: Newman, 1952).

8. Pheme Perkins, "Irenaeus and the Gnostics: Rhetoric and Composition in *Adversus Haereses* Book One," *Vigiliae Christianae* 30 (1976), 193-200.

9. Philip Hefner, "Theological Methodology and St. Irenaeus," *Journal of Religion* 44 (1964), 294-309.

10. P. Perkins helpfully suggests the relevance of W. Ong's research on the correlation among communications media, psychological structures, and cultural stages; this suggestion comes into play when, in *The Gnostic Dialogue: The Early Church and the Crisis of Gnosticism* (New York: Paulist, 1980), p. 9, she remarks that "Gnostics generally use their abstractions in the oral, narrative mode rather than in the philosophic, analytic one." Irenaeus, we are proposing, met the Gnostic challenge in that same mode.

11. John P. Meier offers a complementary view on Irenaeus' originality. In *Antioch and Rome: New Testament Cradles of Catholic Christianity* (New York: Paulist, 1983), which he coauthored with R.E. Brown, Meier concludes a chapter devoted to Ignatius of Antioch with the remark (p. 78) that "Ignatius represents the first attested attempt to blend the major streams of NT thought into a coherent viewpoint that articulates the faith of the church catholic . . . . In this the bishop-theologian Ignatius . . . foreshadowed the much greater synthesis of Irenaeus of Lyons. . . ."

12. Henri Lassiat, *Promotion de l'homme en Jésus-Christ* (Strasbourg: La Maison Mame, 1974), pp. 59-145.

13. Antonio Orbe contrasts Irenaeus' interpretation with that expounded by Origen in *Antropologia de San Ireneo* (Madrid: Biblioteca de autores cristianos, 1969), pp. 7-31.

14. A. Orbe argues that in the final analysis, it is the risen, glorified body of Christ which provides the exemplar for the creation of Adam: "La carne gloriosa de Jesus es imagen perfecta de Dios y paradigma del hombre" (A. Orbe, *op. cit.*, p. 102).

15. Jean-Pierre Jossua offers this interpretation of Irenaeus' usage in *Le Salut: Incarnation ou Mystere pascale* (Paris: Editions du Cerf, 1968), pp. 69-72.

16. Gustav Aulen systematically neglects the significance of this point in his *Christus Victor: An Historical Study of the Three Main Types of the Idea of the Atonement* (ET New York: Macmillan, 1969); On Irenaeus, see pp. 33-34.

BIBLICAL POWER AND JUSTICE:
AN INTERPRETATIVE EXPERIMENT

Alice L. Laffey

The exegetical method most commonly used today to interpret both the Hebrew Bible and the New Testament still remains historical criticism. Most doctoral research in the field of biblical studies, both in secular and religiosly-affiliated universities, is historical-critical in methodology. Most seminary professors teach, almost exclusively, insights derived from this method in their training of future priests and ministers. And finally, almost all manuscripts written to serve as textbooks in courses which introduce the Bible adopt an historical approach.

No one can deny the valuable contributions which historical-critical study has made to our understanding of biblical literature. Most especially, it has helped us to recognize the texts' writers produced literature out of the culture which produced them. They were limited by the knowledge and understanding, yes, even by the cultural prejudices of the milieux in which they lived. If one takes this insight seriously, therefore, one recognizes that to name the Christian Bible as the product of the tenth century B.C. through the first century A.D. is to name writings all of which are permeated by hierarchical and patriarchal biases. No honest historian of religion can deny this.

Yet if one limits one's scholarship to historical-critical methods, and names the author's intention and cultural setting as the hermeneutical key, though that may in some cases allow for cultural diversity (for example, the exclusivist policies of the author of Ezra and Nehemiah in contrast to the more universalist theology of the authors of Second-Isaiah, Ruth, and Jonah) and for a growing moral sensitivity (for example, Jesus' refinement of the Mosaic law in the Beatitudes), one risks arriving at the conclusion that the patriarchal-hierarchical biases which pervade the texts are somehow implicitly atemporally valid. One fears that this is the case with many biblicists who have written textbooks to introduce the study of the Bible from an historical-critical perspective but whose work has omitted any mention of patriarchy and hierarchy, nevermind a critique of these as time-conditioned cultural prejudice.[1]

If the biblical texts are to have meaning today — for the twentieth century believer, for advocates of peace, as well as for women, then these texts must be interpreted beyond the hierarchical-patriarchal culture which produced them. It seems to me, therefore, that a contemporary hermeneutical task, for both scholars and teachers of the Scriptures, is to find ways to interpret the biblical texts which acknowledge that these prejudices are time and culture conditioned.[2]

Moreover, although the hermeneutical task cannot ignore the writer's intention, it must go beyond it. One brings his or her own questions to a text, in the very real culture of which he or she is a part. Like the base communities of Latin America, the contemporary American woman seeks to dialogue both with the texts which are normative for Christians and Jews, and with her own religious experience in a male-dominated church. Can the texts which promise justice to the oppressed, to captives, to the poor, to widows, to orphans, that is, to all the powerless, foreshadow a new way of structuring society, both political and religious society, which is non-hierarchical and non-exclusivist, one in which power is shared, one in which domination gives way to cooperation and subordination to mutuality?

The paper which follows is an attempt to answer this question.[3] Methodologically, it collects those biblical texts which describe and evaluate political and religious power as it was exercised in ancient Israel. But not satisfied to stop there — it would be equally unsatisfactory to collect the many female biblical characters who are victimized by male dominance and stop there — I have sought out, in addition, those texts which point toward a new way of relating to power as well as a new way of relating to women.

Power in the Old Testament

In the earliest Old Testament sources, the Yahwist and the Elohist, God is the Ultimate Power. God is the Redeeming Power of the Exodus (Exod 3:7-11) and the Creative Power of Genesis (Gen 2: 4b-22). Yahweh is the Giver, giving to Abraham, for example, a name, and a nation, and a land. Yahweh's, too, is a Delegating Power; the Lord empowers Moses and makes promises of progeny and prosperity to the patriarchs; the Lord is with them, and they are Yahweh's servants.

This delegated power, however, is tamed by covenant law. Yahweh's people must always exhibit the fullness of fidelity. There are to be no other gods besides Yahweh (Exod 20; cf. Dt 5), and they must always exercise justice toward their neighbor (Exod 20; cf. Dt 5: 12-26).

The Deuteronomistic history continues the emphasis on divine power. The Lord's Word is effective, the Lord fights for Israel and the Lord, through his servant Joshua, leads the Israelites into the land (Dt 34; Jos 1); the judges arise, as the Lord's delegated power, to act as military leaders and to arbitrate disputes, to maintain justice in the community (Deut 16:18-20); the kings, heirs to the Davidic covenant, promise the people peace and security in the land.

But delegated agents of the Lord's power must, like the people themselves, be subordinate to convenant fidelity. Their leadership is meant to guarantee the appropriate worship of Yahweh and the exercise of justice. Anything else is abuse of this delegated power. Such power, unrestrained by justice and covenant law, is consistently condemned throughout the Deuteronomistic history. 1 Sam 8, an anti-monarchic source, warns, for example, of the king who will

> . . . take your sons and appoint them to
> his chariots and to be his horsemen . . .
> appoint commanders of thousands and
> commanders of fifties,
> and some to plow his ground and
> to reap his harvest, and
> to make his implements of war and
> the equipment of his chariots.
> . . . take your daughters to be perfumers
> and cooks and bakers.
> . . . take the best of your fields and
> vineyards and olive orchards and give them
> to his servants.
> . . . take the tenth of your grain and
> give it to his officers and to his servants.
> . . . take your menservants and
> the best of your cattle and your
> asses and put them to his work.
> . . . take the tenth of your flocks —
> . . . who will, in fact, make you his slaves.
>
> (vv. 11-17)

Here the king, meant to represent the delegated power of God, has become the tyrant. The rendering of just judgment (1 Kgs 3) has given way to domination. One recognizes this attitude in, for example, the Deuteronomist's condemnation of Rehoboam (1 Kgs 12:27-33).

The Deuteromonistic historian also names the practice of idolatry as a distortion of power, a denial of the truth, that the kings' power is delegated by Yahweh. Such, for example, was the cause of Solomon's downfall (1 Kgs 11). And Manasseh "erected altars for Baal, and made an Asherah, and worshiped all the host of heaven, and served them" (2 Kgs 21:3). In the last analysis, it was, for the Deuteronomistic historian, abuse of power which led to the downfall of both the Northern and Southern kingdoms.

The prophetic literature is replete with oracles of the Lord. Many of these, especially the oracles of Deutero-Isaiah, reaffirm Yahweh's creative power (Is 40:26,28) and his redeeming power (Is 50:2-3; cf. Jer 10:12; 27:5; 32;17). Many, too, written during the time of Israel's monarchies, reassert the importance,

both for the leadership and for the people, of fidelity to covenant law, adherence
to monotheism, and the exercise of justice. They condemn rampant covenant
violations, especially those of which the leadership are guilty.

Micah, for example, announces Yahweh's own power and God's response to
the abuse of power by Judah's leadership:

> I am full of strength, of justice and of power,
> to denounce his crime to Jacob
> and his sin to Israel.
> Listen to this, leaders of Jacob,
> rulers of Israel, you who make justice hateful,
> building Zion in bloodshed and
> Jerusalem in iniquity. Her rulers sell justice,
> her priests give direction in return for a bribe,
> her prophets take money for their divination . . .
>
> (Micah 3:8-11)

Note that leadership at every level — rulers, prophets, and priests — is here
condemned.[4]

Jeremiah warns vehemently against prophetic abuse of delegated power:[5]

> Thus says the Lord of hosts:
> "Do not listen to the words of the prophets
> who prophesy to you, filling you with vain hopes;
> they speak visions of their own minds,
> not from the mouth of the Lord.
> They say continually to those who despise
> the word of the Lord, 'It will be well with you';
> and to everyone who stubbornly follows
> his or her own heart they say,
> 'No evil shall come upon you.'
>
> For who among them has stood
> in the council of the Lord
> to perceive and to hear God's Word
> and listened? . . .
>
> I did not send the prophets yet they ran;
> I did not speak to them, yet they prophesied.
> But if they had stood in my council, then
> they would have proclaimed my words
> to my people,

and they would have turned them
from their evil way,
and from the evil of their doings."
(Jer 23:18-22; cf. Micah 3:5)

Ezekiel laments:

In you, Jerusalem, the princes of Israel,
one and all, have used their power to shed
blood; people have treated their fathers and
mothers with contempt; they have oppressed
the alien and ill-treated the orphan
and the widow.
You have oppressed your fellows for gain
and you have forgotten me.
(22: 6-12)

A similar rebuke of Israel's princes can be found in Hos 5:10; 7:16; 9:15;
Micah 7:3; Is 1:23; Zeph 1:8; 3:3; and Ezek 22:27.

Yahweh reasserts divine power when Jeremiah names Nebuchadnezzar the
Lord's servant and Yahweh's instrument in leading Judah to exile.

A major power shift takes place after the Exile. Israel's Shepherd-King had
been replaced. Yahweh would shepherd the people since the kings had shown
themselves devouring shepherds (Ezek 34); Yahweh would again reign as King
(Zeph 3:15).

In fact, Israel's post-exilic community developed into a theocracy; priests
replaced the king as Israel's leaders. One needs to note here only the books of
Ezra and Nehemiah and the priestly editing of the Pentateuch. Membership
in the covenant community had become, more than ever, the basis of national
identity.

It is here that the canonical Old Testament effectively ends. Though the
Roman Catholic tradition claims the canonicity of 1 and 2 Maccabees, their
theology, including that relating to power, is at best obscure. For all practical
purposes, the leadership of Israel is now in the hands of the official religionists,
and that is precisely where we find it in the New Testament.

Power in the New Testament

The New Testament strongly reaffirms the absolute power of God. (e.g.,
1 Cor 2:5; 2 Cor 4:7; 13:4; Rom 1:20; Mk 9:1; 12:24; Mt 22:29; 26:64; Lk
1:35; Acts 1:7). Therefore, the relationship of God to people is often depicted
as one of Master-Servant, especially in several parables. Happy is the servant who

is found at his or her task when the master comes (Mk 12:35-38; Mt 24:45).
Happy the servant who used her or his talents well (Matt 25:16ff.; Lk 19:12-27).
Even the servants who arrive at the twelfth hour will be amply rewarded (Mt
20:1-13) while those who mismanage and act cruelly toward what is entrusted
to them — the wicked husbandman and the unmerciful servant, for example —
will be punished.

The literature of the New Testament[6] also presents a Palestine in which
political power is held by Rome and religious power by contending groups,
including the pharisees and the saducees.

We derive from the texts, first of all, an understanding of political power as
delegated by God and exercised for the purpose of insuring good conduct:
Paul tells the Romans:

> Let every one be subject
> to the governing authorities.
> For there is no authority except from God,
> and those that exist have been instituted
> by God. Therefore,
> the one who resists the authority
> resists what God has appointed, and
> those who resist will incur judgment.
> For rulers are not a terror to good conduct,
> but to bad.
> Would you have fear
> of the one who is in authority?
> Then do what is good and
> you will receive approval,
> that one is God's servant for your good.
> But if you do wrong, be afraid,
> for the person does not
> bear the sword in vain;
> the person is the servant of God
> to execute God's wrath on the wrongdoer.
>
> Therefore one must be subject
> not only to avoid God's wrath
> but also for the sake of conscience.
> For the same reason you also pay taxes,
> for the authorities are ministers of God,
> attending to this very thing.
> Pay all of them their dues, taxes to whom
> taxes are due, revenue to whom

revenue is due, respect to whom
respect is due, honor to whom
honor is due.

(Rom 13:1-7)

In both Mark's and Matthew's gospels, in answer to a question about the appropriateness of Jesus' disciples paying taxes, Jesus responds, "Render to Caesar the things that are Caesar's, as well as to God the things that are God's" (Mk 12:17; Mt 16:13). And John's gospel names Pilate's power over Jesus as given from God (Jn 19:10-11). Though these last texts from Mark, Matthew, and John are consistent with Paul's extensive exhortation to the Romans, one may conclude that the Pauline text was occasioned by the peculiar circumstances of Jewish Christians in Rome.[7]

Yet the passage from Romans has been used, more than any other biblical text, to legitimate persons in power. Matthew's infancy narrative, in contrast, describes this delegated political power abused: Herod slaughters the male children in Bethlehem and seeks to kill Jesus.

When one turns to the religious leadership of first century Palestine as portrayed in the New Testament[8] one again sees delegated power gone astray. The Law, which had originally functioned as a guarantor of monotheism and a guideline for the exercise of justice, had degenerated into countless human traditions, the observance of which was a way of gaining prominence and influence, that is to say, power, in the religious community. It is this avenue to power among the religious leadership which Jesus condemns. They worshiped God in vain; in truth, they were honoring themselves. As Matthew, for example, points out, "They taught as precepts of God merely human doctrines" (Mt 15:8-9); they were "blind guides" (Mt 15:14; 23:16); they tithed, but they neglected justice, and mercy, and faith, the weightier matters of the law (Mt 23:23).

Moreover, the pharisees did not practice what they preached (Mt 23:2-4). They did all their deeds to be seen by other people; they loved to stand and pray in the synagogues and at the street corners, that they might be seen (Mt 6:5); they looked dismal and disfigured their faces when they fasted, to be seen (vs. 16); they made their phylacteries broad and their fringes long, and they loved the places of honor at feasts and the best seats in the synagogues and salutations in the market places, and being called rabbi. Pretending to lead people to God, they intended to lead people to themselves! Is this a New Testament version of idolatry?

Luke points to this sense of self-righteousness and false superiority when he tells the parable of the two men who go to pray in the temple (18:9-14). The men, a pharisee and a publican, experience themselves very differently and this difference is reflected in their prayer. The one, knowing his dependence on God and his unworthiness, remains at a distance and prays for God's mercy.

The other, an arrogant pharisee, no doubt influential in the society, protests his worthiness.

Jesus warned, too, against false prophets. They came in sheep's clothing, but inwardly were ravenous wolves. Just as grapes cannot be gathered from thorns or figs from thistles, neither can healthy fruit be produced on rotten trees. The quality of the fruit indicates the health of the tree (Mt 7:15-20)!

Jesus condemned all abuse of prestige and delegated power with a reordering of the power structure: the greatest is the servant; whoever exalts herself or himself will be humbled, while who ever humbles herself or himself will be exalted (Mt 23:5-12).

The power which Jesus brings is very different. His is the power of God to forgive sins (Mk 2:10; Mt 1:21; 9:6; Lk 5:24; Jn 1:29); this power he shares with those who would follow him (Mt 6:12; 18:22; Lk 11:4; 17:3-4).

Just as Jesus' power liberates from the bondage of sin, it frees, too, from the bondage of pain. The Christian communities of Matthew's gospel, for example, record that he cured a leper (Mt 8:3) and a centurion's paralyzed son (vs. 6); he relieved the fever from Peter's mother-in-law (vs. 15) and expelled devils from two men possessed (vs. 30). He cured another paralyzed man (9:2) and raised the daughter of a synagogue official back to life (vs. 18). He stopped a woman's hemorrhage (vs. 20) and restored sight to two blind men (vs. 27). He cast out another devil (vs. 31), restored a man's withered arm (12:10), and restored the speech and sight of a man blind and dumb (vs. 22). Jesus cured the possessed daughter of a Canaanite woman (15:28), an epileptic (17:16), and another blind man (20:34). Though the healing described in these episodes is a physical one, the texts are symbolic of Jesus' power and his willingness to use it for good.[9] The historical certitude of the miracles is of far less importance than the fact that the early Christians remembered Jesus as a man whose power was always put at the service of the suffering and oppressed. The power of Jesus is re-creating; there are no traces here of domination and control. Delegated by his Father (1 Cor 1:24; Mt 9:8; 28:18; Jn 17:2; Acts 10:38), Jesus' power stands in judgment on the perverted power of the pharisees. And the power which Jesus delegates to those who would follow him is "for building up and not for tearing down" (2 Cor 13:10).[10]

But the New Testament evidence is complex. The letter to the Philippians represents Jesus, the fullness of the revelation of God (cf. Jn 1:1,14; 14:9), as choosing to forego power and calling those who would believe in him to do likewise:

> Your attitude must be that of Christ:
> Though he was in the form of God,
> he did not deem equality with God
> something to be grasped at. Rather,

> he emptied himself
> and took the form of a slave,
> being born in the likeness of humans.
> He was known to be of human estate and
> it was thus that he humbled himself,
> obediently accepting even death,
> death on a cross.
>
> (Phil 2:5-8)

Jon Sobrino comments, "There came a time for Jesus when his all-conquering power — that power which symbolized his mastery over the negative powers operative in the world — was not enough to get across the message that God is love in a concrete historical situation where sin and injustice triumphed. The sin-ridden concrete situation robbed Jesus of his power — except for the power of truth, the power to sacrifice his life for others out of love"[11] (cf. Col 2:15; Jn 10:18).

The New Testament literature records also, however, that hierarchical structures emerged in early Christian communities. Though the Acts of the Apostles refers frequently to the "apostles and elders" (for example, 15:2,4,6,22-23; 16:4), these terms so used do not necessarily imply hierarchy. In fact, Luke describes all those who believed as being "together" and "having all things in common" and selling their possessions and goods and distributing them to the needy (cf. Mk 10:21; Mt 19:21), and attending the temple together and breaking bread in their homes and praising God and having favor among the people (Acts 2:44-47). There is no mention here of hierarchy. Those who believed were a company, of one heart and one soul, no one claiming personal possessions but everybody sharing everything with the others. The function of the apostles was to testify to Jesus' resurrection. No one was needy in the community because the "have's" shared with the "have not's" (Acts 4:32-35).

However, both the letters to the Ephesians and to the Colossians, attributed to Paul though their true authorship is unknown, presume some kind of hierarchical order between husbands and wives, parents and children, masters and slaves (Eph 5:21-6:9; Col 3:18-25). Yet each of these relationships bears mutual responsibilities: there is no partiality with God.

The Pastorals, especially the so-called letters of Paul to Timothy and to Titus, also presume a hierarchical structure in their exhortations regarding appropriate attitudes and behavior for the elders (Tit 1:5-9), the bishops (1 Tim 3:3-7), and the deacons (1 Tim 3:8-23). The Philippian letter also alludes to the existence of elders and bishops in its greeting (Phil 1:1). What the "powers" of this community leadership were, we, in fact, do not know. Their appointment may have been by the participatory will of the community. Those whose authority came from first proclaiming the gospel to the community may have functioned as the group's representatives in ratifying the communities' choices of leadership.

Summary of Power from a Biblical Perspective

Summarizing all this evidence, and what is presented here is only part of the story but consistent with the whole, one discovers that the Old Testament presents power as good — in creation, the promise of land, of progeny, of prosperity, and of deliverance from slavery. Delegated power is also good; one thinks of the leadership of Moses, Joshua, the judges, David, Hezekiah, and Josiah. However, delegated power which does not recognize Yahweh's supremacy, and act in accord with God's law, is sinful; the kings of Israel and the kings of Judah abused power and perverted justice by practicing idolatry, by trusting in foreign alliances instead of in Yahweh, and by disregarding the rights of widows, orphans, and the oppressed of their society.

The Lord was constantly testifying to the divine power, by the warnings of the prophets, by Josiah's restoration of Covenant Law, and eventually, by the Exile. Yet the Lord's power which banished Israel was also the power which recreated the people, as the effective word of Second-Isaiah promised; the priests became the new delegates of Yahweh's power.

But the gospel testimony regarding the pharisees details that, here again, delegated power became perverted. Jesus confronted this abuse of power, and for that he would die. Yet Jesus had the power of his Father,[12] the power to bring justice, the power to overcome death, the power of his Spirit (for example, Lk 4:1,14; Mt 3:16); it is this power which Jesus delegated to those who would follow him.

From the biblical texts studied historically and linguistically, therefore, one can conclude that power is meant to be exercised for justice and for good, faithful to the Source of power.

But because power can and has become perverted, the "king" cannot be trusted "just because" he is king; the "prophet" cannot be trusted "just because" he claims to be a prophet; nor can the "priest" be trusted "just because" he is priest. Delegated power is never absolute. Its legitimacy must constantly be tested against greater criteria: fidelity to God and God's call to justice!

Alternatives and the Restructuring of Power

One might think that the conclusions reached in the first part of this paper are quite sound and applicable today. But victims of the perverted use of power, as well as oppressors, must go further. As Americans, we participate in a powerful political structure, which many consider directly delegated by God (one recalls the new "Promised Land" imagery or the "Right Reverend Ronald Reagan's" speech to Evangelicals),[13] a structure which presumes the superiority of this nation over others, a structure which even justifies the domination, manipulation, and control of others, in the name of national security. And yet Roman Catholic women — like all non-clerics — are devoid of power, lacking the possibility of participation in the Church's policy-making; female inferiority and incompetence are taken for granted.

And so it becomes necessary to look now at biblical perspectives on justice. The Old Testament repeatedly affirms God's concern for the powerless and for the oppressed:

> In God the orphan finds mercy.
> (Hos 14:4)

> The Lord shows no partiality
> and takes no bribes.
> God executes justice for the fatherless,
> and the widow, and loves the sojourner,
> giving her or him food and clothing.
> (Dt 10:17-18)

> The Lord watches over the sojourners
> and upholds the widow
> and the fatherless.
> (Ps 146:9)

> The Lord is a stronghold
> for the oppressed.
> (Ps 9:10)

Similar assurances of God's benevolence toward the weak and forlorn can be found in Jud 9:11; Ps 10:18; 103:6; 146:7; and Job 34:28.

Moreover, the Old Testament literature also asserts the responsibility of the community, including the leadership, toward the powerless and oppressed of the society. The powerless, that is, the widows, the orphans, the aliens in the land, are the very ones by which Israel's fidelity to God is measured.

> O house of David! Thus says the Lord:
> Execute justice in the morning,
> and deliver from the hand of the oppressor
> the person who is robbed . . .
> (Jer 21:12)

> Is not this what I require of you as a fast:
> to loose the fetters of injustice,
> sharing food with the hungry,

taking homeless poor into your house,
clothing the naked . . .
(Is 58:6-7)

She or he who oppressed a poor person
insults her or his Maker,
but the one who is kind to the needy
honors God.
(Prov 14:31)

Incline your ear to the poor,
and answer them peaceably and gently.
Deliver one who is wronged from the hand of the
wrongdoer, and do not be fainthearted
in judging a case.
Be like a father to orphans,
and instead of a husband to their mother . . .
(Sir 4:9-10)

One need mention here, in addition, only Exod 22:21; 23:11; Dt 24:12,14-15, 17,19-21; and 27:19, but the texts are legion.[14] The Lord's servant according to Second Isaiah, the one who is God's chosen, is precisely the one who bears others' misery and suffering, others' afflictions and torments; it is through the servant that others are healed (Is 53:4-5). Finally, the servant is the one who will faithfully bring forth justice to the nations (42:1-4).[15]

Is it any wonder then that Luke begins his gospel with Jesus' announcement that he has come to "preach good news to the poor, to proclaim release to the captives and sight to the blind, and to set at liberty the oppressed . . ." (Lk 4:18; cf. Mt 11:4-6; 12:17-21; Lk 7:21-22). Matthew tells us that whoever gives a cup of cold water to any one of the lowly will not lose his or her reward (10:42). Further, Matthew's criteria for the great judgment are expressed explicitly in terms of the oppressed: food and drink for the hungry and thirsty, clothing for the naked, welcoming for the stranger, visiting for the sick and the prisoner (Mt 25:35f.).

But one cannot ignore the re-orientation of power to which other biblical texts refer. A radical restructuring is implied which takes those who are subordinate, those who are dominated, and raises them in stature. The Lord saves lowly people but brings down the haughty (2 Sam 22:28; Ps 18:28; 138:6). The Lord raises the lowly to the heights (Job 5:11). God raises them from the dust and lifts the needy from the ash heap (Ps 113:7; cf. 1 Sam 2:8). The bows of the mighty are broken, but the feeble gird on strength (1 Sam 2:4). And the New Covenant which Jeremiah promises is one by which all, from the least to the greatest, will know the Lord (Jer 31:34).

The New Testament writers pick up the threads of this reordering of hierarchical power and make it an integral part of Jesus' person and an essential part of Jesus' teaching.

Jesus' own personal relationships, as the evangelists describe them, are non-hierarchical. He is among them as one who serves (Lk 22:24); in fact, he washes their feet (Jn 13:13-15); he calls them not servants but friends (Jn 15:15). Moreover, many with whom he associates are social outcasts – publicans, tax collectors, and sinners (Mt 9:10; Mk 2:15; Lk 15:1). He names Matthew an apostle (Mt 9:9) and eats in Zaccheus' home (Lk 19:1-18). He shows no less regard to the Samaritan woman at the well (Jn 4) than to the prestigious pharisee, Nicodemus (Jn 3).

In chapter 12 of the first letter to the Corinthians, Paul assures the members of the community that, though they have different gifts, it is the same Holy Spirit who empowers them all. Though their functions in the community are diverse, they all serve the same Lord. It is the same God who inspires them all in the varieties of work which they do. Their source of unity, therefore, is far superior to their diversities; the differences are not a source of hierarchy. His comparison with the human body further illustrates this point. It is the parts of the body which seem to be weaker which are, in fact, indispensable, and the parts we think less honorable that we invest with greater honor (vs. 22). God has so adjusted the body as to give greater honor to the inferior part precisely to prevent discord in the body and to guarantee that the members may have the same care for one another. If one member suffers, all suffer together; if one member is honored, all rejoice together (vs. 24).[16]

In this same letter Paul understands resurrection as "the end, when Christ delivers the kingdom to God his Father after destroying every rule and every authority and every power." Paul looks toward a time when all creation is subject to Christ and Christ subject to God, "that God may be everything to everyone" (1 Cor 15:24-30; cf. Col 2:10; Eph 1:21).

The author of Colossians envisions as a goal of Christian community the non-hierarchical relationships between people which Paul had intimated: "If you have been raised with Christ, seek the things that are above and set your mind on the things which are above . . . . Put to death passions and evil desires and covetousness, which is idolatry. Here there cannot be Greek and Jew, circumcized, and uncircumcized, barbarian, Scythian, slave, free, but Christ is all, and in all" (3:1-11).

Mark's gospel asserts that anyone who would be first must be the last of all and the servant of all. Competition with one another among the members of the community to outdo the other, to outrank the others, has no place among those who would follow Jesus. In fact, it is the one who caters to the child rather than to the influential of society who receives Jesus (Mk 9:34-35). Many who are now first will be last, and the last first (Mk 10:31); that one who would be great among the people must be the servant, and the one who would be first must be the slave of all (Mk 10:43-44).

Matthew's and Luke's gospels reiterate this same teaching.[17] The Lord has put down the mighty from their thrones and has exalted the lowly (Lk 1:52; cf. Mt 11:25). It is the lowly who will inherit the earth (Mt 5:5). In answer to his disciples' query regarding the greatest in the kingdom of heaven, Jesus responds that whoever humbles herself or himself like a child is the greatest in the kingdom of heaven (Mt 18:1; Lk 9:46-8). "Many that are first will be last, and the last first" (Mt 19:30; Lk 13:30).

The parable of the laborers in the vineyard is about this same reversal; those who arrived last to work received their wages first, to signify that the last will be first; whoever would be great among Jesus' disciples must serve the needs of all (Mt 20:8,16,27).

Many of the parables,[18] in fact, are precisely about a reversal of the traditional hierarchical structures. One need mention only the parable of the Good Samaritan, where official religious leadership is replaced by the religious outcast (Lk 10:29-36), or the parable of the Rich Man and Lazarus, where abused economic prosperity leads to hell and abject poverty, to the bosom of Abraham (Lk 16:20-23), or the parable of the Pharisee and the Publican which, again, effectively displaces traditional religious leadership (Lk 18:9-14), or the parable of the Wedding Banquet, where the invited guests are replaced by the "sojourner" (Mt 22:2-10), or the parable of the Prodigal Son, where the seemingly less-deserving younger son is rewarded (Lk 15:11-24). Another parable of a vineyard explains that tax collectors and harlots will enter the kingdom of heaven before the chief priests and elders (Mt 21:28-32). Of the ten lepers cured only a foreigner, a Samaritan, returned to give thanks (Lk 17:18).

Nor can we ignore such texts as Matthew's which instructs Jesus' disciples to call no one father since they have only one father, who is in heaven. Nor are any of them to be called masters, for they have one master, Christ. The one who is greatest among them is the servant; the one who exalts herself or himself is the one who will be humbled, whereas the one who humbles herself or himself is the one who will be exalted (23:9-11; cf. Lk 14:11).

Luke deals with this same temptation for power, understood as over others, in his account of Jesus' last supper. There Jesus tells his disciples that whereas the kings of the Gentiles exercise lordship over their subjects and their subjects regard the kings as benefactors, it is not to be that way among them. The greatest among them is to become as the youngest, and the leader as one who serves. One normally expects that the one who sits at table is greater than the one who serves. And yet, Jesus, their example *par excellence,* is among them as one who serves (Lk 22:24; cf. Mt 20:25-28).

Even the Master-Servant relationship between God and the people is transformed. We are no longer slaves but children and heirs (Gal 4:6-8; cf. Jn 1:12).

In Christ Jesus we are all children of God. There is neither Jew nor Greek, there is neither slave nor free, there is neither male nor female (Gal 3:26,28; cf. Rom 10:12).

Conclusion

A study of power in the biblical texts has rendered an understanding of its Source, and its purpose, and how delegated power is to be exercised in the service of justice and good conduct. However, the power which the biblical texts describe is always a hierarchical one due to the patriarchal culture which produced the texts. Once one has admitted this cultural bias, however, one must move beyond that context and worldview to a more adequate interpretation of justice and the locus of power for our times. Both the Old Testament's concern for the liberation of the oppressed, and the New Testament's reversals of traditional hierarchical structures demand that believers work to abolish those structures in society and in the churches which support the superiority, influence, and power of one nation, one race, one sex, or one class over another, the patriarchal and hierarchical structures which breed domination and control rather than equality and services, mutual cooperation, shared responsibility and freely-chosen interdependence.

Just as the works of mercy were for too long interpreted as expressions of personal generosity rather than as demands for systemic change, so also for too long have the hierarchical-patriarchal biases of the biblical texts been interpreted as atemporal, and the reversal texts been understood as directed only to individuals rather than to structures. For too long have they been merely a call to humility or an affirmation of the relativity of delegated power; that they well may be. But I am convinced they hold more: in them lies a vision of a peace-filled global village and a truly just Church.

NOTES

1. E.g., Bernard Anderson, *Understanding the Old Testament*, 3rd ed., (Englewood Cliffs, New Jersey: Prentice-Hall, Inc., 1975); John H. Hayes, *An Introduction to Old Testament Study* (Nashville: Abingdon Press, 1979); H. Jagersma, *A History of Israel in the Old Testament Period* (Philadelphia: Fortress Press, 1983); Eugene H. Merrill, *An Historical Survey of the Old Testament* (Grand Rapids: Baker Book House, 1966); James King West, *Introduction to the Old Testament*, 2nd ed. (New York: Macmillan Publishing Co., Inc., 1981).

2. I am very much indebted to the work of Elisabeth Schüssler Fiorenza, especially *In Memory of Her* (New York: Crossroad, 1983), for historical reconstruction of Christian origins.

3. This paper on power and justice emerged out of several situations which have recently touched my life and work: a Lenten talk I gave to a parish on power and powerlessness; a comment made by Sandra Schneiders at the 1982 CTSA meeting ("I regard it as a fact that the male hierarchy and women in the Church are involved in a power struggle!"); and finally, an article by Paul Hansen, "God Metaphors and Sexism in the Old Testament," *Ecumenical Review*, 27 (Oct., 1975), 316-324 which does acknowledge the biblical texts' patriarchal biases and looks to the prophetic proclamations of justice for the vindication of the oppressed, especially women.

4. Cf. Jer 2:26-27.

5. The Revised Standard Version is, for the most part, the translation used throughout this paper. Occasionally, for the sake of inclusive language, the translation is the author's own.

6. A careful historical approach to this literature moves through Paul to Mark, and then to the other synoptics, and finally to John, taking into consideration the redactional activity within each of the texts. However, for our purposes, such a careful scrutiny of the time frame and circumstances of each of the texts is unnecessary, since the same complementary attitudes toward power are present in most of the first century literature.

7. When one notes the verses which follow Rom 13:1-7, "Owe no one anything except to love him or her . . .," one suspects that, in that particular historical situation, subservience was the most appropriate form of love.

8. This picture differs widely from how the pharisees are depicted by Josephus and the rabbinic tradition. Cf. J.M. Cook, "Jesus and the Pharisees," *Journal of Ecumenical Studies* 15 (1978), 441-460; J. Neusner, *From Politics to Piety*, (Englewood Cliffs, New Jersey: Prentice-Hall, 1973). However, it is the literary statement of the New Testament with which we are here concerned.

9. Cf. Lk 4:36; 5:17.

10. Cf. Rom 5:13,19; Mk 3:15; 6:7; Mt 28:18; Lk 9:1; 10:19; 24:49; Acts 3:12; 4:7.

11. Jon Sobrino, *Christology at the Crossroads*, (Maryknoll, New York: Orbis Press, 1978), p. 359.

12. See the related article by Bernard Cooke, "Non-Patriarchal Salvation," *Horizons*, 10 (Spring, 1983), 22-31.

13. *Time Magazine*, February 7, 1983.

14. Additional texts include Prov 22:16; Ezek 18:12; Job 29:12; 31:16; and Sir 10:7.

15. Similar texts include Is 33:15; Jer 7:7; Ezek 18:7,16; 45:9; and Is 58:9.

16. The verses which follow have been interpreted so as to legitimate a hierarchical model i.e., "apostles first, second prophets, third teachers, and then . . . ," but one recognizes in

what follows immediately that love is the "highest gift." This seems to be Paul's consistent judgment of hierarchical structures. (The same exhortation to love occurs after the hierarchical description in Rom 13!)

17. I recognize that these texts may be derived from a common tradition but that has no bearing on this presentation. In fact, the very fact that each gospel writer repeats the tradition highlights the importance of this posture among the early Christian communities.

18. Cf. Dominic Crossan, *In Parables: The Challenge of the Historical Jesus* (New York: Harper and Row, 1973).

KINGDOM SPEAKING AND KINGDOM HEARING: MATTHEW'S INTERPRETATION OF JESUS' KINGDOM TRADITION

Gary A. Phillips

Have you understood all this? They said to him, "Yes." And he said to them "Therefore every scribe who has been trained for the Kingdom of Heaven is like a householder who brings out of his treasure what is new and what is old."

—Mt. 13:52[1]

Rabbi Akiba he called a "well-stocked storehouse." To what might Rabbi Akiba be likened? To a laborer who took his basket and went forth . . .[2]

—Rabbi Judah the Prince

With Jesus' brief question and parable of the scribe (Mt 13:50-52), the first evangelist brings to a close the third of five major discourses by Jesus in the gospel, the central Parables Discourse on the Kingdom. Having begun by addressing four kingdom parables to the crowd, Jesus turns mid-way through the discourse (v. 36) from the crowd to the disciples, now his exclusive audience, and offers three more kingdom parables. At the end of his discourse Jesus asks in a twofold manner whether they have understood what his parable speaking has been all about. First, he puts the question, "Have you understood all of this?"; then he offers a parable that equates the successful hearer or "scribe trained for the kingdom of heaven"[3] with a "householder who brings out of his treasure what is new and what is old."

For the most part, critical discussion of the scribe and accompanying parables in the Parables Discourse has concentrated attention on the form and function of the individual parables or on the development of the parables in Chapter 13. Form critics attempt to locate the kingdom parables within the context of Jesus' prophetic ministry,[4] while tradition critics seek to describe the interpretive forces that led the early Church to allegorize and ultimately moralize Jesus' prophetic words.[5] It has been left to redaction critics to describe the overall structure of the chapter as a discourse[6] and to offer an explanation of the historical significance of the evangelist's consistent presentation of Jesus as rabbi engaged in midrash upon Pentateuchal and Mosaic traditions.

Recent redaction criticism has seen in the change of audience from crowd to disciples in v. 36 and in the concluding scribe parable concerning the disciples' interpretive competence — a parable which, we will argue, differs in significant ways from the other seven kingdom parables in the discourse — a key for understanding Matthew's theological purpose.[7] Jesus' change in audience is taken as narrative evidence of a redirection on the part of Matthew's early Christian community away from an exclusively Jewish mission to one that is open to and encompasses all nations (Mt 28:19). From this perspective, what is new and what is old in 13:52 signifies two different audiences within the scheme of salvation history, two successive if not conflicting missions during the crisis period that followed upon the destruction of the Temple.[8] The larger historical context proposed for the missionizing redirection in the Parables Discourse and for the gospel as a whole is that of rabbinic and Jewish-Christian communities locked in a post-Temple destruction interpretive battle over the true understanding of Jewish tradition, namely the meaning of Torah. This conflicting relationship is reflected not only in the acute anti-pharisaic tone of the gospel (especially Chapter 23), but is most dramatically presented in Jesus' Sermon on the Mount Discourse. Here Jesus says in formulaic terms regarding the Law, "You have heard it was said . . . but I say to you . . ." (cf. 5:17, 27, 31, 33, 38, and 43).[9] Scholars identify the parties to the conflict between the Mosaic interpretation of Torah and Jesus' interpretation of Torah as Jamnian Jews who, like Ezra and the scribes some six centuries before, are engaged in building an interpretive "fence around Torah."[10] On the other side are Matthean Jewish-Christians who, following the interpretive strategy laid down by Jesus some two generations before, propose a revision of Torah and alteration to the tradition and Torah's place within it.

For purposes of this essay, however, we would focus the critical attention in a somewhat different way upon Matthew's Parables Discourse to see what it has to say about the relationship of tradition to interpretation. What we will say about the traditional questions of textual form, rhetorical function, or historical context of the discourse then will be informed by an understanding of the dialectical relationship between tradition and interpretation in rabbinic Judaism.[11] From this critical vantage point, the Parables Discourse emerges as an effort on the part of the evangelist to engage the reader/hearer in a dialogue with Jesus' interpretation of the Kingdom tradition in its parabolic form.

Our strategy will first be to describe the rabbinic understanding of the relationship between tradition and text, focussing in particular upon the distinctive relationship of Torah to commentary upon Torah. For this purpose we will rely upon Gershom Scholem's essay on revelation and tradition as religious categories in Jewish thought. Secondly, we will discuss the distinctive parabolic tradition associated with Jesus, namely his peculiar way of speaking in parables about the kingdom of heaven. On the basis of Scholem's categories, we will propose an explanation of the way Matthew appropriates and reinterprets the tradition of Jesus' speaking in parables about the kingdom in Matthew 13. Our contention is that Matthew transforms the tradition about Jesus by providing a model for continued speaking and hearing of the Kingdom parables on the part of the Gospel reader. Finally, we will conclude with some observations about the significance of the rabbinic understanding of interpretation for the contemporary reader that underscore the ongoing dialectical and textual character of tradition and interpretation.

Revelation, Tradition, and Interpretation in Rabbinic Thought

In his book of collected essays entitled *The Messianic Idea in Judaism and Other Essays Upon Jewish Spirituality*,[12] Gershom Scholem offers a provocative essay, "Revelation and Tradition as Religious Categories in Judaism." In this essay, he proposes an explanation of the relationship between revelation and tradition and the importance of interpreting Torah in rabbinic Judaism. Scholem contends that the rabbinic understanding of revelation and of Torah underwent a significant development over the period of six centuries extending from the fourth century B.C.E. to the second century of the common era. Initially, revelation was understood to be "the concrete communication of positive, substantive and expressible content,"[13] a content set down in written form in Holy Scripture or Torah. By the end of this time, a dramatic change in understanding had taken place. Revelation was now viewed as comprising "everything that will ever be legitimately offered to interpret its meaning,"[14] and Torah was understood to include not only written texts but oral texts and commentary upon both oral and written texts ss well. It was over this period of time that tradition became established as an important religious category. Scholem suggests that under the pressure of changing historical circumstance renewed expressions of God's revelation in Torah were called for and that what was viewed as both revelation and Torah grew to include these new interpretations in the form of oral and written texts.[15] This expansion of the notion of revelation in Torah beyond its original scope thus signaled the birth of tradition as the embodiment of the "realization of the effectiveness of the revelatory Word in every concrete state and relationship entered into by a soeiety."[16] Tradition is neither fixed nor complete. Tradition is more than

> the totality of that which the community possesses as its cultural patrimony and which it bequeathes to its posterity; it is a specific selection from this patrimony, which is elevated and garbed with religious authority. It proclaims certain things, sentences, or insights to be Torah, and thus connects them with the revelation. In the process, the original meaning of revelation as a unique, positively established, and clearly delineated realm of propositions is put in

doubt — and thus a development as fruitful as it is unpredictable
begins which is highly instructive for the religious problematic of
the concept of tradition.[17]

Two important conclusions are to be drawn from Scholem's argument. First,
revelation and tradition stand in a complementary and dynamic relationship;
revelation and its concrete expression in the written Torah calls for tradition in
the form of further interpretation to unfold and to disclose the significance of
the revelation of the Holy One within history. Secondly, and perhaps more
importantly, tradition itself acquires a religious authority of its own. The very
existence of tradition as authoritative corollary to revelation in Torah challenges
the notion of a single, self-evident, and univocal expression of revelation; revelation
is manifold in form and changing in content.

As a vehicle for the continuing revelation of God, tradition continues to
unfold Torah in the form of new interpretation. This dynamic relationship of
revelation to tradition is to be seen in the relationship of oral interpretation
to written text.[18] The notion of what constitutes Torah expands to include
both written and oral Torah (Mishnah); whether written or oral in form, ancient
or modern in origin, Torah is Torah. Like written Torah upon which it is based,
Torah in its oral form as interpretation possesses revelatory power for Judaism
as a word which illumines, interprets, or otherwise expands the meaning of
God's revelation in Torah. Mishnah thus continues the revelatory Word found
in the canonical texts as part of a tradition that "turns revelation," as the
Talmud puts it, "Turn it [revelation] and twist it again, for everything is in it."[19]
And Mishnaic commentary upon oral Torah enters into the tradition and becomes
a means by which revelation continues to address new audiences in new historical
situations. In language that brings to mind the scribe parable in Mt 13:50 Scholem
remarks:

> Out of the religious tradition they bring something entirely new,
> something that itself commands religious dignity: commentary.
> Revelation needs commentary in order to be rightly understood
> and applied.[20]

The rabbinic understanding of revelation and tradition operates, however,
with an inner tension. On the one hand, tradition, which includes oral Torah
and subsequent commentary upon Torah, is part of an incomplete process of
revelation; on the other hand, revelation already includes within itself as sacred
tradition all subsequent interpretation. In characterizing this "patently absurd
position," Scholem says in paradoxical terms that "Revelation comprises everything that will ever be legitimately offered to interpret its meaning."[21] All later
interpretaion, including even that which conflicts with previously written Torah,

was given to Moses at Mt. Sinai. As Rabbi Joshua ben Levi is reported to have said, "Torah, Mishnah, Talmud and Aggadah — indeed even the comments some bright student will one day make to his teacher — were already given to Moses on Mount Sinai."[22]

What makes this so-called "fiction" possible is the view that "truth is given once and for all, and it is laid down with precision. Fundamentally, truth merely needs to be transmitted" . . . "everything that can come to be known has already been deposited in a timeless substratum . . . ."[23] In contrast to Hellenistic modes of thinking,[24] Rabbinic thought does not conceive of revelation in transcendental and systemic categories but rather in historical and textual forms, as commentary, as new interpretation. To use a term current in contemporary literary criticism, tradition is an instance of "intertextuality," an unending process of text in relation to text in relation to text. Tradition is to be seen as a "living organism,"

> . . . concerned with the realization, the enactment of the divine task which is set in the revelation. It demands application, execution, and decision, and at the same time it is indeed, 'true growth and unfolding from within'.[25]

As the embodiment of revelation in ever-new texts, tradition requires a hearing in order to succeed. A hearing, however, can take either of two forms. On the one hand, the hearer can function as a mere receptacle of preserved tradition (i.e., of previous texts and interpretations), one who does not actively augment the tradition in any way with his/her own questions and experiences. Tradition for this type of hearer is petrified and closed. On the other hand, the hearer can press the tradition in and through his/her questioning, thereby making "Torah concrete at the point where he stands . . . Applicable *hic at nunc,* fashioning his specific form of concretization in such a manner that it may be transmitted. . . ."[26] Tradition demands this second type of active, dialectical hearing that is responsive to previous interpretation out of a present, concrete historical moment. By its nature idiosyncratic and argumentative, tradition engages in a revelatory function through dialogue of past with present in an oftentimes conflicting extension of oral and written commentary upon Torah. In this way, tradition can be seen as "the force within which contradiction and tensions are not destructive but rather stimulating and creative."[27] For example, even though Hillel interpretation comes to be considered decisive, the contradictory Shammai commentary is nevertheless preserved with great care. Tradition is a unity of conflicting interpretations.

Scholem thus exposes within the historical development of rabbinic Judaism two major tensions inherent within the rabbinic understanding of revelation, tradition, and interpretation. First, the notion that revelation is "consistently unified and self-enclosed" gives way to a view in which it becomes diversified, multifold, and full of contradictions; the content of revelation is in the process of development. A second tension is present in the conflict of texts and inter- pretations which takes the form of commentary within the tradition. The varied possibilities for interpreting written Torah and giving expression to the truth about the Word are all contained and preserved within the tradition, namely within Torah itself. Witness, for instance, the interpretive debates between the first century schools of Hillel and Shammai.

In the second part of his essay, Scholem goes on to describe the dynamic power of tradition and the necessarily conflicting character of commentary within the kabbalist tradition ("kabbalah" means "receiving the tradition"). It is Scholem's concern to show the connection between kabbalist thinking and the dialectical and unfolding dynamic contained within rabbinic thought. Indeed, the kabbalist tradition preserves the very vitality and creative force of rabbinic thought in two respects: first, in the central notion of the Word of God (Torah) as possessing infinite meaing, as being infinitely interpretable; and second, in the understanding of tradition as founded upon the dialectical tension of Torah as at once "absolutely complete" and "simply unfulfillable" revelation.

In summarizing Scholem's arguments we may say the following:

(1) Revelation gives rise to tradition; tradition is an essential outgrowth of and complement to revelation. Tradition is the process by which revelation, codified in the form of Torah, is experienced in ever-different interpretive forms in ever-different historical moments.

(2) Tradition is at one and the same time a process of textual production and the end product of that process. Tradition calls for a dialectical response on the part of the hearer of Torah. Tradition demands renewed interpretation, questioning, and expression to meet new situations. Like revelation, tradition too is unfolding and incomplete.[28] In this way the hearer of the tradition plays an integral role in the unfolding of revelation.

(3) Commentary is the textual manifestation of tradition and a "legitimate form through which truth is approached."[29] Tradition lives in the multiplicity of texts. The productive hearer/scribe of Torah inserts himself/herself within the developing flow of the tradition — what we might call a labyrinth of texts — and through interpretation as commentary unfolds the truth of the Word.

(4) Finally, tradition is a dialectical relationship of text with text. Containing within itself even mutually exclusive interpretations, tradition makes a place for both the orthodox and the heretical, the Hillel and the Shammai. Were it otherwise tradition would be a dead letter, a monologue, silence.

The Kingdom Tradition and the Parables of Jesus

After more than two centuries of investigation into the life of Jesus, contemporary biblical scholarship, for the most part, recognizes that the gospels are not modern-style biographical reports of the life and times of the historical Jesus but kerygmatic expressions of the Church's belief in Jesus as Messiah. As kerygmatic statements, however, the meaning of these narratives about Jesus is properly understood only insofar as they are read as a word about *God* and God's salvific action in history. While the gospel narratives do share certain formal features with the biographical genre of antiquity,[30] their major function is that of restating the good news of God's conclusive, salvific action in history.

One way to speak of the relationship between the gospel narrative and the story of God's saving action in history is in terms of the contrast between "mundane" and "sacred" stories. As mundane stories, the gospels are particular narrative expressions arising at different historical moments for different believing communities. The gospel narratives in this sense are pertinent and peculiar ways of telling the basic story of God's saving presence in history. The sacred story that the gospels as mundane stories give expression to is the controlling foundation myth, to use Norman Perrin's language, of God's creation, revelation, and restoration of history.[31] It is this sacred story that in one form begins with "Hear O Israel; The Lord our God is one Lord" (Dt. 6:4) with its centering of attention upon God that informs, sustains, and directs Jewish consciousness and belief; it is the framework, as it were, within which God's revelation and human history are made sensible. Jewish articulation of that sacred story, however, is never direct and unmediated, but comes to expression necessarily in multifold ways in the narratives of Israel's creation and salvation, in her recounting of the escape from Egypt, in her apocalyptic reflections on a glorious time to come, in Torah and its halakic and haggadic commentary, in its symbols such as "kingdom of God/kingdom of heaven." For Jewish-Christians in particular, the gospel narratives articulate in unique narrative forms the sacred story of God's revelation as king by telling the story of the life, ministry, death, and resurrection of Jesus.

An important outcome, therefore, of the search for the historical Jesus has been the recognition of the historical character of the Gospels themselves as unique expressions of the founding sacred story. This discovery, however, has not put a halt to the search for what is historically ascertainable about Jesus and his message; on the contrary, it has refined that search by placing it upon sound historical-critical footing. Under the scrutiny of historical investigation, the gospel texts, to use an archeological methaphor, disclose the stratified character of the immensely varied materials and traditions that went into their making. With the aid of the criteria of dissimilarity, multiple attestation, and coherence the "bedrock" tradition,[32] if not the actual texts produced by the historical Jesus, is identifiable: that bedrock tradition is the prophetic proclamation of the kingdom of God, and the particular textual form that it takes is the parables of the kingdom.

Source and form criticism of the gospel texts have made an indisputable case that the central theme of Jesus' prophetic message is the coming of the kingdom of God/heaven (cf. Mt 4:23; Mk 1:14-15; Lk 4:42-43).[33] The kingdom of God/ heaven is the apocalyptic language from Israel's tradition that symbolizes the sacred story of God as active and revealing, taking charge of human history and making God present in human affairs. Though the symbol "kingdom of God/ heaven" admits of a static spatial or territorial meaning (e.g., in the sense of God's "realm"), within the preaching of Jesus, this symbolic language appears to have functioned in a much more dynamic way.[34] In this respect, Jesus transmitted the Hebrew sense of *Malkut Shamayim* as God's governance, reign, authority, power, kingly presence. This is the sense of kingdom found in Mt 6:33, "But seek first his kingdom and his righteousness, and all these things shall be yours as well;" and Mt 20:20-21, "Command that these two sons of mine may sit, one at your right hand and one at your left, in your kingdom."

The Hebrew concept of *Malkut Shamayim* is expressed in a variety of traditional images: for instance, as military success (Ps 45:6ff.), political control (Dan 4:3, 34; 7:27), and national reconstruction (Ps 145:11). The significance of the figurative language that explains the symbol becomes clear, however, only when read against the backdrop of the sacred story of God revealed in history as creator, as giver of Torah and the one who definitively transforms human history in the coming of Messiah. Psalm 145:10-13 offers one mundane expression of this sacred story:

> All thy works shall give thanks to
>   thee, O Lord,
> and all thy saints shall bless thee.
> They shall speak of the glory of thy
>   kingdom
> and tell of thy power
> To make known to the sons of men
>   thy mighty deeds,
> and the glorious splendor of thy
>   kingdom.
> Thy kingdom is an everlasting
>   kingdom,
> and thy dominion endures
>   throughout all generations.

The apocalyptic text of Dan 5:25 provides another:

for he is the living God, enduring for ever; his Kingdom shall never
be destroyed, and his dominion shall be to the end. He delivers and
rescues, he works signs and wonders in heaven and on earth . . .

As particular narrative expressions of the symbol "kingdom of God," these
texts invoke Israel's memory of God's acts of creation, sustenance, deliverance,
and salvation — the sacred story — and the recognition of God's kingly presence
in and through them. So too Jesus' prophetic enunciation of the kingdom of
God/heaven in the narrative form of the parables is a reminder of God's dynamic
reign and an interpretation as well of its significance for a new time. In traditional
prophetic style, Jesus, the spokesperson of and for God's eschatological reign,
uses the unusual narrative form of the parable to call Israel's attention to the
past/present/future of God's control.[35] It is the tradition of speaking about
God in parabolic language that the gospel writers inherited and preserved in
their own efforts to express the meaning of God's presence in history.

Jesus' distinctive understanding of the kingdom of God emerges in his
interpretation of the great commandment of Torah in Matthew 22:36-40. In
response to the lawyer's question in v. 36, "Master, which is the greatest
commandment in the Law?," Jesus cites a portion of the Shema (Dt 6:4-6):
"You shall love the Lord your God with all your heart, and with all your soul,
and with all your mind." Jesus continues "And a second like it is you shall love
your neighbor as yourself. On these two commandments depend all the law and
the prophets." Jesus' response to the lawyer's question is interpretation of
Torah in the form of midrash upon the Shema. It is an expression of what it
means to say that "God is one", i.e., the meaning of the story of God's creation
and control. Not only does Jesus stand within the prophetic tradition that
proclaims God as King, he also reflects those very attributes characteristic of the
learner/hearer/scribe of the tradition who actively takes up Torah and extends it
through interpretation. The peculiar nature of Jesus' midrash, however, goes
beyond the mere fact that he reaffirms God's control (i.e., that God is one,
Dt 6:4). What distinguishes this radical affirmation is the way Jesus extends it
to interpret the relationship with the brother and sister. The significance of
"God is one" is that at one and the same time the brother and sister are at the
center too. Commonly regarded as an expression of Jesus' radical love ethic, we
have an indication here of what is meant when Jesus speaks of God as king.

Jesus' message is distinctive not only with respect to its content, the Kingdom
of God, but also with respect to the form of that teaching, namely *en parablais.*
In the Septuagint *parabole* translates the Hebrew word "mashal."[36] Mashal
encompasses a wide variety of literary types, including proverbs (I Sam 24:13),
satire (I Kg 9:7), riddles (Ezek 17:2; Ps 49:4), story or allegory (Ezek 24:2-5).
Similarly, within the Gospel tradition *parabolē* is used in a broad way to
designate metaphors or figurative expressions (Mk 7:14-16), proverbs (Lk 4:23),

story parables (Mt 21:28), example parables (Lk 12:16-21), and allegories (Mt 22:2-14). Hence, when defining the parable form we would do well to remember Stein's advice:

> It might be useful to limit parable to story and example parable, but the New Testament does not do so. It might be more reasonable, on the other hand, to list all similies and metaphors as parables, since every metaphor presupposes a simile, a similitude and a story parable result from the expansion of a simile, and an allegory results from running together several metaphors.[37]

In the case of Jesus' parables of the kingdom, it is not simply his use of the mashal tradition, or his speaking about God as king, or the metaphorical character of his language that sets his speaking apart. What is distinctive is the combination of all three of these elements and the collective impact that they have upon the reader/hearer. Dodd's oft-quoted definition of the parable puts it best:

> At its simplest the parable is a metaphor or simile drawn from nature or common life, arresting the hearer by its vividness or strangeness, and leaving the mind in sufficient doubt about its precise application to tease it into active thought.[38]

Key to the success of the parable's narrative development is the strangeness or oddness that the reader/hearer perceives. Jesus' kingdom parables stand out with respect to the twist that he gives to the events of common life described in the parables and the effectiveness of this distortion in leading the hearer to a perceptual and behaviorial change with regard to his/her understanding of what it means to call God king. Jesus' parables thus work as disturbing narrative expressions of Israel's sacred story.[39]

As we have said before, the use of the mashal tradition by Jesus is not and in and of itself unique. What makes the parable singularly distinctive is its metaphorical use in communicating something about the kingdom of God/heaven. In terms of its imagery, Jesus' kingdom parables stand out because of the commonplace language used to speak of God as king. A cursory look, for instance, at the parables of Matthew 13 shows the following images of the kingdom: harvesting grain (vv. 3b-9), seed growth (vv. 31-32), baking bread (v. 33), weeding fields (vv. 24-30), finding treasure (v. 44), locating merchandise (v. 45), and fishing the sea (vv. 47-50). This language contrasts with traditional honorific language used to describe God's kingly presence (cf. Is 33:22, Ps 145:12-13 as military power and national reconstruction). The congruence of parabolic form and atypical or non-traditional kingdom of God/heaven content lies at the heart of Jesus' kingdom tradition which the gospel writers preserve and historical criticism identifies in clear terms as deriving from the historical Jesus.

From the perspective that we have developed so far, Jesus' prophetic kingdom message stands within the heart of the Jewish tradition both in terms of content of discourse (God's reign as king) and its form *(parabole)*. The unique combination of form and content functions to provide a distinctive mundane story whose narrative action proves to be odd and unexpected. The effect upon the reader/hearer is one of drawing his/her attention through disruption to the "normal" patterns of nature and the common life in the story. The metaphorical effect is thus to say something provocative and unsettling about the expectations, assumptions, language, and tradition ordinarily employed when speaking about God's kingly presence, God as one. For just as the extravagance of an extraordinary harvest, the selling of everything to buy an ordinary treasure, or the impossible catch of every kind of fish does not fit with respect, to ordinary harvesting experience, buying/selling practices, or fishing behavior, so too does the ordinariness or non-traditional character of Jesus' language about God's kingly presence not fit with the normal images, language, and mundane stories traditionally used to describe the sacred story of God's reign. Jesus' parables of the kingdom function iconoclastically to disturb by undermining the tradition of mundane stories about God's kingly presence, all the while making use of traditional symbols and literary forms to do so. In using the kingdom tradition to undermine the tradition about God as king so as to reinterpret what is central to the kingdom tradition, Jesus extends through his interpretation that very tradition, thereby opening it up rather than sealing it off through commentary. In this respect Jesus' kingdom discourse in parables points to an interpretive practice that is suggestive of the later rabbinic understanding of revelation, tradition, and text.

To summarize, in his distinctive understanding and interpretation of the kingdom tradition, Jesus unfolds and continues that very tradition through its displacement, distortion, and critique, through an iconoclastic word about what was then held to be the mundane way of speaking of the kingdom of God/heaven. The gospels preserve Jesus' mundane word as seen in his commentary upon Dt 6:4-5 (cf. Mt 22:36-40) and in different parabolic mundane stories (such as seed harvest, finding treasure, baking bread, etc.) that give expression to the sacred story of God's creative control of and presence within history. Traditional and *atraditional* interpretation are inextricably bound together: mashal with Shema, parable with kingdom symbol, text with text. Indeed, it is the paradoxical and dynamic quality of this relationship that makes Jesus' kingdom proclamation unusual and, as we will see in the case of the evangelist Matthew, authoritative.

Matthew's Interpretation of Jesus' Parabolic Tradition

Redaction criticism has long recognized the influence of Jewish tradition and thought upon the first evangelist.[40] The Jewish provenance of the gospel can be detected in any number of ways, but the most obvious one is the christological presentation of Jesus as Rabbi, the authoritative teacher and interpreter of Torah. We observe this in the contrast between Jesus and Moses over the matter of the interpretation of the Law (Chapters 5-7), the underlying theme of prophetic promise and fulfillment of Scripture (5:17-20), Jesus' overt connection with the Davidic throne and kingship (Chapters 1-3), and Jesus' overt conflict with pharisees over righteous living (Chapter 23). Throughout the gospel Matthew's portrait of Jesus betrays the evangelist's deep familiarity with rabbinic Judaism.

The influence of rabbinic thought and practice upon the evangelist is evident especially in Chapter 13. Jesus' rabbinic stature is established in the opening scene where Jesus is described as sitting (like the great scribes and judges of the past) and speaking to the great crowds gathered about to hear him. Throughout the chapter, Jesus displays his authority not only through his spatial relationship with the crowd and the disciples (vv. 2, 36), but also in his mastery of word, story, and explanation. After enunciating the sower parable (vv. 3b-9) to the crowds and to the disciples who are also present, the disciples ask Jesus to explain why he has chosen parabolic teaching to speak to the crowd (v. 10). Their unstated question, of course, is why he should want to confuse them. Jesus responds in a twofold way by explaining what he has said with the use of scriptural interpretation. He does so first by making appeal to Isaiah the prophet (Is 6:9-10) — "You shall indeed hear but never understand, and you shall indeed see but never perceive. For this people's heart has grown dull, and their ears are heavy of hearing, and their eyes they have closed, lest they should perceive with their eyes, and hear with their ears, and understand with their heart, and turn for me to heal them" (vv. 14-15). Secondly, he offers an allegory of the parable (vv. 18-23) that makes explicit what was hidden, mysterious, and secret about the kingdom of God. The parabolic text is illumined then by way of commentary in two forms — scripture and allegory — through a process that unfolds the meaning of the sower parable narratively as explained by Isaiah's text and Matthew's allegory. The rabbinic intertextual and interpretive practice is clearly evident.

In the remainder of the first half of the chapter Matthew's Jesus offers three additional kingdom parables: the parables of the wheat and tares (vv. 24-30), the mustard seed (vv. 31-32), and the leaven (vv. 34). Immediately following the leaven parable the narrator of the story inserts an interpretive comment into the narrative to explain Jesus' parabolic speaking to both crowd and disciples. Whereas in vv. 11-13 the disciples were the stated beneficiaries of the interpretation regarding Jesus' speaking habits, now in vv. 35-36 the reader of Matthew's text emerges as the direct recipient of the explanation. And as before in Jesus' explanation to the disciples of speaking in parables to the crowd (vv. 10-17), the explanation here also makes appeal to scripture. Jesus spoke *en parabolais* in order to fulfill what was spoken by the prophet:[41] "I will open my mouth in parables. I will utter what has been hidden since the foundation of the world" (v. 35). The similarity in explanation masks an important difference in level of explanation. In the first instance, it is directed to the disciples inside the story, and in the second it is to the readers outside the story. Furthermore, the Psalm 78:2 text functions for the reader of Matthew's text not just as commentary upon one or another of Jesus' parabolic texts about the kingdom but instead in a more general way as an interpretation of the overall character of Jesus' kingdom speaking. In short, and if the reader did not already perceive this, Jesus' parabolic speaking is subject to two levels of scriptural interpretation: scripture is used to explain the what and the way of Jesus' kingdom speaking. And from Matthew's commentary upon Jesus' discourse, we can infer that Jesus' kingdom discourse has entered the tradition and has now become part of the intertextual, revelatory process; they are traditional and, hence, authoritative texts. Like Isaiah's text that illumines and is illumined by Jesus' parable speaking, so Jesus' parables illumine and are illumined both by the psalms and now by Matthew's own narrative in a never-ending fabric of intertextual and circular connections of text upon text upon text.

In the second half of the Parables Discourse Jesus addresses the disciples in and about parables. However the narrator's comments in vv. 34-36 make it clear that we the present readers of the text are also privy to this "private" exchange; we too are the beneficiaries of the interpretive prowess demonstrated by Jesus in illumining the Isaiah texts and the prophetic tradition concerning the word which has been "hidden since the foundation of the world" (v. 35). The readers "outside" the text are the recipients of the word to the same degree as — if not more than — the disciples "inside" the story. Inside and outside, disciples and readers, parables and prophetic texts are all linked by way of interpretation and discourse.

As part of the overall chiastic [42] organization of the chapter, Matthew presents an allegorical interpretation of the wheat and tares parable (vv. 24-30) that correlates with the allegorical interpretation of the sower parable (vv. 36-43).[43] The allegory functions effectively to unite the first half of the Parables Discourse directed to the crowd with the second half of the discourse directed to the disciples. Moreover, the second allegory parallels the interpretation offered to the disciples in vv. 18-23 upon the Sower parable (vv. 3b-9) in two respects: in the agricultural image developed and in the discursive injunction "He who has ears, let him hear," vv. 9, 43. Next follows the twin parables of the treasure (v. 44) and the pearl (vv. 45-46) that correspond to the twin parables of the mustard seed and leaven in the first half of the chapter (vv. 31-33). As for the net parable, it is evidently a hybrid text made up of parable (vv. 47-48) and allegorical commentary upon the parable (vv. 49-50). The union of parable and allegorical interpretation here suggests, as Crossan and Wilder have fully discussed,[44] the unstable nature of the metaphorical image of the kingdom and the community of faith's penchant for "stabilizing" the parable by way of allegory.[45] Within the context of a rabbinic understanding of text and interpretation, however, the allegorization at two levels — that of the net parable at some moment early on in the development of the oral tradition and later of the sower and wheat and tares parables by the evangelist — points to the on-going interpretive process of commentary upon text and tradition characteristic of Jewish thought and practice.

The final parabolic discourse in vv. 51-52, the so-called scribe parable, presents a special problem for redaction critical readings of Matthew 13. But within the framework of rabbinic commentary upon tradition we can explain its function by appeal to the notion of text and interpretation. First of all, the scribe parable disrupts an otherwise near-perfect chiastic pattern of four parables in vv. 1-33 and four in vv. 34-52. Indeed, some critics have raised doubts about whether this is an authentic Jesus' parable since it does not have as its referrent the kingdom of God/heaven. Unlike the other seven parables in the discourse, the scribe parable sets up the comparison between the hearer/learner/scribe trained in the kingdom and the householder who is able to bring from out of his/her storehouse or treasure both the new and the old. The parabolic comparison has shifted from saying what the kingdom of heaven is about to saying something about the nature of the learner of the kingdom of heaven.

Secondly, with the first seven parables what is in view is the *meaning* of the kingdom of God/heaven as enunciated by Jesus, that is particular mundane stories that draw attention to the meaning of God's saving presence. In the case of the scribe parable, what is in view is the meaning of Jesus' *manner of commentary upon kingdom texts and tradition* and the interpretive significance of that method for Matthew and Matthew's reader, i.e., learning how to speak and hear the kingdom. The tradition of speaking about God's kingly reign which lies at the heart of Jesus' message and its meaning has been displaced by commentary upon the *interpretive process itself* — that is, upon the tradition — which enabled Jesus to voice his disorienting, atraditional and iconoclastic word, upon the very process by which the kingdom tradition stays alive and speaks to the learner in Matthew's historical context.

Thirdly, the scribe parable then is evidence of Matthew's *own* interpretive practice — Matthew and Matthew's reader/hearer as a learner/scribe. Through the juxtaposition of parable with prophetic interpretation, Matthew the narrator unfolds not only the tradition associated with Jesus of speaking about God's kingly presence through a telling of the parables; Matthew also comments upon

Jesus' interpretation of that tradition, and through the use of the Psalm and Isaiah texts comments himself/herself upon both the kingdom tradition and Jesus' distinctive interpretation of that tradition. In this fashion Matthew has enlarged the kingdom tradition of Jesus now to include elements that were not originally part of Jesus' commentary (e.g. the allegories upon the sower and wheat and tares parables). Commentary upon commentary, midrash upon midrash, text upon text upon text. All enter into the tradition.

Some Concluding Interpretation

What stands out about Matthew's midrash[46] upon Jesus' kingdom speaking in the use of the scribe parable in Chapter 13 is that Matthew does what Jesus does and also does something different. Matthew reports Jesus's kingdom parables and interpretation of the tradition and also offers his own interpretation. Whereas Jesus speaks about God as king in parabolic ways that are unusual and disorienting, Matthew incorporates those texts and that imagery into the narrative, adds to it allegory and then tops it all off with a comprehensive parabolic evaluation that puts all into "proper" perspective (Matthew's perspective, of course). This peculiar Matthean perspective, however, is concerned with developing an interpretative competence on the part of the readers/hearers of the gospel, to show them how to become kingdom speakers and kingdom hearers for their own day, a day rich with interpretive conflict with pharisaic counterparts.[47]

If Matthew's effort in Chapter 13 (and the gospel as a whole) is any indication to be a scribe trained in the kingdom of Heaven is not simply a matter of miming Jesus through the repetition of his atraditional interpretative strategy (i.e., using parabolic form and kingdom of God content), which has now become traditional and as such an authoritative way. Nor is following Jesus' lead necessarily a rekindling of apocalyptic expectation or prescription of a millenarian ethics. Rather, as the scribe parable shows, retelling Jesus' kingdom parables in narrative form is one way of affirming one's place within the larger tradition of which Isaiah, Jesus, and Matthew are a part, and a playing of the interpretative game competently and persuasively. Interpretation is in this sense a game, a serious game that is in no sense frivolous. It is an effort to win[48] by entering into dialogue with the tradition, and that means engaging in argument and using the images and literary forms that are part of the tradition. The aim is to bring from out of the tradition the older elements of the tradition that will allow the tradition to come alive in a new way and thereby speak to the present believing community in a way that counts. To play is, in Scholem's words, to be that kind of hearer who presses the tradition in and through his/her questioning, who makes "Torah concrete at the point were he stands".[49]

Thus, Matthew's Parables Discourse is far more than a simple historical description or an imaginative reconstruction of the way Jesus was as speaker for God's kingdom. Matthew 13 is a manual[50] for scribal or interpretive self-development, a working template for becoming a competent scribe and interpreter of the tradition oneself. It is a text that instructs the reader by providing a narrative example of the way Jesus spoke about God's kingly presence, and the way that Matthew the narrator did, and the way that the reader can and must do in order to keep the tradition alive. But does the reader/hearer have ears to hear and to listen? The question remains as unanswered and as open ended as the interpretive question itself. Furthermore, Matthew's text also says by its narrative example that the reader of this text — be he/she an original first century reader or a twentieth contemporary reader — cannot interpret exactly as either Jesus or Matthew did. Becoming a learner/scribe/hearer of the kingdom of Heaven means finding one's own way of speaking through dialogue with predecessors and that requires interpretation that may take the form of conflict, reversal, undermining, challenging, contesting, and the like.

Finally, what is the point of all this interpretive effort? Certainly the play of dialectic itself can provide a rush of excitement. The essential reason, however, is to keep alive the tradition and one's part in it, and thus to unfold God's revelation in the present moment. As Scholem insists, to interpret the tradition is to participate in the revealing action of God in the world; it is to assert in an ever-fresh mundane way the sacred story that God is One, by saying God is king, and perhaps, even one day soon, God is Queen.

NOTES

1. Translations of Biblical text, unless otherwise indicated, follow the Revised Standard Version.

2. The saying continues: "...When he found wheat, he put some in the basket; when he found barley he put that in; spelt, he put that in; lentils, he put them in. Upon returning home he sorted out the wheat by itself, the barley by itself, the beans by themselves, the lentils by themselves. This is how R. Akiba acted, and he arranged the whole TORAH in rings" (Avot de R. Natan, ch. 18). Cited in Susan Handelman, *The Slayers of Moses: The Emergence of Rabbinic Interpretation in Modern Literary Criticism* (Albany, New York: State University of New York Press, 1982), p. 45.

3. This is the expression preferred by O. Lamar Cope in his monograph *Matthew: A Scribe Trained for the Kingdom of Heaven,* Catholic Biblical Quarterly Monograph Series no. 5 (Washington, D.C.: The Catholic Biblical Association of America, 1976).

4. Most notably C.H. Dodd, *The Parables of the Kingdom* (New York: Scribner's, 1961), pp. 85-156.

5. See J. Jeremias, *Rediscovering the Parables* (New York: Scribner's, 1966), pp. 54-71.

6. See in particular David Wenham, "The Structure of Mt XIII," *New Testament Studies* 25 (1974), 516-522.

7. Along with Cope's monograph two significant redaction critical treatments of Mt 13 should be mentioned: Jack Kingsbury, *The Parables of Jesus in Matthew 13: A Study in Redaction Criticism* (Richmond: John Knox, 1969); and Jean Dupont, "Le point de vue de Matthieu dans le chapitre des paraboles" in *L'Evangile selon Matthieu: Rédaction et théologie,* ed. M. Didier, Bibliotheca Ephemeridum Theologicum Lovaniensium no. 29 (Gembloux: J. Duculot, 1972), pp. 221-260.

8. Matthew is drawing a quite different distinction from that made by Paul in Gal. 2: 7-8. In the latter case the division of labor (Peter to the Jews, Paul to the Gentiles) goes on simultaneously, whereas for Matthew, if Norman Perrin is corect, the division is a successive one between Jewish and Gentile audiences. See Norman Perrin and Dennis Duling, *The New Testament: An Introduction,* 2nd ed. (New York: Harcourt, Brace, 1982) pp. 263-274.

9. A number of scholars contend that the hermeneutical conflict is reflected in Benediction 12 of the "Eighteen Benedictions" (Shemoneh 'Esreh):

> "For the renegades let there be no hope, and may the arrogant kingdom soon be rooted out in our days, and the Nazarenes and the *minim* perish as in a moment and be blotted out from the book of life and with the righteous may they not be inscribed. Blessed art thou, O Lord, who humblest the arrogant."

(Cited in C.K. Barrett, *The New Testament Background: Selected Documents* (New York: Harper, 1961), p. 167.

10. Mishnah Aboth, 1.1.

11. We take the position that a Jewish provenance for the gospel is most probable. For a discussion of the various critical options, however, see W.G. Kümmel, *Introduction to the New Testament,* trans. Howard C. Kee. rev. ed. (Nashville: Abingdon, 1975), pp. 119-120.

12. Gershom Scholem, *The Messianic Idea in Judaism and Other Essays upon Jewish Spirituality* (New York: Schocken, 1971), pp. 282-303.

13. Ibid., p. 289.

14. Ibid.

15. Scholem does not directly take up the issues of these historical pressures. While admittedly a weak spot in his overall argument, we could offer support of his position from the point of view of discursive practice. An historical assessment, therefore, would have to take into consideration the changing rules for speaking and the linguistic practices that can be documented for the time in question, discursive changes resulting from the incursion of hellenistic culture into Jewish Temple worship, the growing sense of despair in general, the rise of apocalyptic speculation, etc. Such an approach is developed in the historical work of Michel Foucault, *An Archeology of Knowledge* (New York: Pantheon, 1963).

16. Ibid., p. 284.

17. Ibid., pp. 285-286.

18. While Scholem is essentially correct in arguing that tradition functions as an authoritative force in second-Temple Judaism, it would be incorrect to see the development of Torah in oral form as a post-written phenomenon alone. From one point of view, it could be argued that the written form of Torah, symbolized by the tablets at Sinai, was a post-dated response to oral traditions and practices already in force. Indeed, the hypostatizing of Torah undermines the notion of an antecedent and privileged written Torah.

19. Ibid., p. 287.

20. Ibid.

21. Ibid., p. 289.

22. *Midrash Tanhuman*, ed. Solomon Buber, II, 60a., cited in Scholem, p. 289.

23. Scholem, p. 289.

24. See Thorlief Bowman, *Hebrew Thought Compared with Greek* (Philadelphia: Westminster, 1960), especially pp. 17-26.

25. Scholem, p. 291.

26. Ibid., p. 297.

27. Ibid.

28. Ironically, the closure of the canon is evidence of the incomplete character of tradition. The need to exclude certain texts and interpretations points to the fact of continued interpretation. Of course, the development of the oral tradition that eventuates in the Talmud also clearly indicates the ongoing character of the interpretive process. See Handelman, pp. 51-82.

29. Scholem, p. 289.

30. See Charles Talbert, *Literary Patterns, Theological Themes, and the Genre of Luke-Acts* (Missoula: Scholars Press, 1974).

31. For more on the distinction between mundane and sacred story see Stephen Crites, "The Narrative Quality of Experience," *Journal of the American Academy of Religion* 39 (1971), 291-311. Crites develops the contrast in phenomenological terms and establishes the pair in relation to the notions of time and space.

32. For a detailed discussion see Norman Perrin and Dennis Duling, *The New Testament: An Introduction*, pp. 400-406.

33. For a detailed discussion see Norman Perrin, *Rediscovering the Teaching of Jesus* (New York: Harper, 1967), pp. 54-108. Also see Robert Stein, *The Method and Message of Jesus' Teaching* (Philadelphia: Westminster, 1978), pp. 60-79. "Kingdom of heaven" is a synonym for "Kingdom of God." Given Matthew's Jewish sensibilities, the evangelist prefers the former expression as a circumlocution for the name of God.

34. For a different view, see S. Aalen, " 'Reign' and 'House' as the Kingdom of God in the Gospels," *New Testament Studies* 8 (1962), 224ff. My thanks to John Koenig for bringing this article to my attention.

35. Cf. Micah 2:12ff; 4:1-7; Is 24:21-23; 33:22; 52:7-10; Zeph 3:14-20; Obad 2.

36. See Stein, pp. 35-39.

37. Ibid., p. 39.

38. Dodd, p. 5.

39. See Jan Lambrecht, *Once More Astonished: The Parables of Jesus*, (New York: Crossroad, 1981), pp. 1-22.

40. Perrin and Duling, *The New Testament: An Introduction*, pp. 262-273.

41. It is worth noting that some textual authorities read "the prophet Isaiah" at this place in obvious parallelism with vv. 14-16.

42. Chiastic structure refers to organization or material in which the first half of the text is mirrored inversely in the material of the second half. A simple chiastic pattern might follow the form A/B/C/B'/A'. A and A', and B and B' may be related to one another by similarity of grammatical structure, vocabulary, or theme. See W.W. Lund, *Chiasmus in the New Testament: A Study in Formgeschichte* (Chapel Hill, North Carolina: University of North Carolina Press, 1942) and Wenham, p. 514.

43. Wenham, pp. 517-520.

44. See J. Dominic Crossan, *In Parables: The Challenge of the Historical Jesus* (New York: Harper, 1973), pp. 13-22; Amos Wilder, *Early Christian Rhetoric* (New York: Harper, 1964), pp. 71-88.

45. See Jeremias, pp. 36-53.

46. For a specific discussion of midrashic technique in Matthew's gospel see M.D. Goulder, *Midrash and Lection in Matthew* (London: SPCK, 1974), pp. 3-46.

47. Perhaps the conflict between Jamnian Jews and Matthean Jewish Christians is therefore to be seen in more positive terms as a conflict of interpretive strategies not unlike other conflicts of interpretation experienced in the growth of the tradition.

48. In a commentary upon the interpretive process, Rabbi Eliezer is said to have been arguing against a majority interpretation: "Then he said: "If the *Halakhah* always agrees with me, let it be proved from Heaven." Thereupon a heavenly voice was heard saying: "Why do you dispute with Rabbi Eliezer? The *Halakhah* always agrees with him." But Rabbi Joshua arose and said (Deut. 30:12): "It is not in heaven." What did he mean by that? Rabbi Jeremiah replied: "The Torah has already been given at Mount Sinai [and thus is no longer in Heaven]. We pay no heed to any heavenly voice, because at Mount Sinai You wrote in the Torah (Exod. 23:2): 'One must incline after the majority.' " Rabbi Nathan met the prophet Elijah and asked him: "What did the Holy One, blessed be He, do in that hour?" He replied: "God smiled and said: My children have defeated Me, my children have defeated Me." (Baba Metzia 59b, cited in Scholem, p. 292.)

49. Scholem, p. 297.

50. Cf. K. Stendahl, *The School of St. Matthew and its Use of the Old Testament* (Lund: Gleerup, 1953).

III

SHIFTING HORIZONS

INTERPRETATION OF TRADITION
IN A GLOBAL CONTEXT

Ewert H. Cousins

It is a challenge to address such a profound and broad topic as the theme: Traditions and Interpretations. And it is doubly challenging to address this theme in a global context, as I have chosen to do, perhaps foolheartedly. Yet I am consoled by the fact that I can draw support from the topic itself. For tradition itself can come to my aid since it is a storehouse of resources, containing the accumulated wisdom of the great minds of the past — a wisdom that has been handed down to aid us in our inadequacy. This sense of tradition was summed up in the Western Middle Ages in the famous observation of Bernard of Chartres: that we are dwarfs, but we stand on the shoulders of giants.[1] Bernard's statement is consoling in that it assures us of powerful assistance from the past. But it can also function as a mythic image opening to us tradition as an archetype. By this I mean that tradition can be seen as an archetypal, or primordial, structure of consciousness which establishes our roots in history, which links us to the great minds of our past, and which opens a channel for their wisdom to flow into our lives. The significance of Bernard's image as archetypal can be seen if we invert his formula: We are giants, but we stand on the shoulders of dwarfs. Not only does this minimize the wisdom of the past and render us guilty of hubris, but it undercuts tradition as an archetype; it closes the door upon the flow of wisdom from the past. For tradition to function as an archetype, it must be evoked and cultivated by an attitude of reverence and respect; it must be received with humility and gratitude.

Granted its benefits, tradition — like all archetypes — has a dark side. It can be heavy and oppressive, a dead weight, a lifeless corpse, a prison of the human spirit. Even at its best, when it is alive and nourishing, it can present obstacles to innovation and stifle creativity. It is here that interpretation must enter to transform the dark side of tradition. Interpretation must retrieve the past and bring it to life in the present, but it must be critical and discriminating. It must be critical in recovering the past with accuracy, but it must also be discriminating in bringing the past into our lives; for not all of the past is worthy to live in the present. In addition to these demands, it must be sensitive to the direction of the future. It must have a tenacious and accurate memory of the past, a sense of vitality in the present, and a creative impulse towards the future. These, then, in brief are some of the challenges of our theme: Traditions and Interpretations.

Jean Leclercq and Global Mutation

In treating such a challenging topic, I will follow the suggestion of Bernard of Chartres. Aware of my dwarf-like stature, I will stand on the shoulders of a giant — a great historian who has done perhaps more than anyone else to interpret the religious traditions of the Middle Ages — Jean Leclercq, the chief editor of the critical text of Bernard of Clairvaux, author of *The Love of Learning and the Desire for God,* along with more than twenty other books and more than eight hundred scholarly articles. Through his research he has retrieved a major portion of the medieval tradition — the monastic theology which preceded the scholastic theology of the universities, which had been forgotten by modern historians, and which lay buried by the massive scholarship on medieval philosophy during the era of the Neo-Scholastic revival. Like an archeologist at an excavation, he has unearthed monastic theology as a dimension of the medieval monastic tradition.

In 1976, when I was the director of the Graduate Program in Spirituality at Fordham University, I invited Jean Leclercq to give a lecture entitled: "The Role of History and Tradition in Contemporary Spirituality."[2] When I met him at the airport, he told me that his talk would be more abstract than I might have anticipated. As I listened to his lecture that evening, I realized why he had said that; for he was presenting his own theory of the nature of history and tradition — a theory that had grown out of more than forty years of dedicated scholarly work. He defined tradition as the past alive in the present, and history as the hermeneutics of tradition. In so doing he has provided us with a formula for understanding the nature of tradition and the relation of hermeneutics, or interpretation, to tradition. In describing tradition as the past alive in the present, he was highlighting the positive side of the archetype I described above. From this perspective, historical research, as interpretation, helps us retrieve the past as a vital force in the present. It is not a cataloging of dead events recorded on the graves of a previous age, nor the assembling of lifeless exhibits in a museum. Rather it reaches into the past and taps its energy for the present and the future. As memory and interpretation of the past, history makes available the vitality of tradition.

So far Leclercq's shoulders have supported me with the concepts of tradition and interpretation. But what of the second part of my topic: in a global context? On this Leclercq had something startling to say. For he claimed that we are in a radically new period in history that calls for a new stance toward tradition and interpretation. According to Leclercq history may proceed by way of an organic unfolding or by way of mutation — a quantum leap in which a new context is produced by a break with the past and a leap into the future. In the case of organic unfolding, each generation passes on its values to the next. Of course, this is not necessarily a smooth process, but involves changes, new discoveries, revolutions, rejections of elements of the past. Granted these fluctuations, the changes in a continuous tradition are not so radical as those of a mutation.

As examples of mutation, Leclercq cited the barbarian invasion of Europe and the Westernization of Japan. These he characterized as regional since they affected only a limited area of the earth and a limited number of the earth's population. In contrast, he claimed that between the end of World War II and the sixties a mutation occurred on a global scale. Science, technology, communication, and other forces, which had been building up for centuries, finally reached a point that produced a global matrix for culture. This worldwide mutation has brought about the convergence of cultural traditions and the encounter of world religions. This mutation is global not only in its extent but in its very content; for it is producing a global consciousness: a consciousness that is open to traditions other than our own and, in fact, to the traditions of the entire human community.

How does this mutation affect tradition and interpretation? What effect will this have on the archetype of tradition? On the religious level, we are now encountering many traditions: the Hindu, Buddhist, Islamic, and others. What is the task of interpretation in relation to these traditions — and in relation to our own Western traditions in the light of this mutation? At this point, Bernard of Chartres can no longer come to our aid since this global mutation is unique in history; there are no giants who have faced this situation before and on whose shoulders we can stand. And yet there is much that we can learn from the past and from those giants who emerged at the time of regional mutations.

These, then, are the issues I would like to explore with you on the theme: Traditions and Interpretations. Keeping in mind the global mutation described by Leclercq, I will examine, first, the issues of interpretation within our own tradition, taking as my example the 60-volume series being published by Paulist Press: The Classics of Western Spirituality. Secondly, I would like to explore the role of interpretation of traditions in a global context, as seen in the 25-volume series to be published by The Crossroad Publishing Company: *World Spirituality: An Encyclopedic History of the Religious Quest.* Thirdly, I would like to propose a way of understanding the present global mutation through my own theory of the Second Axial Period.

The Classics of Western Spirituality

Before moving into the global context, I will examine the interpretation of tradition within Western culture through The Classics of Western Spirituality. This series provides a remarkable example of an attempt to recover a forgotten tradition. In its own way it is comparable to Leclercq's retrieve of monastic theology within the Middle Ages. For many reasons during the first part of this century, the great spirituality traditions of Western culture had slipped into forgetfulness. It is true that they were alive on the level of religious practice and devotion, in large communities and in specific religious orders, but they did not enter substantially into our general collective memory, nor ironically into theology or the academic study of religion. The academic community and its educational programs did not manifest an awareness of the great spiritual writers and their classical works in any way comparable to the discipline of philosophy, with its familiarity with Plato, Aristotle, Aquinas, Descartes, and Hegel; or English literature, with Chaucer, Shakespeare, and Milton. In other words, in the case of spirituality the past was not alive in the present. We spiritual dwarfs of the twentieth century did not have giants on whose shoulders we could stand. The archetype of tradition in our psyche was not functioning in relation to spirituality in a comprehensive way.

Then came the sixties, with its consciousness explosion, its critique of the scientific mind-set, its turn to Eastern ways of the spirit. By the seventies many Westerners had discovered the spiritual quest — not from their own traditions, but in psychotherapy, in the human potential movement, in yoga, or Zen. Simultaneously, in the academic world the history of religions was making available data from the Orient and from archaic cultures. In this ferment many felt the need to discover their own spiritual roots: as Westerners, as Jews, as Christians. They found themselves asking many questions: Does Judaism or Christianity have a spiritual wisdom? Techniques of meditation? Spiritual practices and disciplines? If so, where can they be found? Not likely in theology, it seemed, which for decades and even centuries had been expending much of its energy to reconcile traditional belief with the scientific world view. The present need sprang from a deeper level of the person — not from his or her adjustment to scientific culture, but from the depths within, from the spiritual center that had been awakened in a new way. It was clear that an entire tradition had to be recovered, that an archetype had to be evoked, that giants had to be awakened, that their shoulders had to be brought to the support of our searching, stumbling feet.

It was at this point in the mid-seventies that the idea of The Classics of Western Spirituality was conceived by Richard Payne, then an Associate Editor of Paulist Press. Clearly discerning the need to retrieve the Western spiritual tradition, he realized the necessity of having classical spiritual writings available in readable English translations based on the finest critical scholarship. Following the general lines of the Great Books of the Western World, he designed a 60-volume series of the spiritual classics of Judaism, Christianity, Islam, of the American Indians and black Americans. In this he was taking the term "Western" in a combined historical and geographical sense, including those traditions that trace their origins from Judaism, along with the primal traditions of North and South America. He chose — rightly, I believe — a closed series of 60 volumes, rather than an open-ended series with an unspecified number of volumes. This made the selection of volumes difficult, it is true; but it assured that the authors chosen were among the tallest giants with the broadest shoulders.

Extensive market research confirmed that there was a large group of potential readers in church ministry, in the academic community, and in the increasing number of spiritual seekers. With the support and direction of Father Kevin Lynch, President of Paulist Press, the series was launched. The first volume, *Julian of Norwich: Showings* was published in 1978;[3] and since then over half of the volumes have appeared. Among the Christian authors are Origen, Gregory of Nyssa, Bonaventure, Meister Eckhart, Catherine of Siena, Teresa of Avila, Jacob Boehme, Johann Arnt, John and Charles Wesley. The remaining volumes in the series have been commissioned and will appear over the next several years. Response to the series — both critical and popular — has been so positive that Paulist Press has commissioned an additional 20 supplemental volumes.

It would be interesting to analyze the Classics of Western Spirituality as a case study in traditions and interpretations. In a literate society writings are among the most powerful means of transmitting tradition. It follows, then, that the interpretation of these spiritual classics is a major means of retrieving the tradition. Under the term "interpretation" I wish to include not only the intellectual re-presentation of the past, but the more comprehensive process of remembering, understanding, and evaluating the past. In this I am explicitly drawing from Augustine's analysis of the mind, or *mens,* as including memory, understanding, and will.[4] In this process, the editors of the Classics of Western Spirituality first remembered the past by searching out the critical texts if these had been edited. In the case of the *Showings* of Julian of Norwich, the editors and translators, Edmund Colledge and James Walsh, had been working for a number of years to establish the critical text, which appeared in print not long after the volume in the Classics.[5] Thus their modern English translation reaped the benefit of their long research in the historical immediacy of the critical text. Once the critical text of a work has been retrieved by memory and meaningfully translated, the interpretaion process continues. Each volume in the Classics contains an introduction which situates the spiritual writer and the work in its historical setting, analyzes the major spiritual themes, and evaluates the work's contribution from a critical perspective. Each work, then, is retrieved from the past for the present by this complex process of interpretation, which includes memory, understanding, and evaluation. Through this hermeneutical process, in terms of Leclercq's formula, the past is brought to life in the present.

Has the interpretive process at work in the Classics of Western Spirituality actually retrieved the spirituality tradition? Has the spiritual wisdom of the past, in Leclercq's phrase, become alive in the present? In its initial phase, in the academic community, I would say yes. The volumes are being used widely in courses, not only in religion programs, but in literature, history, and other disciplines. Certain courses are now possible for the first time because of this series. The spirituality tradition is being taken more seriously by various disciplines within religious studies: theology, history, psychology of religion, biblical studies. Individuals are reading the classics for spiritual nourishment. Efforts have been made to bring them into workshops, study groups, prayer groups, and other community settings. Since the effect of the series will undoubtedly be cumulative, its ultimate success in retrieving the tradition — on the academic and religious levels — will have to be judged in the future.

World Spirituality

We have seen an example of the retrieve of a tradition through the interpretative process within Western culture. This fits the category of the continuous transmission of tradition described by Leclercq. But what of his other category: that of mutation, and specifically the global mutation he believes has occurred at the present time? I would like to address this from the standpoint of a second publishing project, the 25-volume series *World Spirituality: An Encyclopedic History of the Religious Quest,* which is in progress now and which is scheduled to be published — all volumes simultaneously — in 1984.

When Richard Payne developed the idea of The Classics of Western Spirituality, he conceived it as part of a threefold project. The Classics of Western Spirituality would be complemented by a similar 60-volume series: The Classics of Eastern Spirituality, including English translations of the classics of Hinduism, Buddhism, Taoism, Confucianism, and other Oriental traditions. A third project consisted of a history of world spitituality, a series of volumes containing essays by contemporary scholars covering the entire history of the human spiritual quest from prehistoric times, through the great traditions, into the present and future. The Classics of Eastern Spirituality are still in the early planning phase; but when Richard Payne moved from Paulist Press to the Crossroad Publishing Company, he brought with him the plans for the history of world spirituality, which was developed under the direction of the Crossroad Publisher, Mark Linz, into a 25-volume series entitled *World Spirituality: An Encyclopedic History of the Religious Quest.* For the most part the volumes are organized according to major traditions, e.g., two volumes on Hindu spirituality, two on Buddhist spirituality, and so forth. Each volume will be 500 pages in length, containing about 25 articles on aspects of the tradition's spirituality written by specialists in the field. There will also be photos and illustrations. Each volume has an editor who plans its content and commissions articles. The general policy has been to choose editors and contributors both culturally and spiritually from the traditions. This means that Hindus are writing on Hinduism, Buddhists on Buddhism, etc. At present there is a netword of some 500 scholars around the world writing articles for this project.

As you can see, this series is a microcosm of our theme, reflecting the global mutation described by Jean Leclercq. Each tradition is attempting to retrieve the wisdom of its past by the complex process of interpretation I described above. What is unique about the series is that it is global in scope. It is a concrete attempt to deal with the problem of traditions and interpretations in a global context, not merely by retrieving the traditions in their historical continuity, but by contributing to the encounter of traditions at the present time. The fundamental problems are different from those of the mere transmission of a tradition. What happens when spiritual traditions encounter each other? Volume 23 deals with this issue, with articles on the regional encounters in the past between the various traditions: for example, Buddhism with Taoism and Confucianism in China. Volume 24, however, deals with the global encounter in the mutational context of the present and future. What happens when the traditions meet in this context? I will attempt to explore this complex problem, in the light of my work on the project as General Editor. In this capacity, in compensation for the burdens of coordinating the project, I have a privileged vantage point to observe the tensions and creative energies as these emerge. What I will say will be my own observaitons and may or may not be shared by our editors and contributors.

The fundamental issue, as I see it, is that traditions are meeting which have not only diverse content but diverse historical conditioning. The archetype of tradition within individual and collective consciousness has a different historical memory among Hindus, Christians, Buddhists, and Muslims. This is, I believe, the primordial fact we are facing: we must deal with this fact personally, collectively, and academically. Is it possible for me to share another's tradition? Can I share his or her memory? His or her understanding? What of my evaluation of that tradition? Is it to be judged according to the criteria of my own? Of the other's tradition? Of some norms that are emerging in our global context? I certainly do not have answers to these questions, but I can venture some observations.

First, I tend to take a positive view: that we can assimilate the heritage of other traditions. My colleague Thomas Berry has said that for the first time in history each person can become heir to the spiritual heritage of mankind.[6] Prior to the present period, this has not been possible since geographic, historical, and cultural barriers have kept us apart. How will we receive this inheritance? Certainly not by sharing the different historical conditioning. Not by the memory of traditions, but by the convergence of traditions. In this convergence we must do two things: evoke a sense of belonging to the whole human race and cultivate an empathetic consciousness towards other traditions. Our first task is to associate our own sense of tradition with the traditions of the human community as a whole. This means to link our psychic archetype of tradition not only with our own history but with that of the human race, as somehow sharing a common tradition, even though this has been historically diversified. This means to globalize our archetype of tradition; by so doing, we will enhance our openness to other traditions and render our interpretation of them more effective.

The second task is to cultivate an empathetic consciousness toward the other traditions. In John Dunne's words, we must "pass over and come back;" or in Raimundo Panikkar's terms, we must develop "dialogic dialogue," which is open to the values of other traditions, in contrast to "dialectical dialogue," which seeks to argue against the others.[7] I have claimed that on the theoretical level we must develop a "shamanistic epistemology" and on the practical level we must activate our "shamanistic faculty."[8] By this I mean that like the shaman who in spirit leaves the body, goes to distant places, and returns enriched with new knowledge, so we have the capacity to leave the horizons of our own consciousness and enter into the consciousness of another tradition, returning to our own with a new awareness of the values of the other. In relation to the process of interpretation described above, "passing over" substitutes for memory. In effect, we "pass over" into the other's memory and share his or her tradition in that way. Then we can activate our understanding and evaluation, thus bringing to completion the process of interpreting traditions.

I would like to point out how important the memory of tradition has been in the design *World Spirituality: An Encyclopedic History of the Religious Quest.* In principle, we have commissioned Hindus to write on their own spirituality, Buddhists to write on theirs, etc. This means that the volumes will have the power of the collective archetype of traditions as these are evoked by their editors and contributors, Of course, it is not easy for an individual or group to come to a reflective, self-critical consciousness of their own tradition. On a recent trip to India, in Varanasi and Madras, I had the privilege of sharing in that process as the Hindu editors and contributors attempted to interpret their own traditions.

At this point I would like to make a suggestion which has grown out of this work and also my participation in the research seminar organized by Peter Berger in 1978, which produced the book *The Other Side of God: A Polarity in World Religions,*[9] and which is presently working on another book. I believe that the time is ripe for fruitful work to be done in the academic community by combining the model of the history of religions with that of ecumenical dialogue. By that I mean to develop collaborative research projects by scholars who share the living tradition on which they work. For example, I have been attempting to develop a research project on Mysticism: Hindu and Christian, by having Hindu scholars writing on Hindu mystics and Christian scholars writing on Christian mystics. They can strive to use a common methodology and to study together the evidence from both traditions. The history of religions in the West has relied heavily on texts and histories written by Westerners, without always tapping the living traditions studied. On the other hand, ecumenical dialogue has proceeded by testimony of traditional faith, without always bringing to bear the controls of critical academic scholarship. It may well be that such collaborative research projects would be the most effective means of helping us bridge through interpretation the gap that exists between diverse traditions in this period of global mutation.

The present situation would be complex enough if all we had to deal with were the diverse religious traditions. But the problem is compounded by the impact of the secular. At the same time that the spiritual traditions are meeting in a mutually supportive atmosphere, each of them is struggling with the growing secularization of culture. Western religion has been dealing with this for centuries, but it is now a Buddhist problem, a Hindu problem, a problem for all the spiritual traditions. Each will encounter the secular out of its own traditional resources. But there is emerging a consciousness that the problems evoked by the secular are common human problems: nuclear destruction, the pollution of our enviroment, widespread injustice and poverty.

Jaspers and the Axial Period

The encounter of the traditions with the secular brings us to our third point. How do we interpret traditions when they themselves are being transformed? The very secular developments in culture that produced a global enviroment have not left the religious traditions unaffected. In fact, both the secular and religious trends in culture may be caught up in a larger transformation which is having its effect on both. I would like to explore this possibility of a larger transformation, taking my point of departure from Leclercq's notion of mutation, enlarging it by drawing from Karl Jasper's concept of the Axial Period, and extending it by my own theory of the Second Axial Period.

If we were to take a long-range view of history, we would observe that the world religions as we know them today were shaped in their fundamental dimension during a single period in the first millenium B.C. In three geographic areas: China, India, and Persia and the Eastern Mediterranean including Israel and Greece, a striking transformation of consciousness occurred, without a discernible influence of one area or another. This phenomenon has been studied by Karl Jaspers in his book *The Origin and Goal of History*.[10] He calls this era the Axial Period because it "gave birth to everything which, since then, man has been able to be." He continues: "It would seem that this axis of history is to be found in the period around 500 B.C., in the spiritual process that occurred between 800 and 200 B.C. It is there that we meet with the most deep-cut dividing line in history. Man, as we know him today, came into being. For short we may style this the 'Axial Period.'"[11]

In the Axial Period, great spiritual teachers appeared who through their lives and doctrines helped effect the transformation of consciousness. It was during this period that Confucius and Lao-tze taught in China; the Upanishads,

Mahavira, and the Buddha appeared in India; Zoroaster in Persia; the prophets — Elijah, Isaiah, and Jeremiah — in Israel; and Socrates, Plato, and Aristotle in Greece. These teachers heralded a transformation of consciousness from mythic to self-reflective thought, from fusion with the cosmos and the tribe to independent individual identity. The emergence of individual identity is most characteristic of the Axial Period and the basis for analytic, self-reflective, critical consciousness. No longer fused with nature or the tribe, Axial people could, with their newly developed analytic skills, criticize collective consciousness politically and religiously. Like Socrates they could criticize the Athenian establishment, or like the Hebrew prophets present moral excellence as superior to ritual observance, or like the Buddha set out on an individual spiritual path that would culminate in personal enlightenment.

It was during this period that the great religions of the world, as we know them today, came into being; for they all contain as central to their spiritual message the characteristics of Axial Consciousness. This is true of the religions that were shaped in this period: Hinduism, Buddhism, Jainism, Zoroastrianism, Taoism, Confucianism, and Judaism. And it is true also of those religions that appeared later in continuity with roots in this period: Christianity, Islam, and Sikhism. It is safe to say that we are products of the Axial Period: for as Jaspers observes, "in this age were born the fundamental categories within which we still think today, and the beginnings of the world religions, by which human beings still live, were created."[12]

In the Axial Period the possibility of an individual spiritual path emerged. In primitive cultures spirituality was cultivated through cosmic, ritualistic, and mythic consciousness. Although these modes of consciousness remained in the religions of the Axial Period, they were subordinated to the new forms of individual, analytic, and critical consciousness. The newly emerged individual consciousness made possible the spiritual path of monasticism, which appeared for the first time in the Axial Period: in Hinduism, Jainism, and Buddhism, and later in Christianity. In the Axial Period the monk appeared as a marginal person in society. By becoming a beggar, he could free himself from the tasks of the tribe and by sexual abstinence, from the fertility cycles of nature. Thus liberated from attachment to material things, he could pursue his spiritual path either as a hermit or in a community of monks who had made the same radical break from nature and the collectivity.

The first Axial Period released enormous spiritual energy, but at the same time it tended to alienate human beings from their roots in the cosmos and from their organic relation to the community. Individual consciousness freed them from immersion in nature, but it tended to set them over against the phenomenal world and to launch them on a spiritual ascent which drew them far above their roots in matter. Axial consciousness tended to produce an otherworldly attitude in religion which directed attention away from the social, economic, political dimensions of the human person.

Second Axial Period

If we turn our gaze from the first millenium B.C. to the present, I believe that we can discern that we are going through a Second Axial Period. The mutation of which Leclercq speaks is producing not only a common global context, but is transforming religious consciousness itself. Like the first, this Second Axial Period is effecting a radical change in consciousness; and like the first it is bringing about a transformation of the religious sphere. In this Second Axial Period, there is emerging a new global consciousness and a new global spirituality. It is global in two senses: a horizontal and a vertical. On the horizontal plane, the religions are meeting each other and developing a more complex form of consciousness through dialogue. In this sense religion is becoming more collective in its scope because it is encompassing the fulness of human religious experience in its historically diverse traditions and is sharing the fulness of the human spiritual quest. In this sense it can be called global. And in this sense it can be seen to overcome the separation from the collectivity that was characteristic of the First Axial Period. In a certain sense we are rediscovering the values of the collective consciousness of the primitive Pre-Axial Period without abandoning the distinctive values of the Axial Period.

This new consciousness can be called global in another sense. This is the vertical sense, for it plunges down into the earth and the material level of life. In the Pre-Axial Period, consciousness was rooted in this level, for primitive peoples possessed a cosmic awareness that linked them to the totality of life — to their roots in nature, to the vegetative and animal world, and to the cosmic cycles. In the Second Axial Period consciousness must not only encompass the entire human community; it must also root itself again in the earth. Problems have developed on a global scale that call for a global solution. It is as if the earth itself were calling for help; for the pollution of our environment, the depletion of natural resources, the threat of nuclear war are threatening life on our planet. In addition to this, there is widespread injustice, with the unequal distribution of material resources, with the consequent problems of hunger and poverty in large areas. Already these problems have reached a global scale and call for a global solution.

It is this vertical dimension of global consciousness that presents the greatest challenge to religions at this time and to the interpretation of traditions. Religions must move fully into the Second Axial Period, tap the spiritual energies released in the First Axial Period, and channel these toward the solution of human problems. They must deal with the fulness of human life: not only the spiritual, but the economic, social, and political dimensions as well — not in an isolated fashion, but in the dialogic, global consciousness of the Second

Axial Period.

It follows, then, that the religions cannot merely draw from their past wisdom — merely retrieve their traditions by sophisticated interpretation — since these traditions reflect the distinctive horizons of First Axial Period consciousness. Does this mean that the third point of my presentation undercuts my first two points, which dealt with the recovery of traditions? Not at all! On the contrary, I believe that the Second Axial Period calls for the full richness of the traditions that were born and developed in the First Axial Period. These traditions must be recovered. But it calls for more. It calls for a sensitivity to the pre-Axial forms of consciousness, to the challenges of the present, and the possibilities of the future. In brief, it calls for the creative interpretation of tradition. That is a creativity that is rooted in the past but not bound by the past — a creativity that draws from the past, present, and future. This creative interpretation must retain the wisdom of the past, it is true, and build upon it; but it must also transform the past to open to wider and deeper horizons. Each of the traditions, in its own way through creative interpretation, must enter into the horizontal and vertical dimensions of the global consciousness of the Second Axial Period. They must discover the point of intersection between the cosmic, the human, and the transcendent. They must develop an integral view of life in a global context. Most of all, they must bring the spiritual resources of their distinct heritages to bear on the creative solution of common human problems.

In conclusion, I would like to suggest that the most appropriate image of the interpretation of tradition in this mutational Second Axial Period is not that of dwarfs standing on the shoulders of giants — although this image has its place within the separate traditions described in my first two points. A more appropriate image, I believe, is that of the earth as it was seen by the astronauts when they first moved into outer space. Looking back, they saw the beautiful blue globe shining against the black background of space. They were overwhelmed by its beauty; and although they were far distant, they felt their rootedness there in the earth. From this distant point of view, they could see the earth as a whole and feel that they belonged to the earth as a whole. This image of the earth, then, seen from outer space, can symbolize the two dimensions of global consciousness that I described above. It can be the symbol of the archetype of the common tradition that underlies all diverse tradition; and it can be the symbol of a spirituality that integrates the cosmic, the human, and the transcendent. It is, I am sure, not by chance that the emergence of global consciousness has coincided with the first time that humans have had a concrete sense experience of the earth as a single sphere; for this type of sense experience is the quarry of archetypal symbols. Furthermore, the great distance required for the astronauts to obtain such a view can symbolize the perspective that is required for our interpretation of the many traditions that have flourished on this planet.

Instead of dwarfs on the shoulders of giants, then, we have been transformed into astronauts in outer space — overwhelmed, it is true, by the size of the universe and the task it enjoins, but simultaneously supported by the clarity of vision it affords and stimulated to take up the challenging task of the creative interpretation of traditions in a global context.

NOTES

1. Bernard of Chartres, as cited by John of Salisbury, *Metalogicon*, III, 4; *P.L.* CXICX, 900 c: "Dicebat Bernardus Carnotensis nos esse quasi nanos, gigantium humeris incidentes, ut possimus plura eis et remotiora videre, non utique proprii visus acumine, aut eminentia corporis, sed quia in altum subvehimur et extollimur magnitudine gigantea."

2. Jean Leclercq, O.S.B., lecture delivered at Fordham University, November 30, 1976, unpublished; a slightly longer summary of the contents of the lecture appears in my article "Raimundo Panikkar and the Christian Systematic Theology of the Future," *Cross Currents*, 29 (1979), 142-143.

3. *Julian of Norwich: Showings*, trans. Edmund Colledge, O.S.A., and James Walsh, S.J. (New York: Paulist Press, 1978).

4. Cf. Augustine, *De Trinitate*, VII-XV.

5. *A Book of Showings to the Anchoress Julian of Norwich*, ed. Edmund Colledge, O.S.A., and James Walsh, S.J., 2 vols. (Toronto: Pontifical Institute of Mediaeval Studies, 1978).

6. Thomas Berry, "Contemporary Spirituality — Its Global Content, Its Historical Dimensions, Its Future Vision," *Riverdale Studies* 1 (1975), 1.

7. John S. Dunne, *The Way of All the Earth: Experiments in Truth and Religion* (Notre Dame: University of Notre Dame Press, 1972), p. ix; Raimundo Panikkar, *Myth, Faith and Hermeneutics* (New York: Paulist Press, 1979), pp. 241-245; cf. also *The Intrareligious Dialogue* (Paulist Press, 1978).

8. Cf. Cousins, "Raimundo Panikkar and the Christian Systematic Theology of te Future," 153-154.

9. Peter Berger, ed., *The Other Side of God: A Polarity in World Religions* (Garden City, NY: Anchor Books, 1981).

10. Karl Jaspers, *The Origin and Goal of History*, trans. Michael Bullock (New Haven: Yale University Press, 1953).

11. Ibid., p. 1.

12. Ibid., p. 2.

IMAGES, INTERPRETATIONS, AND TRADITIONS:
A STUDY OF THE MAGDALENE

Diane Apostolos-Cappadona

If one studies the history of any major image of Christian iconography, one will find a traceable development not only in artistic images but in theological interpretations. Central images are the "classics" of the Christian artistic and theological tradition.[1] The great "classics" of art transcend time and history, and represent eternal human truths in such a way as to make them universals. However, they need to be re-interpreted for successive generations. Sometimes, one particular painting or sculpture is not so much the "classic" as is its central theme: for example, all paintings of the repentent Magdalene are not "classics", but the artistic image of her repentance is a "classic"

A study of the transformations and interpretations of Mary Magdalene in art will make open to us not merely a series of visual "classics" but an understanding of the different cultural and theological shifts that have occurred in the 2000 years of Christian history and which are ways of keeping the "classic" alive.[2] This examination of the image of the Magdalene offers changing reflections on the interpretations of woman as saint and sinner in Christian theology.[3] This analysis will be divided into three sections: (1) the formative scriptural and theological traditions of the Magdalene; (2) the traditional symbolism of the Magdalene; and (3) a general survey of the Magdalene images in Christian art.[4]

Scriptural and Theological Tradition

The essential scriptural materials reveal that Mary of Magdala was one of the early followers of Jesus of Nazareth (Luke 8:3), that he cast seven devils from her (Luke 8:2), that she was one of the "holy women" who went to the tomb of the crucified Jesus to anoint his body (Mark 16:1f.), and that the resurrected Christ appeared to her first of all his followers (Matthew 28:9; John 20:11f.). Mary is introduced as the woman from Magdala (Greek form of Migdol or watchtower). Magdala lies at the south of the Plain of Gennesaret, where the hills reach forth to the Lake of Galilee. Among the Galileans, Magdala had an unsavory reputation.[5] It is this association that supports the Magdalene's eventual identification with the nameless sinner of Luke 7:37, the woman taken in adultery of John 7:53-8:11, and the theory that the Magdalene's "seven devils" were the devils of unchastity in Luke 8:2.

The confusion over the Magdalene's identity is evident in that neither the evangelists nor the church fathers are clear or in agreement as to who the Magdalene is.[6] Tertullian's discussion of the unction scene suggests that the two women who wipe the feet of Jesus of Nazareth with their hair are one and the same woman. Gregory the Great identifies the Magdalene with Mary of Bethany and the repentent sinner. Ambrose is not clear in his discussion of the Maries, but Jerome makes a sharp distinction between the sinful woman and the unnamed woman of the anointing scene. Origen clearly delineates between the two women involved in the unction scenes, while Augustine argues for the composite Magdalene image.

In the *Litany of All Saints*, Mary Magdalene is invoked as a virgin: her name stands at the beginning of the list of the holy virgins.[7] There is no indication that she may be a widow or that this title is an honorific or that the term, "virgin", may not necessarily have sexual connotation. This text serves as significant liturgical testimony for the distinction between the sinful woman and the Magdalene coinciding with her designation as a virgin by Ambrose and Modestus of Jerusalem. Since the sixth-century decree by Gregory the Great, the western Christian tradition has accepted this composite image of repentant sinner and devoted follower of Jesus of Nazareth primarily based upon the similarities of the two unction scenes.

Following the writings of Origen, the eastern Christian tradition honored three women, who are often confused, as distinct and separate individuals by celebrating the feasts of the Converted Sinner, March 21; Mary, the sister of Lazarus, March 18; and Mary Magdalene, July 22. The western Christian tradition celebrates the feasts of Mary and Martha, January 19; and Mary Magdalene, July 22. The identity question has never really been resolved by either the eastern or western Christian traditions, and remains a point of puzzlement and debate among scholars.[8]

The question and discussion of Mary Magdalene's life has been popular with the Christian faithful and confusing to theologians. Her early popularity is signified by the many legends which emerged to fill the biographical lacunae. For example, a French legend speaks of her evangelical mission to France, her ministry of teaching and healing, her years of penance in the French woods, and the ministry of angels at her death. The Roman martyrology states that she evangelized Provence, a view that is now accepted as legendary. The eastern Christian tradition teaches that after Pentecost, Mary Magdalene, John the Evangelist, and the Virgin Mary travelled together to Ephesus where they remained until their deaths. Other early legends and Egyptian gnostic texts account for the Magdalene's last days as spent with Thomas the Apostle in India or with the risen Christ in the desert. The volume of literary and visual artworks of the Magdalene image increases in successive centuries. The metamorphoses of the Magdalene through the Ages of Early Christianity, the Medieval Period, the Renaissance, the

Counter-Reformation, the Enlightenment, and Romanticism to the Ages of Angst and Aquarius deepen our understanding of symbols, spirituality, and the human imagination.

Traditional Iconography of Mary Magdalene

The basic iconography of the Magdalene consists of a young woman with long flowing hair who holds an ointment or unction jar.[9] The central referent is to the understanding of the Magdalene as the one who anointed the feet and/or who attempted to anoint the crucified body of Jesus of Nazareth. Many popular representations find the Magdalene portrayed as one deep in contemplative penance with a skull and/or scourge nearby or held by her.[10] This symbolism refers back to her conversion experience. And when she is pictured as deep in contemplation and gazing into a mirror, this is not a reversion to her previous narcissicism but rather an introspective moment as she looks into her own soul. She has also been represented as a dishevelled, wan, and distraught older woman in preparation for her death.

Usually, the Magdalene is dressed in violet, the color which traditionally signifies penitence and mourning, passion and suffering, and love and truth. Her red mantle signifies love, and the occasional wearing of blue indicates constancy and devotion.[11] All of the characteristics attributable through traditional color symbolism indicate the composite identity of the unnamed women of the scriptures with Mary of Magdala.

Flowing, beautiful hair is a major motif of the Magdalene, representing her role as the anointer of Jesus of Nazareth, and as a repentant and converted sinner. Hair has multivalent symbolic qualities. Traditionally, the Magdalene is imaged with red hair which is symbolic in classical culture of prostitution.[12] Copper-colored or red-hair implies a venereal character [hence, the connection with prostitution]. Hair also represents energy and fertility. A full head of hair represents *elan vital* and *joie de vivre*, linked with the will to succeed. Hair on the head symbolizes spiritual energy. So, abundant, beautiful hair signifies spiritual development. Artistic representations, of the Magdalene with long flowing tresses indicate her spiritual development after her conversion experience.[13]

In the ancient world, it was customary for unmarried women (virgins) to wear their hair long and unbound, a style which becomes synonymous with images of sacred love, whereas courtesans braided or piled their hair high on their heads as seen in artistic images of profane love. The Magdalene's long flowing hair refers to this custom and symbolically to the writings of the early church fathers and the *Litany of All Saints* where she is invoked as a virgin.[14]

Survey of Images of the Magdalene

Early Christian art does not deal with the questions of who Mary of Magdala was or how all these female figures became identified as one. In early Christian art, one basic fact or idea takes preeminence in the representation. It was not the saint who was important as an individual, but the miracle or episode in the life of Jesus of Nazareth to which the saint stood as witness. Just as the "classic" emphasizes universality through the particularity of its continuous reinterpretations, so for the Magdalene, "her dignity lies in her proximity to the mystery of salvation."[15] Early Christian art was concerned with expressions of faith.

In early Christian art or in Byzantine iconography, one would search in vain for individual representations of the Magdalene, finding instead representations of those miracles and episodes in which she played a part, i.e., the Casting Out of the Seven Devils, and the Resurrection. There are also several representations of the Magdalene within the contexts of those scriptural stories which involved the unnamed women such as the Awakening of Lazarus, the Anointing at Bethany, and the Woman Taken in Adultery. Sarcophagi from Milan and Servanne, ivory tableaux from Milan and Munich, the wooden doors of Santa Sabina, and a mosaic at San Apollinare Nuovo attest to early artistic interest in the Magdalene. In the Rabula Codex (sixth century, Zagba), there are unmistakable representations of the Magdalene with the apparition of the risen Christ (presaging the *Noli Me Tangere* which first appears in the early Renaissance) and in prayer for the Awakening of Lazarus (early identification with Mary of Bethany).

The transitional period between early Christian and Medieval art develops the composite image of the Magdalene. Mosaics, frescoes, manuscript illuminations, and miniatures evidence the common identification of the Magdalene with the converted sinner. Representations of the anointing scenes are blended together as the Magdalene becomes identified with Mary of Bethany. Images of the Magdalene reading symbolize the contemplative and meditative path which exacerbates this eventual confusion with Mary of Bethany.[16] This acceptance and identification of the Magdalene with the repentent sinner and Mary of Bethany solidified the composite scriptural image. This confusion of stories and images results in a folk understanding of who the Magdalene was and what she represents to the Christian tradition.[17] Such image development is not unique either to the Magdalene or the Christian tradition.

During the medieval period, the Magdalene begins her metamorphoses from part of the composition of traditional saintly female figures in Romanesque and Gothic art to become a major independent artistic topic. Representations of the Magdalene are prevalent in the cycles depicted in medieval cathedrals, carved or painted on arches and/or in the walls of their portals. During this time, the Magdalene received great veneration as a penitential saint. This period of great faith recognized the power of sin, and enforced penance. The fourteenth-century was the age of the great plague which underlined with daily expediency human suffering, misery, and the fragility of human experience.[18] As the great sinner who received love and forgiveness from Jesus of Nazareth, the Magdalene symbolizes encouragement and solace for her fellow sinners.

The medieval age was also the age of the liturgical drama or Passion play, and of Franciscan spirituality. The figure of the Magdalene loomed large in the traveling plays, particularly in the lamentation and Resurrection scenes. A direct result of these plays was a change in the Magdalene's hair: no longer covered by a mantle or veil, as had been characteristic in earlier art, her beautiful tresses flow loosely around her shoulders. This was a theatrical attempt to humanize the saintly and matronly Magdalene and to make her visually appealing to the audience.

Legendary and theological texts were important sources for this medieval metamorphosis of the Magdalene. For the emerging Franciscan spiritual tradition, she becomes a symbol of penitence, humility, and love. Pseudo-Bonaventura's *Meditations on the Life of Christ* contains many important references to the Magdalene. Several medieval commentators affirm the legend which revealed the true identity of the bridal couple of the Marriage at Cana: Mary Magdalene and John the Evangelist.[19] Bernard of Clairvaux's sermons on the *Song of Songs* (especially Sermon #57) follows the tradition established by Origen in his *Commentary on the Canticle of Canticles* of linking that bride with the anointer of Jesus of Nazareth, Mary Magdalene. She now becomes a symbolic source of the merging of earthly love with spiritual love, *eros* with *agape*.[20] The Magdalene is transformed from saintly matron to a heroine of the great Christian virtues.

Medieval France developed an important devotion to the Magdalene, who was understood as France's Christian missionary and penitent saint.[21] The elaborate legends of her preaching, life, and miracles in France resulted in special veneration. In the thirteenth-century, a chapel to the Magdalene was built and dedicated over the site of a ruined Temple to Diana in Marseilles.[22] The Magdalene has obviously assimilated (not only in France) characteristics of the classical goddess who was protectress of women and human life. Perhaps, the most important French legend which would strengthen the Magdalene's supplanting of Diana is that of the miraculous birth of a son to the queen of Marseilles. As recorded in the *Golden Legend*, the Magdalene assisted in the miraculous conception and birth of a son to the previously barren queen, restored the queen's life after she dies in childbirth, and later preserved the lives of both the queen and her young son.[23] The Magdalene is no longer merely an actress in the drama of salvation; she becomes the heroine.

The Magdalene's new prestige is evidenced by the following transition. During the late medieval period, the illustrations of the Magdalene found in the mysteries of salvation which had previously been located on the cathedral front portals were removed. The representations of these mysteries, including those of the Magdalene, moved inside the cathedrals to decorate the windows and walls, and later the carpets and the altar tableaux. With this change, those who prayed within the confines of the ecclesial structure may have found a new closeness to the Magdalene.

The Magdalene "was one of the favorite subjects of Renaissance paintings, and pictures of her abound. Some are devotional, but many show scenes from the Gospel and her legendary life."[24] During the Renaissance, representations of the Magdalene come into their own and her popularity was in full prominence. "She hardly appears with any distinct prominence till the period of the Renaissance, being confounded with the other Maries in the art of the previous centuries."[25] At this time, the Magdalene came to the forefront as an individual — she no longer needed to be represented within the confines of a narrative.

From medieval times through the Renaissance, the Magdalene is represented under the cross and within the context of those scriptural sequences related to the converted sinner.[26] There can be little doubt that the artists took both women to be one. And such an artistic direction would reflect and nurture the legendary associations of the Magdalene for the Christian faithful. From both an artistic and a spiritual perspective, such an identification would have practical and profound motives: visual expression of the power and meaning of the expiatory death of Jesus of Nazareth for fallen humankind. The crouching figure of this distraught and "fallen" woman at the foot of the cross offers a thematic association for the Christian to the promise of redemption. Such representations visualize two scriptural images that come to represent the Magdalene: first, the woman kneeling at the feet of Jesus of Nazareth — the same feet she earlier anointed and wiped with her hair; and secondly, she who stands like the sentry of the watchtower (Migdol) by the body of Jesus of Nazareth as he hangs from the cross. This image of her kneeling at the feet of Jesus of Nazareth becomes a major artistic convention in representations of the Magdalene, an association begun as early as the fifth-century in western art.

During the early Renaissance, the theme of the *Noli Me Tangere* (representations of Christ's appearance to Mary Magdalene after the resurrection, John 20:17) appears in art, an image which further advances the growing importance of the Magdalene. She becomes a symbol of penitence, humility, and love. The development of Franciscan spirituality, particularly through the writings of Bonaventure and Jacobus de Voragine, firmly establish this theological symbolism of the Magdalene. Her popularity waxes with the Christian's desire to understand and experience the concept of forgiveness: the Magdalene was the great sinner who repented, was forgiven by Jesus of Nazareth, became his devoted disciple, and was the first person to whom he appeared after the Resurrection. Just as the liturgical drama emphasized this image of the Magdalene, Giotto gave artistic expression to the *Noli Me Tangere* in the Arena Chapel frescoes.[27]

The great Italian and Spanish Baroque painters exalted the Magdalene in art.[28] Along with Peter, she became a symbolic defender of the sacrament of penance. This sacrament was as heartily denounced by the Reformers as it was defended by Roman Catholic theologians. During the Baroque period, representations of the penitent Magdalene in the desert, the last communion of the Magdalene, and the contemplative Magdalene were popular.[29]

The Counter-Reformation was a time of intense emotional spirituality, so the Magdalene's appeal and popular position was understandable. The artists highlighted the sensual and voluptuous nature of the Magdalene through the use of color, natural lighting, flowing drapery, and provocative poses. However, these images never lost the impact of the religious and spiritual motivation which brought them into being. Many Baroque artists represent the Magdalene as a beautiful young woman with long flowing hair who wears a revealing garment and who tearfully contemplates her fate. The Magdalene's nakedness symbolized not wantonness, but the innocence and purity of the human spirit once it had experienced repentance and forgiveness.[30]

The Magdalene's popularity was due in part to her position as a defender of the faith, a symbolic crusader for the Roman Catholic tradition, which promised salvation through the sacramental mysteries of the church.[31] Thus one of the reasons for the Magdalene's popularity during the Baroque period was the contemporary religious situation which was one of great sacramental intensity, and images of the Magdalene always seem to be popular at such times.

The rise of science and the decline of Christianity occurred in the centuries after the Counter-Reformation. This secularization of western culture touched all aspects of life, including the arts. Later representations of the Magdalene evidence this growing division as she begins to live as a major personality in Christian spirituality, and as a secular symbol for a reformed prostitute in art, literature, and common parlance. In the seventeenth and eighteenth centuries, her descendents often replace her in literature and the arts as the "whore" — honest or wicked, good or evil, pathetic or comic.[32]

Several nineteenth-century art movements initiated a revival of interest in the Magdalene. The Romantic Movement found the fictionalized image of the Magdalene as the great heroine of the Christian story to be of particular attraction.[33] Crypto-religious art movements like the Pre-Raphaelite Brotherhood and the Nazarenes have a special affinity for dramatic representations of the composite image of the Magdalene.[34] The Symbolists' images of the Magdalene highlight an important artistic metamorphosis in her image: she is now depicted as the *femme fatale*.[35] She is transformed in a fashion similar to other great female figures like Judith, Salome, and Cleopatra. The emphasis on the abundantly flowing hair, androgynous body, and blatant sexuality characterize the basic iconography of the *femme fatale* image which develops in the nineteenth-century.[36]

The Magdalene's journey into the twentieth century heralded a revival of interest in her in art, literature, and music. The secularization of religious art resulted in those puzzling and haunting images of the female descendants of the contemplative repentant sinner. These portraits of unnamed women are artistic attempts to visualize the Magdalene as Everywoman and Everywoman as the Magdalene.[37] Several significant artistic images of the Magdalene have been created in twentieth-century art movements, most notably in expressionism and abstraction. Each selects a different characteristic of the Magdalene to emphasize. The expressionists favor the forgiven repentant sinner, while the cubists develop the terror and suffering of sinfulness.[38] These twentieth-century artists have retrieved and sought to express the archetypal meaning of the Magdalene in a visual language which speaks with adequacy and appropriateness to the secularized Ages of Angst and Aquarius.

Conclusions

The Magdalene's popularity throughout the last twenty centuries is grounded in the successful transformations of her image which are formed by and reflect changes in Christian and secular spirituality. These reinterpretations have been based on a concern for the archetypal meaning of the Magdalene and an artistic attempt to represent that meaning in a language which speaks with immediacy to each new generation. No one image of the Magdalene reveals or expresses the fullness of the "classic"; rather, all the Magdalene images are independent of but interdependent with each other. It is the fundamental nature of a "classic" simultaneously to transcend boundaries and yet be comprehensible within the parameters of a particular moment in history.

On a personal and devotional level, the Magdalene's appeal has endured as the centuries have progressed with certain key moments of intensity, such as the Counter-Reformation. As enigmatic as the Magdalene's image may be or as interested as scholars are, it is evident that on the popular level of the Christian traditions her role is of great significance. She becomes a "classic" image of the redemptive and transformative nature of Christian love. The average Christian finds him/herself closer to accepting the reality of the otherwise abstract concepts of sin and forgiveness as concrete human experiences when imaged through the Magdalene who comes to represent the fullness of human experience in her journey from sinner to saint.

And in her journey through the centuries, the Magdalene has become a prostitute, a goddess, a preacher, a mystic, a contemplative, a miracle-worker, and a muse inspiring artists and writers as well as the Christian faithful. Several of these images, especially that of prostitute and muse, might initially appear as inappropriate references for the saintly figure that the Magdalene has become.

However it was originally intended, her fusion with the unnamed adultress of John 7:53-8:11 led to her eventual evolution into *the* repentent prostitute. Thus, the Magdalene symbolizes human frailty as her sinfulness is acknowledged and she is then redeemed by the freely given love of Jesus of Nazareth. In this way that which might other appear to be profane becomes a metaphor for spiritual transformation. Similarly, the Magdalene as muse inspiring artists and writers might appear as a curious expression of spirituality. Yet such inspiration even when it produces a secular artwork untimately results in the continued visibility and recognition of the religious "classic".

In her own unique fashion, the Magdalene incorporates several of the paradoxical images and characteristics of woman within the framework of the Christian traditions. For example, she has been characterized as promiscuous, virginal, destructive, creative, maidenly, or maternal. A further study of the Magdalene's "femaleness" would illuminate our understanding of the role of woman in the Christian traditions and in western culture. As suggested earlier, reinterpretations of a "classic" throughout the centuries is as reflective of theological developments as it is of shifts in cultural conventions and artistic styles. Each of these different images speaks to those living at *a* particular moment in history. Each major reinterpretation of the Magdalene explicates *that* particular cultural understanding of woman and her societal role.

The Magdalene has withstood the tests of time and history to remain a central figure in the Christian traditions. These reinterpretations of her image affirm the fundamental reality that she symbolized an identifiable and fallable human being who undeservingly received God's grace. So it is the Magdalene who makes the possibility of *that* grace intelligible and the reality of *that* God approachable for the average believer.

In this brief survey, I have been able only to suggest key elements in the Magdalene's metamorphosis from sinner to saint. An expanded analysis of specific artworks, theological texts, and cultural shifts would offer a definitive examination not only of the Magdalene but also a commentary on the fundamental nature of the religious "classic" and the inter-relationship between religion and art. This essay can only serve as an introduction to one understanding of that inter-relationship. It seems appropriate to conclude with a comment from an artist not from a theologian. George Bernard Shaw was able to relate to both the repentant Magdalene musing before her mirror as well as to one understanding of the inter-relationship between religion and art, when he wrote, "You use a glass mirror to see your face. You use works of art to see your soul."

NOTES

1. The understanding of the "classic" is taken from David Tracy, *The Analogical Imagination: Christian Theology and the Culture of Pluralism* (New York: Crossroad Publishing, 1981), esp. pp. 154-229.

2. My original study of the iconography of Mary Magdalene began as a research project for a graduate seminar under the direction of Dr. Laurence Peirera Leite, Professor Emeritus of Art History and Theory, The George Washington University, in 1971. I am also grateful to Dr. Leo Steinberg, Benjamin Franklin Professor of Art History, University of Pennsylvania, and Dr. Stephen Happel, Associate Professor of Religion, The Catholic University of America, for their comments on this manuscript. Of course, any errors in data and the basic interpretation suggested in this manuscript are my own. I am endebted to the Edward F. Albee Foundation for a residency which provided the necessary time and quiet for the revision of this manuscript.

3. An interesting study could be made of those representations of the Magdalene by women artists. I have located only three specific works on the Magdalene theme by women artists: Lavinia Fontana, Noli Me Tangere *(1581;* Uffizi Gallery, Florence); Artemesia Gentileschi, *The Penitent Magdalene* (1619-1620; Pitti Palace, Florence); and Elizabeth Sirani, *The Penitent Magdalene in the Wilderness* (1660; Private Collection, Bologna). This study is a project-in-process.

4. The most helpful discussion of the transformations of the Magdalene image is Marjorie M. Malvern, *Venus in Sackcloth: The Magdalene's Origins and Metamorphoses* (Carbondale: Southern Illinois University Press, 1975).

5. For a discussion of the tradition of the "unsavory reputation" of Magdala as interpreted in the *Talmud*, see Helen M. Garth, *Saint Mary Magdalene in Medieval Literature*, The Johns Hopkins University Studies in Historical and Political Science, LXVII.3 (1949), (Baltimore: Johns Hopkins University Press, 1950), esp. p. 77.

6. Primary references for all the following patristic discussions of the identity of the Magdalene as well as additional early theological opinions on her identity can be found in the following: J.E. Fallon, "St. Mary Magdalene" in the *New Catholic Encyclopedia* (1965), Volume XXV 387-389; Peter Ketter, *The Magdalene Question* (Milwaukee: Bruce Publishing Company, 1935), pp. 66-79; and Victor Saxer, *La Culte de Marie Madeleine en Occident, des origines à le fin du moyen âge* (Paris: Librarie Claveuil, 1959), Vol. 1, 1-31; Vol. II, 327-350.

7. Peter Ketter, *The Magdalene Question,* translated by Hugo C. Koehler (Milwaukee: The Bruce Publishing Company, 1935), p. 83.

8. *The Jerome Biblical Commentary,* edited by Raymond E. Brown, Joseph A. Fitzmeyer, and Roland E. Murphy (Englewood Cliffs: Prentice-Hall, Inc., 1968), pp. 59, 60, 138, and 462.

9. As images reflective of the basic iconography of the Magdalene, see Roger van der Weyden, *Mary Magdalene* (1450-52; Louvre, Paris); Jan van Scorel, *St. Mary Magdalene* (c. 1529; Rijksmuseum, Amsterdam); and Bernardino Luini, *The Magdalene* (Sixteenth-century; National Gallery of Art, Washington).

10. Examples of this iconography include: Titian, *St. Mary Magdalene in Penitence* (1560; The Hermitage Museum, Leningrad); Caravaggio, *St. Mary Magdalene* (c. 1590; Galleria Doria Pamphil, Rome); Francesco Albani, *Repentent Mary Magdalene* (1605-6; Kunsthist Museum, Vienna); Simon Vout, *Penitent Magdalene,* (c. 1630's; Musée des Beaux Arts, Amiens); Georges de la Tour, *The Penitent Magdalene* (1640; National Gallery of Art, Washington); Tintoretto, *Magdalene in the Wilderness* (Sixteenth-century; Detroit Institute of Art, Detroit); El Greco, *The Penitent Magdalene* (Sixteenth-century; William Rockhill Nelson Gallery, Kansas City); Artemesia Gentileschi, *The Penitent Magdalene* (1619-1620; Pitti Palace, Florence); Orazio Gentileschi, *Repentent Mary Magdalene* (ca. 1626; Kunsthist Museum, Vienna); Perode Mena, *Penitent Magdalene* (1664; Museo Nacional de Escultura, Vallodoid); Charles Le Brun, *Mary Magdalene Penitent* (Seventeenth-century; Louvre, Paris); Adraen van der Werff, *Mary Magdalene,* (active 1659-1722; Private Collection, Dresden); and Baudry, *The Penitent Magdalene* (Salon of 1859; Musee des Beaux Arts, Nantes).

11. For an understanding of traditional color symbolism in Christian art, the reader is referred to any of the basic texts such as George Ferguson, *Signs and Symbols in Christian Art* (New York: Oxford University Press, 1980 [1966]), or James Hall, *Dictionary of Subjects and Symbols in Art* (New York: Harper and Row, 1979).

12. Representations of the Magdalene with red hair are grounded in her confusion with the unnamed adulteress. Such images flow in and out of art; for example, Workshop of Martin Schongauer, *Noli Me Tangere* (c. 1475; Musee d'Unterlinden, Colmar); Carlo Crivelli, *St. Mary Magdalene* (Fifteenth-century; Rijksmuseum, Amsterdam); School of Avignon, *Avignon Pieta* (1460; Louvre, Paris); Tommaso Masaccio, *Crucifixion* (1426; Museo di Capodimonte, Naples); Corregio, *Noli Me Tangere* (1511-12; National Gallery, London); Titian, *Noli Me Tangere* (Sixteenth-century; National Gallery, London); and Bartolomeo Schedoni, *Three Marys at the Tomb* (1614; Galleria Nazionale, Parma). However, several artists have used the symbolism of red hair to identify the unnamed adulteress; see Rembrandt. *The Woman Taken in Adultery* (1644; National Gallery, London); and Emil Nolde, *Christ and the Adulteress* (1926; Private Collection, Cologne).

13. The majority of the aforementioned representations of the "Repentent Magdalene" (and variations thereof) portray the Magdalene with long flowing hair.

14. An interesting point for further study would be the relationship of these early texts and the spirituality of celibacy and virginity. In such a context, the Magdalene might be understood as a symbol of the overcoming of *eros* by *agape*.

15. Johannes H. Emminghaus, *Mary Magdalene: The Saints in Legend and Art*, Volume 5 (West Germany: Aurel Bongers Publishers, 1964), 15.

16. As examples of this iconographic development, see Roger van der Weyden, *The Magdalene Reading* (1450; National Gallery, London); and Studio of Ambrosius Benson, *The Magdalene Reading*, (active 1519-1550; National Gallery, London).

17. My use of "folk understanding" is intended to denote that fusion of history, legend, and superstitution which originated with and was accepted as truth by the common believer.

18. It is interesting that the "Dance of Death" (*la danse Macabre*), developed both as a theatrical and artistic device at this time. See Emile Mâle, *Religious Art from the Twelfth to the Eighteenth Century* (Princeton: Princeton University Press, 1982 [1949]), esp, pp. 142-150,

19. Gertrud Schiller, *Iconography of Christian Art*, translated by Janet Seligman (London: Lund Humphries Limited, 1971 [1966]), Volume I, "The idea that it was the apostle [John] who was married in Cana goes back to Jerome, one of the doctors of the Church; despite the lack of a credible tradition, it gained renewed popularity during the middle ages from the *Golden Legend* — which also identified the bride with Mary Magdalene. The legendary story of the marriage is recounted at length in the *Meditationes* of Johannes de Caulibus, the Franciscan." See also *The Golden Legend of Jacobus de Voragine*, translated by Granger Ryan and Helmut Ripperger (New York: Arno Press, 1969 [1941]), p. 363.

20. During the medieval age, the Magdalene became fused with that other reformed prostitute saint, Mary of Egypt. This confusion affirmed the Magdalene as a symbol of the merging of *eros* with *agape*. Donatello's controversial masterpiece, *Mary Magdalene in the Wilderness* (1454-5; Baptistery, Florence), gives visual affirmation to the confusion of the Magdalene with Mary of Egypt. His unpopular sculpture of the Magdalene as old, haggard, dressed in ragged skins and with long flowing hair is symbolic of the extreme asceticism of repentent sinners.

21. A thorough examination of the development of the Magdalene cult in France would prove fruitful on several levels. Why and how such a devotion to the Magdalene developed in France and its possible relation and/or influence on the mythic emergence of St. Joan of Arc (c. 1412-1431), would be questions to investigate for an understanding of the history of Christian spirituality.

22. Remember that the Temple of Diana of Ephesus becomes the site not only of a Christian church dedicated to Mary the Virgin Mother; but Ephesus is also the site of the Ecumenical Council which decrees that Mary is *Theotokos*. These actions stem out of a symbolic motivation to declare/affirm Christianity's superiority to worship of the pagan Earth Mother/ Mother Goddess. The supplanting of Diana by the Magdalene in France is indicative of the rapid growth of her prestige and position in the Christian tradition.

23. *The Golden Legend*, pp. 357-360.

24. Ferguson, p. 135.

25. Anna B. Jameson (finished as Lady Eastlake), *The History of our Lord as Exemplified in Works of Art* (London: Longmans, Green, and Co., 1872), p. 185.

26. Matthias Grunewald's masterpiece, *The Isenheim Altarpiece* (1515; Musee d'Unterlinden, Cologne), offers a magnificent example of the Magdalene at the Crucifixion, Grunewald's work is suggested as one example of this image of the Magdalene. Another powerful expression is found in Tommaso Masaccio, *Crucifixion* (1426; Museo di Capodimonte). In varying degrees, most representations of the crucifixion after the medieval period would also depict this type of image.

27. Jameson, p. 179. The *Noli Me Tangere* becomes an important and popular artistic image, the following is a selective but not comprehensive list of examples: Fra Angelico, *Noli Me Tangere* (Fifteenth-century; S. Marco, Venice); School of Martin Schongauer, *Noli Me Tangere* (c. 1475; Musee d'Unterlinden, Cologne); Corregio, *Noli Me Tangere* (1511-1512; National Gallery, London); Hans Holbein the Younger, *Noli Me Tangere*, (c. 1520; Collection of Her Majesty, Queen Elizabeth II, London); Jan van Scorel, *Christ Appearing to Mary Magdalene* (c. 1550; City Museums and Art Gallery, Birmingham); Titian, *Noli Me Tangere*, (Sixteenth-century; National Gallery, London); Lavinia Fontana, *Noli Me Tangere* (1518; Uffizi Gallery, Florence); Rembrandt, *Mary Magdalene and the Risen Christ at the Tomb* (1638; Collection of Her Majesty, Queen Elizabeth II, London); Frederico Barocci, *Noli Me Tangere* (1528-1612; Uffizi Gallery, Florence); Albert Pinkham Ryder, *Christ Appearing Before Mary*, (1885; National Museum of American Art, Wahington); and Graham Sutherland, *Noli Me Tangere* (1960; Chicester Cathedral, Chicester).

28. Some of the most notable Southern Baroque images include: Caravaggio, *St Mary Magdalene* (c. 1590; Galleria Doria Pamphili, Rome); Francesco Vanni, *The Last Communion of St. Mary Magdalene* (c. 1600; S. Maria di Carignano, Genoa); Giovanni Lanfranco, *St. Mary Magdalene Being Transported to Heaven* (1605; Galleria, Naples); Jusepe Ribera, *Kneeling Magdalene* (c. 1630; Prado, Madrid); and Gian Lorenzo Bernini, *St. Mary Magdalene* (1661-3; St. Peter's Cathedral, Rome).

29. Anna B. Jameson, *Sacred and Legendary Art* (New York: A.M.S. Press, Inc., 1970), Volume I, 357.

30. For an alternative interpretation, see John Berger, *Ways of Seeing* (New York: Penguin Books, 1979 [1973]), p. 92: "The point of her story is that she so loved Christ that she repented of her past and came to accept the mortality of flesh and immortality of the soul. Yet the way the pictures are painted contradicts the essence of this story. It is as though the transformation of her life brought about by her repentance has not taken place. The method of painting is incapable of making the renunciation she is meant to have made, She is painted as being, before she is anything else, a takeable and desireable woman. She is still the compliant object of the painting-method's seduction."

31. This symbolism is evidenced in any of the works listed in note #29, as well as in the work of Peter Paul Rubens.

32. As the secularization of Christian art removes themes and images from the artist's vocabulary, new adaptations of these key images become standards. So images of harlots (particularly reformed harlots like Thais and Camille) become popular. Their popularity and images are grounded in the Magdalene.

33. The works of several Romantic writers, in one interpretation, not only show them to have been intrigued by the heroine character of the Magdalene, but may also serve as the

link in the later connections of the Magdalene with the *femme fatale*; see Samuel Taylor Coleridge, *Christable* (c. 1797-1801); and John Keats, *La Belle Dame Sans Merci* (1819, and *Lamia*, (1819).

34.   See Dante Gabriel Rossetti, *Mary Magdalene at the house of the Pharisee* (1851; Fitzwilliam Museum, Cambridge); and William Holman Hunt, *Christ and the Two Maries*, (1847/c.1900; Art Gallery of South Australia, Adelaide), as representative of the Pre-Raphaelite Brotherhood's interest in the Magdalene. The Nazarenes are represented by Friedrich Overbeck, *Christ with Mary and Mary Magdalene* (1812-6; National Gallery, Berlin).

35.   For example, see Honore Daumier, *The Magdalene* (1848; Private Collection); Elihu Vedder, *The Magdalene* (1883-4; National Museum of American Art, Washington); and any of the New Testament scenes of Gustave Moreau. An intriguing nineteenth-century interpretation is offered by Jean Beraud, *Mary Magdalene in the House of the Pharisee*, (1891; Private Collection).

36.   The *femme fatale* is particularly intriguing. Patrick Bade's study is a fine beginning towards an understanding of this basic image. I suspect that the relationship of that image to the Magdalene can be helpful in understanding her transformations since the late nineteenth-century. See Patrick Bade, *Femme Fatale: Images of Evil and Fascinating Women* (New York: Mayflower Books, Inc., 1979). Consider that another scriptural heroine, Judith (*Book of Judith*, esp. 16:7, 9-11) who liberates Israel by the guile of her beauty also becomes transformed in nineteenth-century painting into a femmefatale; e.g., Gustav Klimt, *Judith* (1901; Osterreichische Galerie, Vienna).

37.   For example, see George Luks, *Woman from Madrid* (late 1920's; Joseph A. Hirshorn Museum and Sculpture Garden, Washington); and Amedeo Modigliani, *Woman with Red Hair* (1917; National Gallery of Art, Washington).

38.   As examples see Max Beckmann, *Christ and the Woman Taken in Adultery* (1917; St. Louis Art Museum, St. Louis); Emil Nolde, *Christ and the Adultress*, (1926; Private Collection, Cologne); Rico Lebrun, *The Magdalene* (1950; Santa Barbara Museum of Art, Santa Barbara): and Graham Sutherland, *Noli Me Tangere* (1960; Chicester Cathedral, Chicester).

TOWARD DOCTRINAL CONSENSUS

Michael J. Gallagher

According to Robert McAfee Brown, the Christian churches have moved from diatribe to dialogue within the decades of the twentieth century.[1] The pain and anguish of a deeply divided Christianity have become increasingly apparent and determined hopes for restored unity have surfaced. In times past, charismatic individuals often uttered pleas for unity. In this century, however, entire churches have committed themselves to the service of unity. Thus, separated Christian churches have formally entered into "systematic theological conversations"[2] of an ecumenical nature.

The intent of this article is to examine one aspect of these theological conversations, namely, the formulation of statements which attempt to express consensus on questions of faith and order. During the past twenty years, the churches have made significant bilateral and multilateral statements on such topics as the nature of the eucharist and the role of authority in the church.[3] These statements are playing a vital, but limited, role in edging the churches toward a visible expression of unity. The structure of this endeavor is as follows. First, a brief historical overview of the Faith and Order movement is presented because this movement has made an abiding impact upon the struggle for theological consensus. Secondly, consensus statements are analyzed in terms of their nature, function, and contribution to the ecumenical movement. Thirdly, attention is given to the methodology of the Faith and Order movement as it strives to blend the traditions of a divided Christianity into a commonly accepted statement of faith.

Historical Overview

The cradle of ecumenism in this century was the first World Missionary Conference which assembled at Edinburgh, Scotland, in June of 1910. This conference represented a meeting of many missionary societies and leaders of various Christian student movements. These missionaries gathered to discuss the problems which they faced in the mission fields, and to design a strategy for a more effective process of evangelization. Many of the missionaries expressed the conviction that the existing divisions within Christianity hampered their preaching of Christ's message of unity and peace. This missionary conference was not a convocation of the Churches as such. Nonetheless, this meeting marked a step in this direction, and, despite the absence of Roman Catholic and Orthodox delegates, was ecumenical in tone and scope.[4]

Toward the end of the Edinburgh Conference, Bishop Charles H. Brent, the Episcopal bishop of the Philippine Islands, voiced an urgent cry for Christian unity, and reminded the delegates of their obligation to strive for a reunited Christianity:

> During these past few days a new vision has been unfolded to us. But when God gives a vision He also points to some new responsibility. When we leave this assembly, we will go away with fresh duties to perform.[5]

Bishop Brent brought his vision of Christian unity to the 1910 General Convention of the Protestant Episcopal Church. Along with Bishop W. T. Manning of New York, he proposed the formation of an international conference to study doctrinal issues, and thus gave birth to the Faith and Order movement. Soon, thereafter, in 1911, a commission of Faith and Order was established to serve the Churches as a forum for study and discussion. The commision stressed that it had no power or authority to commit any participating church to a particular point of view. Furthermore, the commission envisioned its task as threefold: (1) to draw together the results of various ecumenically-oriented theological dialogues, noting both progress and difficulties, (2) to serve as an occasion for self-examination, and (3) to impart a common direction to the formulation of theological questions.[6]

After years of painstaking preparation, the Faith and Order movement held its first world wide conference in Lausanne, Switzerland, 1927, and a second, ten years later, in Edinburgh, Scotland. From these meetings emerged the conviction that a united Christianity demands a common expression of faith.[7]

Eventually, the Faith and Order movement merged with the Life and Work movement — another offshoot of the 1910 Missionary Conference which focused its attention on humanitarian concerns — to form the World Council of Churches in 1948. The fact of two independent movements, one for "practical" Christianity and another for "doctrinal" Christianity, was no longer viable. In part, this convergence stemmed from the theological conviction the the church itself was an essential element of the primitive *kerygma*, and that the true and ultimate goal of all ecumenical activity was one church united in Christ. Thus, "it became increasingly clear that the primary motive in the ecumenical movement must not be to create a sense of spiritual unity among Christians or to facilitate co-operation between churches, however important these objectives may be, but rather to demonstrate the true nature of the church in its oneness, its universality, and its apostolic and prophetic witness in the world."[8]

Under the auspices of the World Council of Churches, the Faith and Order movement convened two other international conferences, Lund, Switzerland, 1952, and Montreal, Canada, 1963. Much energy at these meetings was directed toward the need for a common understanding of the sacraments of baptism and eucharist. Attention was also focused on the imperative to discover a common perspective on the ordained ministry which would ultimately lead to the full mutual recognition of the ministries of the various churches and open the doors to the possibility of sacramental intercommunion.[9]

During the past twenty years, the Faith and Order movement has sponsored numerous meetings and consultations, most notably, Louvain, 1971, Accra, 1974, Bangalore, 1978, and Lima, 1982. These sessions have explored the diverse expressions of the Christian faith within a variety of traditions, the manifold ways of ordering the Christian church, diverse liturgical practices, and the impact of non-theological factors on the development of Christian doctrine. The outcome of this labor has been the creation of a consensus statement on baptism, eucharist, and ministry. This statement has been endorsed by the Sixth Assembly of the World Council of Churches which met in Vancouver, Canada, during the summer of 1983, and will be the focal point of much ecumenical discussion in the years to come.[10]

The initial reaction of the Roman Catholic Church to the ecumenical movement and to the emergence of the Faith and Order commission was courteous but negative. Christian unity was envisioned as a return to Rome. Ecclesiastical authorities in Rome, moreover, denounced the slogan of the Life and Work movement, "Doctrine divides; service unites." The passing of years and the vision of Pope John XXIII, however, have now brought the Roman Catholic Church into the mainstream of the ecumenical movement. Although the Roman Catholic Church is not a member of the Council of Churches, Roman Catholics, with Vatican approval, do serve as voting members on many World Council committees and commissions, including the Faith and Order commission. Thus, Roman Catholic theologians played a part in drafting the consensus statement endorsed at Vancouver. Moreover, the efforts toward doctrinal consensus within the Faith and Order movement have both influenced and have been influenced by the numerous bilateral conversations between the Roman Catholic Church and other Christian churches and communities which have resulted from the ecumenical spirit of the Second Vatican Council.[11]

Consensus Statements: Nature and Function

As noted in the historical overview, the Faith and Order movement is in the process of nudging the churches toward a consensus on the topics of baptism, eucharist, and ministry. This process raises a number of important questions: what is the precise nature of consensus statements? what is the process of their formulation? for whom are they intended? how will they inter-relate with established confessions, theology, doctrine, and church polity?, and what role will they be expected to play in the reunification of the christian churches?

Not all the churches attach the same significance to agreed doctrinal statements. For instance, consensus on doctrinal matters is a much lower priority for the free churches such as the Salvation Army than for the Orthodox churches. Nonetheless, as Lukas Vischer, a leader in the Faith and Order movement, emphasized: consensus statements are of vital importance since they enable each local church to know that its tradition shares in the tradition of the universal faith.[12]

In Faith and Order discussions, doctrinal consensus in the full sense of the term has been defined "as that articulation of faith which is necessary to enable the establishment of visible unity." [13] Thus, the process of formulating consensus statements aims at empowering the churches to confess together the apostolic faith. This process presupposes that the apostolic faith can be restated according to the demands of changing historical and cultural patterns, and that the various traditions will be able to discover sufficient common ground to make a statement of faith acceptable to all.

Consensus statements, moreover, are envisioned as playing an essential role in the creation of a conciliar fellowship among the churches. Ecumenical theologians describe this fellowship as a communion of local churches which will come together, when needed, to express their faith on national, regional, and universal levels. This fellowship, however, is not conceived in terms of a mere federal structure for co-operation among the churches, but rather in terms of a visible expression of the full unity of the church of Jesus Christ. For the creation of such a fellowship, four conditions must be realized. First, the churches must discover ways of overcoming the prejudice of the past, noting both the theological and the cultural factors which have contributed to the historical hostilities among them. Second, the churches must learn to share their common faith in Christ by transcending the anathemas of the past and by creating common confessional forms. Third, the churches must be able to recognize each other's baptism, eucharist, and ministries. Fourth, the churches must establish a mechanism through which they can make decisions together and act in a united fashion. Thus, the need for a consensus in the content of the apostolic faith and the creation of structures making possible common deliberation and decision have been cited as requirements necessary for visible unity in conciliar fellowship.[14]

In their quest for doctrinal consensus, ecumenical theologians are also quick to point out that consensus statements are not to be identified with complete unanimity or with a uniformity of theological understanding. Furthermore, they continue to grapple with such questions as how much theological diversity may be permitted in the expression of the same faith, and whether or not it is an illusion to insist on a common theological articulation of the one faith. Thus, at this stage of ecumenical development, it is quite evident that the relationship between a theological consensus statement and a common confession of faith has not yet been theologically determined.[15]

Avery Dulles readily admits that conceptually diverse formulations may legitimately exist in different sections of the church. Yet, he also stresses the importance of consensus statements. Furthermore, he maintains that consensus statements should meet three requirements. First, they should include everything considered as essential to the subject matter and should specify matters of non-agreement, if any. Secondly, the statements should be deemed potentially acceptable to church authorities and to the faithful. Lastly, the statements should clearly indicate whether the authors assert that the content of the statements must be held or only may be held by the churches involved in the dialogue.[16]

Theological consensus statements are generated by theologians who have been appointed to a dialogue by their respective churches. These theologians then submit the results of their labor to their churches, and thus initiate the long and arduous process of reception. In a very real sense, these statements are directed to the entire People of God, for it is "generally agreed among theologians today that the meaning and the binding value of conciliar decisions cannot be properly assessed without paying attention to their reception in the community of the Church, at the several levels of government, of theology, and of the *sensus fidelium.*"[17] Moreover, this process of reception, more and more, is being envisioned as a vibrant exchange involving the full participation of the laity rather than as a static, passive acquiescence to conciliar statements.[18] In other words, this process involves "not only official endorsement but profound appropriation through a testing process by which the teaching is digested into the life and the liturgy of the community."[19] This, in turn, raises the question of how the churches today can effectively and authoritatively exercise their teaching function, and how the hierarchy of authorities (scripture, creeds, confessional formulas, oversight, pope, bishops, and so forth) are to be inter-related.[20]

Furthermore, the very fact that consensus statements are directed toward the whole People of God in itself raises some significant difficulties. For professional theologians who read them, consensus statements often seem to lack theological finesse and precision; they appear to be so general that in reality they say nothing. Moreover, some theologians are more apt to point out what the statements do not say in terms of their own theological framework or confession of faith rather than to accentuate the progress which has been made. For the theologians who have prepared the consensus statements, moreover, they often become a source of frustration because the statements do not seem to be given enough serious attention by church authorities. In this regard, William Marrevee asks whether these statements will have an impact on church policy or will they simply "serve as an ecumenical window dressing for Churches that remain more intent on maintaining their confessional identity than on attempting to bridge the differences and the disagreements that have emerged in the course of history."[21] On the other side of the coin, church administrators involved in church mergers often lament the fact that the consensus statements seem to lack any real practical application. Finally, the statements often seem to lack immediate relevance for the ordinary Christian in the pew, presuming that he or she even knows about their existence.[22]

It is evident, therefore, that a greater effort must be made to involve all three segments of the Christian community in the process of reflection upon the present statements and in the formulation of future statements. This is imperative, since "it is from the life and thought of the People of God that the consensus emerges and it is into that life that it must be fed back. Only in this way is it possible to appreciate the living context which gives meaning to the consensus statements . . . ."[23]

Nonetheless, despite the importance of consensus statements, they should never be viewed as final products but as stepping stones as Christians come closer together in their appropriation of the Christian mystery. This point has been forcibly made by John Macquarrie:

> The progress of theology does not consist in moving towards a statement of doctrine that would be final and could be accepted by all as an adequate statement of truth. The dialectical character of theology precludes any such possibility, to say nothing of the historical and social conditioning of any statement . . . In ecumenical theology, as in all theology, the truth is not found in a final consensus in which all can rest — and especially not in a consensus so broad or so vague that it is devoid of interest and almost of meaning. Truth is not something at which one arrives, but more of an ongoing process, involving the interplay of different views which sometimes agree, sometimes conflict, sometimes correct one another, but which defy all attempts to subsume them into a single truth . . . every theological truth is one that we have in provisional form and is capable of correction.[24]

It is also generally conceded that consensus statements alone will never create unity; they must be associated with the total life of the community. The attainment of Christian unity is an intricate process involving all levels of the church's life, including prayer, witness through involvement in justice and peace issues, and theological study. Consequently, "consensus is the *result* of an already existing communion. The object of faith is that communion itself. Texts, doctrines, agreements, and forms of worship may make it explicit, but they are not conditions for *koinonia.*"[25]

In the perspective of some theologians, so much communion already exists because of the ecumenical encounter that doctrinal differences should no longer be viewed as a justification for division within the church of Jesus Christ. Such is the position of Jürgen Moltmann who argues that now is the time for church authorities to approve the theological work that has been done and to start making some binding decisions which will enhance the process of conciliar church fellowship.[26] In the same vein, the Jesuit ecumenist, P. De Letter, although he recognizes the value of agreed statements and ongoing theological dialogue, insists that doctrinal differences should not be allowed to obscure the basic unity of faith which has already been achieved by a common belief in Jesus Christ as God-man and Savior.[27] Furthermore, no less a theologian than Karl Rahner has challenged the churches to create a new form of institutional unity in the present and to await a closer doctrinal unity as the result of this institutional unity.[28]

These arguments, moreover, are reinforced by the developments presently taking place within post-ecumenical Christianity.[29] Within this phenomenon, doctrinal clashes are rapidly becoming transdenominational. Avery Dulles has pointed out that a pluralism within each tradition is eroding the older unanimities and that increasingly disputes are found within separate communions rather than between them.[30] Along the same lines, Arthur Crabtree has insightfully written that the "principal methodological contrast today is not between Catholics and Protestants but between those, whether Catholic or Protestant, who think historically and dynamically and those who think unhistorically and statically."[31] Consequently, it appears all the more urgent for ecumenical theologians to clarify, if possible, what is and what is not essential to the Christian faith through the construction of theological consensus statements, which, in turn, can then be related to the historic creeds of the past.

Concluding Reflections on Methodology

The Faith and Order movement has made a noteworthy contribution to the ecumenical thrust of the twentieth century. In light of its often stated goal, to bring churches from isolation to dialogue, the Faith and Order movement has met with remarkable success. Through the efforts of this movement and the World Council of Churches, all major Christian churches — Protestant, Orthodox, Roman Catholic, and Anglican — are now in the process of dialogue, and are moving together on the various levels of prayer, witness, and theological reflection to promote the cause of Christian unity.[32]

In recent years, the dialogue striving for theological consensus has been dubbed as "multilateral conversation." The aim of these conversations is to create a new theological and ecumenical language which can be shared by all the participants. These conversations are characterized by a common point of departure, for there is the cogent realization that it is otiose to attack the factious elements head-on and in isolation whether they are discovered in the creeds of the churches, in their rites of worship, or in their general attitudes.[33] Thus, this method attempts to break new ground, and it has been well described by the noted ecumenist, George Tavard:

> Although the formulations from which they start (as formulated in their creeds, dogmas, and doctrines) may be divergent and at times opposed, their connections with the revelation in Christ are considered, at least hypothetically, as being equivalent. This is precisely what constitutes the parity of dialogue: one recognizes the language of the other as a possible system of expression of the metalanguage of Revelation. The purpose of the dialogue is then to discover in what way and to what depth one can enter in the intentionality of this language, analyze its value, gauge its validity, share it, incorporate it in one's own ways of speaking, thinking, seeing, living, and eventually use it as one's language.[34]

This method has been enhanced by studies on the nature of religious language which conclude that all faith statements are grounded in history and are thus culturally conditioned. It has also been aided by scriptural and ecclesiological research which has demonstrated the pluralism discovered in the New Testament and in the early Christian church. Bolstered by these studies, the method of multilateral conversation has made substantial progress by placing controversial issues in new contexts.Using language which resembles that of the Scriptures and the patristic period, which is part of the common heritage of all Christians, rather than the polemical language of late medieval and reformation theology, these conversations have cast ancient truths in a fresh mold.[35] Moreover, in these dialogues, there has not been the creation of an entirely new theology. Rather, these conversations have facilitated the rediscovery and restoration of theological insights which have been claimed almost exclusively by one or another particular tradition.[36]

In conclusion, the Faith and Order movement has enabled the Christian churches to make significant strides toward the discovery of a new unity for the future rather than the recovery of the lost unity of the past. And, in this process of interpreting anew the traditions of the past, ecumenical theologians are in the process of forging the beginnings of a new tradition. Much has already been accomplished; yet, much remains to be done. This is especially true with regard to the reception of the theological consensus statements on all levels of the churches' life. The challenge remains to make the ecumenical hope for a united Christianity part of the lived experience of all those who have been baptised into Christ and pray the Lord's prayer that all may be one.

NOTES

1. Robert McAfee Brown, *The Ecumenical Revolution* (New York: Doubleday and Company, 1967), pp. 1-84.

2. Lukas Vischer, ed., *A Documentary History of the Faith and Order Movement, 1927-1963* (St. Louis: Bethany Press, 1963), p. 8.

3. For a collection of these statements, see Lukas Vischer, ed., *Growth in Agreement* (New York: Paulist Press, 1982).

4. For a detailed description of this conference, see Ruth Rouse and Stephen Charles Neill, eds., *A History of the Ecumenical Movement, I: 1517-1948* (Philadelphia: The Westminster Press, 1967), 353-62.

5. As quoted in Rouse and Neill, *History of the Ecumenical Movement*, I, 407.

6. Vischer, *Documentary History*, pp. 10-11.

7. For an account of these conferences, see Herbert Bates, ed., *Faith and Order: Proceedings of the World Conference* (New York: Doubleday and Company, 1927) and Leonard Hodgson, ed,. *The Second World Conference on Faith and Order* (New York: Macmillan Company, 1938).

8. Rouse and Neill, *History of the Ecumenical Movement*, I, 701. See, also, David P. Gaines, *The World Council of Churches: A Study of Its Background and History* (Peterborough, N.H.: Richard R. Smith Noone House, 1966).

9. For commentary, see Oliver Tomkins, ed., *The Third World Conference on Faith and Order* (London: SPCK, 1953), and P. C. Rodgers and Lukas Vischer, eds., *The Fourth World Conference on Faith and Order* (London: SCM Press, 1963).

10. For the minutes, reports, and proceedings of these meetings, see Faith and Order Papers, new series, nos. 59, 60, 72, 73, and 113.

11. For the story of the Roman Catholic Church and the ecumenical movement from 1910 until the formation of the World Council of Churches in 1948, see Rouse and Neill, *History of the Ecumenical Movement*, I, 677-93. See, also, George Tavard, *Two Centuries of Ecumenism: The Search for Unity* (New York: Mantor Omega Publishers, 1962). For Roman Catholic statements since the Second Vatican Council, see Thomas Stransky and John Sheerin, eds., *Doing the Truth in Charity: Statements of Pope Paul VI, Popes John Paul I, John Paul II, and the Secretariat for Promoting Christian Unity 1964-1980* (New York: Paulist Press, 1982).

12. Faith and Order Paper, new series, no. 84, p. 23. For an enlightening discussion on the nature of common faith statements and their role in the Christian community, see Glenn C. Stone and Charles LaFontaine, eds., *Exploring the Faith We Share: A Discussion Guide for Lutherans and Catholics* (New York: Paulist Press, 1980), pp. 1-24.

13. Faith and Order Paper, new series, no. 96, p. 9. See, also, David Willis, "Catholic-Ecumenical Theological Consensus? A Reformed Perspective," in *Consensus in Theology?* ed. Leonard Swidler (Philadelphia: The Westminster Press, 1980), pp. 88-89.

14. Faith and Order Papers, new series, no. 92, pp. 28-33; no. 107. pp. 8-17.

15. Faith and Order Paper, new series, no. 96, pp. 10-11.

16. Avery Dulles, "Reflections on Doctrinal Agreement," in *Episcopalians and Roman Catholics: Can They Ever Get Together?* ed. Herbert Ryan and J. Robert Wright (Denville: Dimension Books, 1972), pp. 64-65. Also, see Dulles, *The Survival of Dogma* (New York: Doubleday and Company, 1971), pp. 163-70.

17. George Tavard, "The Anglican-Roman Catholic Agreed Statements and Their Reception," *Theological Studies* 41, no. 1 (1980), 74. See, also, Faith and Order Paper, new series, no. 93, p. 41.

18. Franz Wolfinger, "Theological Reception and Ecumenism," *Theology Digest* 25, no. 3 (1979), 243-47.

19. Faith and Order Paper, new series, no. 91, pp. 87-89.

20. This topic was the subject matter of a consultation sponsored at Odessa by the Faith and Order Commission in 1977. For the report, see Faith and Order Paper, new series, no. 91, pp. 77-93. See, also, Faith and Order Paper, new series, no. 96, pp. 11-12, as well as Carnegie Calian, "Is There a Common Authority for Christians? A Protestant Perspective," and Thomas O'Meara, "Is There a Common Authority for Christians? A Roman Catholic Perspective," *The Ecumenical Review* 22, no. 1 (1970), 16-35.

21. William Marrevee, "Emerging Ecumenical Consensus on the Ordained Ministry, Part II," *Eglise et Theologie*, II, no. 3 (1980), 419.

22. According to Arthur Gouthro, "There have been numerous ecumenical agreements on theological issues but they have tended to be the best kept secrets in town. Unless the contents of the theological statements do not filter down to the person in the pew, they will remain merely academic exercises which the churches as a whole will not take seriously." "The American Church Dialogues on Ministry and Ordination: Roman Catholic Dialogue with Lutherans, Presbyterians, and Anglicans," *Chicago Studies* 16, no. 3 (1977), 327.

23. Faith and Order Paper, new series, no. 69, pp. 127-28.

24. John Macquarrie, *Christian Unity and Christian Diversity* (Philadelphia: The Westminster Press, 1975), pp. 29-30.

25. Faith and Order Paper, new series, no. 92, p. 207. The emphasis is in the original text. Also, see Faith and Order Paper, new series, no. 96, p. 8.

26. Jurgen Moltmann, "The Unity We Seek," *Theology Digest* 27, no. 3 (1979), 247.

27. P. De Letter, "Our Unity in Faith," *Theological Studies* 38, no. 3 (1977), 526-35.

28. Karl Rahner, *The Shape of the Church To Come* (New York: Seabury Press, 1972), pp. 104-05.

29. For a variety of opinions on this phenomenon, see Hans Küng, ed., *Post-Ecumenical Christianity* (New York: Herder and Herder, 1970). In this volume, Yves Congar writes that post-ecumenism is essentially a post-ecumenism of belief, and that "the differences among Christians will no longer be differences among the Churches, but differences among Christians within each church" (p. 16).

30. Avery Dulles, "Ministry and Intercommunion," *Theological Studies* 34, no. 4 (1973), 677.

31. Arthur Crabtree, "Methodological Consensus? A Protestant Perspective," in *Consensus in Theology?* pp. 79-80.

32. Yves Congar, "The Search for Unity: 1927-1977," *Theology Digest* 27, no. 3 (1979), 249-54. Also, see Avery Dulles, *The Resilient Church* (New York: Doubleday and Company, 1977), pp. 173-90.

33. Marrevee, "Emerging Ecumenical Consensus, Part I," p. 210.

34. George Tavard, "The Bilateral Dialogues," *One in Christ* 16, nos. 1-2 (1980), 27.

35. Regarding the nature of religious language and dogmatic statements, see Dulles, *The Survival of Dogma*, pp. 171-184. For an excellent study of New Testament pluralism, see James Dunn, *Unity and Diversity in the New Testament* (London: SCM Press, 1977) as well as Raymond E. Brown and John P. Meier, *Antioch and Rome: New Testament Cradles of Catholic Christianity* (New York: Paulist Press, 1983).

36. A good example of this is found in the Anglican-Roman Catholic dialogue on ministry. Concerning this, Gouthro writes: "The participants did not occupy themselves with trying to answer the question usually raised by Catholics: are their orders valid or invalid? A new and more creative question was posed by the theologians: in what ways is Jesus Christ present and active in the diverse kinds of ministries of the various churches? This question assumes that authentic ministries are carried on and provoke us to describe their gifts and functions and within the communities of faith they serve. The Christological emphasis here also indicates the strong biblical perspective which this whole study of ministry and ordination has. The new approach has been made possible because the conversations between our churches have been dialogues and not monologues . . ." Gouthro, p. 341.

ORIGINAL SIN AND PSYCHOANALYSIS

James Forsyth

A story carried in the Aug. 20, 1980 issue of the *National Catholic Reporter* tells of the cessation of an agreement whereby the Catholic archdiocese of Chicago supplied priests and funds for the mission parish of San Miguelito in Panama. The story implies that the real reason for the breaking of this cooperative link was "the contrast between the apathetic tradition-bound local churches and the socially apostolic activism"[1] of the mission team. Native Panamanian priests are quoted as questioning the doctrinal orthodoxy of the mission team which allegedly "doesn't believe in the real presence or in the virginity of Mary and teaches that original sin is not transmitted by physical generation."[2] Such accusations are painful examples of that kind of dogmatism by which one believer, by clinging to a narrowly interpreted doctrinal formulation, can question the orthodoxy of a fellow believer. It also highlights the dilemma of Catholic theologians in particular who, in attempting to make traditional church teaching intelligible and relevant for their times, must often work within the framework of a doctrinal formulation which is deeply entrenched in the Catholic tradition but suffers all the limitations imposed by the historical and cultural context of its authorship.

Theological reflection on the Catholic doctrine of original sin in recent years has had to face just such a dilemma, namely, how to incorporate contemporary situational, existential, and evolutionary insights into the meaning of the doctrine while remaining faithful to the formula of Trent which states that original sin is transmitted to the descendants of Adam *propagatione non imitatione.*[3] Because the more obvious implications of this formula, namely the association of sin with the sexual procreative act and the notion of a biological connection of the human race with an historical Adam are unacceptable to the mainstream of contemporary theology, Catholic theologians have attempted to discover the authentic meaning and intent of the Tridentine formula by assigning to the word "generation" *(propagatio)* a wider meaning than mere physical procreation.

Andre-Marie Dubarle justifies such an attempt at reinterpretation by pointing out that the main point of doctrinal definition of the canons in which the formula appears is the meaning of justification, not the transmission of original sin. The formula of transmission through generation, therefore, does not belong to the strictly defining part of any canon but appears in a relative clause or in a chapter of doctrinal exposition.[4] Therefore, Dubarle concludes, "a certain latitude for theological interpretation remains possible."[5] The purpose of this paper will be: (1) to examine briefly the theological reinterpretation of the term generation in terms of the concept of the "sin of the world"; and (2) to suggest that a psychoanalytic interpretation might be helpful in clarifying the traditional meaning of the doctrine, and the original intent of the Tridentine formula.

I

The most obvious intent of the formula *propagatione non imitatione* is that by rejecting the Pelagian doctrine that individuals are drawn into sin by the example of Adam (i.e. by imitation), it preserves the idea of the universality of sin and of the appropriateness of infant baptism.[6] Such an explanation, however, gives no positive meaning to the term generation. In attempting to do so, some Catholic theologians have offered an interpretation which goes beyond the idea of physical generation in a narrow sense. In this view, generation refers not merely to the isolated procreative act, but to the entire process (including both birth and one's ongoing interpersonal relationships) by which each individual enters the human world.[7] But the human world with which one attains solidarity is a sinful world. Original sin, therefore, "is not a static given at birth, but an intrinsically historical dimension of being human in a sinful world," and "grows as our participation in sinful humanity grows."[8]

In such a "situational" view, sin is "original" because it is a given not of individual human nature through physical procreation, but of the situation into which one is born and of which one becomes a part. Moreover, one's participation in the "sin of the world" is not, in the first instance, a conscious decision *(non imitatione)*. Rather, sin works its influence upon the individual before he or she is able to make responsible moral decisions. Dubarle states:

> Because he comes from a race and an environment contaminated by sin, he is himself tainted by this contagion, which enters his being through all the avenues of intrapersonal influence, before he is able to offer the least resistance.[9]

It is perhaps true that this situational view gives a more satisfactory account of the involuntary aspect of sin than does the more "personalist" view which appears to be based on the gratuitous assumption that every individual inevitably falls into personal sin. Yet the situational view seems to make an equally gratuitous assumption concerning the inevitability of harmful psychological and social influences. Dubarle, for example, states:

It is inevitable that there should be some injurious and deforming contacts among the multitude of human relationships in which a young child becomes involved, and which he needs absolutely for his formation, just as he needs food to build up his body.[10]

A realistic view of the human condition, no doubt, but does it really account for the universality of sin?

Other authors take a similar situational view of original sin.[11] Louis Monden argues that a child, before the conscious experience of freedom, is profoundly influenced by "all the greed, the cupidity, the pride, the divisions, quarrels and jealousies"[12] of the human community. For Monden, original sin is a situation,

. . . brought about in mankind from the very beginning, an initial option which keeps spreading more widely as mankind expands and growing stronger with the individual sins of each person. On the other hand, each man, even before he is able to use his freedom, is by the very fact of being historically situated within mankind unavoidably caught up in the sphere of influence of that evil, as an area of darkness which he cannot conquer by his own power and which holds him back from the meeting with God.[13]

According to Sharon MacIsaac, the doctrine of original sin conveys the truth that the human person "is formed by his environment at a level anterior to choice,"[14] and asks whether such an explanation of sin in terms of environmental influences can adequately convey the meaning of the traditional formula *propagatione non imitatione.* She answers in the affirmative.

It can, surely, if environmental influences are understood not in the superficial Pelagian sense of examples that are freely chosen for imitation, but in the profound sense brought into fresh prominence by the investigation of Freud and the social sciences. In this sense, the child is born into a situation which is sinful (as well as wholesome), and one which forms him before he can choose with respect to it. It is operative from the moment of birth.[15]

Christian Duquoc describes the "sin of the world" as "the tangle of responsibilities and errors which constitute human reality in its reciprocal interdependence as deaf to the appeal from God."[16] Duquoc identifies this tendency to interpret original sin as the "sin of the world" along with a shift in emphasis from "historical antecedence" to "eschatological dynamism" as the two main lines of approach in the current reinterpretation of the Catholic doctrine of original sin. The latter tendency involves a more processive, evolutionary view which sees original sin not so much as the unhappy residue of some past event but as "the opposition at present between our history and the dynamism of the ultimate,"[17] i.e. the contradiction between what one is and what one is called to become in Christ.

The theology of the sin of the world raises at least two questions. In the first place, when original sin is identified as the sin of the world does it really provide an adequate reinterpretation of the word "generation"? In trying to expand the meaning of generation so as to avoid the unacceptable association of sin with the procreative act, have we ended by branding as sinful the whole process of nurturing and educating our children? Moreover, the expanded understanding of "generation" in the authors quoted above sounds suspiciously more like imitation than generation. Unless, of course, one restricts the meaning of imitation to conscious, freely chosen imitation. This may indeed be true to the intent of the Tridentine formula to condemn a Pelagian view of original sin. But could one not argue also that another obvious intent of the formula was to identify, in the terms it had available to it, original sin as a given of individual human nature rather than something contracted from the enviroment?[18]

Secondly, perhaps one could be forgiven for wondering whether the two lines of reinterpretation mentioned above (the situational and the evolutionary) are entirely compatible. Does not the concept of the sin of the world, inviting as it does the vision of an increasingly sinful situation in which the individual must live, come into conflict with the more optimistic vision of eschatological fulfillment as the culmination of the historical process of human striving? If people see themselves as hopelessly enmeshed in a sinful world, their options would appear to be: (a) to turn away from the world and seek a very individualistic type of salvation, or (b) to pursue a path of idealism in which their own self-authentication and the salvation of the world become matters of human achievement — an attitude which is the antithesis of faith. I want to suggest that the "consciousness of sin" which is the necessary precondition of faith comes not so much from the realization of one's solidarity with sinful humanity but from the realization of the inadequacy of one's own and human civilization's "good works" to authenticate or justify one's existence. For St. Paul, faith becomes possible only when one is convinced of the inadequacy of the "works of the law."

The view, therefore, that humanity's need for redemption becomes convincingly apparent only at the highest point of religious, moral, and cultural achievement seems to me to fit best with the evolutionary view of original sin mentioned above. Only such a view finds a place for human progress and initiative (as the necessary preamble to faith), for salvation is then seen not merely as the rescue of individuals from a hopelessly sinful world, but as the eschatological achieving of the transcendent goal of human striving, i.e. the goal which is beyond human achievement. It is this ambiguity of all human achievement which makes the individual aware of the need for redemption, and which Theodore Roszak describes as the "terrible paradox of progress which gives us this world where things get worse as they get better."[19] According to Karl Barth, making us aware of this paradox is the function of "religion."

> Religion compels us to the conception that God is not to be found in religion. Religion makes us to know that we are competent to advance no single step. Religion, as the final human possibility, commands us to halt. Religion brings us to the place where we must wait, in order that God may confront us — on the other side of the frontier of religion.[20]

In this view the formula which best describes the human condition would not be, the more sinful the individual the more he or she realizes the need for redemption, but rather the more religious the individual becomes the more he or she realizes the need for redemption, or, in Roszak's words "things get worse as they get better." The "sin of the world" concept, on the other hand, seems to give us a vision of the world in which "things get worse," without reminding us of the paradoxical truth that this happens precisely "as they get better."

II

It is at this point, I believe, that a psychoanalytic interpretation of the word "generation" might prove helpful to the discussion. Whereas the sin of the world concept accounts for the inevitability and universality of sin in terms of the injurious enviromental influences brought to bear on the child before that child is capable of conscious moral choices, the psychoanalytic view of human growth locates the origins of guilt precisely in the attempts of those in the child's environment to transmit moral values. Applying this insight to the doctrine of original sin, involves reinterpreting the word generation in the light of a concept such as Erik Erikson's "generativity." There can be no question of the appropriateness of the use of psychological data for an understanding of a word such as "generation." It is obvious that the reinterpretation of generation as a process in the concept of the sin of the world is based on psychological insight into the nature of human development. But psychological theory can also be used as an interpretive tool for a fuller understanding of theological concepts such as God, justification, sin, grace, and redemption if we remember that, whatever else they might be, these words are conceptualizations of human experiences which are accessible to psychological analysis. In the dialogue between psychology and theology, what one is trying to discover is the common experiential substratum of both psychological and theological discourse. In the words of Seward Hiltner:

> If the study of theology consists of God, man, sin, and salva-
> tion — then the kind of psychological understanding which is now
> becoming possible is related to all four fields. In other words, there
> is a sense in which psychological knowledge is an aspect of all
> theological knowledge.[21]

It should be pointed out, however, that this dialogue takes place at the level of psychological and theological anthropology — the fundamental view of human nature and of the human condition which is implicit in psychological and theological discourse. At this level psychological and religious language intersect in describing certain types of human experience. In the context of our present discussion, the theological concept the experiential meaning of which we are trying to rediscover is the concept of original sin. Whatever else this concept might mean, it certainly refers to our experience of the tragic dimension of human existence. It seems entirely appropriate, therefore, to put this concept into dialogue with the Freudian and psychoanalytic analysis of that same experience.

For Erikson, the term "generativity" represented a logical extension of Freud's psychosexual model of human development. For Freud, the culmination of that development was the achieving of genital sexuality in young adulthood. Erikson expands this view of human becoming by pointing out that sexual intimacy "leads to a gradual expansion of ego interests and to a libidinal invest-ment in that which is being generated."[22] This "libidinal investment" is what Erikson calls generativity and which he defines as "the concern in establishing and guiding the next generation."[23]

Like the concept of the sin of the world, the concept of generativity calls for an interpretation of the word generation, not as the isolated procreative act but as a process. In this case, however, the process is no longer the negative one of being gradually assimilated into a sinful environment with the resulting evil consequences, but rather the process of parenting, nurturing, and educating in which humanity does not do its worst to corrupt the child, but its best to transmit moral principles and values. But in keeping with our previously stated paradoxical view of the human condition, psychoanalytic theory suggests that it is precisely in the process of internalizing such moral principles that the child first experiences guilt or, in religious language, the consciousness of sin.

To understand this paradox, it is helpful to recall the final formulation of Freud's instinct theory in which the dualism he saw as characteristic of the human condition is described as the conflict between Eros, the life instinct, and the death instinct. In this final formulation, Eros is no longer identified simply with sexuality; sexuality is but one expression of a more basic instinct whose function is "to preserve living substance and to join it into ever larger unities."[24]

Eros, therefore, is a unifying force, which is served, in Freud's view, by the process of civilization "whose purpose is to combine single human individuals and after that families, then races, peoples and nations into one great unity, the unity of mankind."[25] The death instinct, on the other hand is a divisive force whose function is to dissolve the unity achieved by individual units of life. It is operative, therefore, in physical death which dissolves the unity of the multicellular organism and returns it to an inorganic state, as well as in those mechanisms such as self-preservation, self-affirmation, aggression, and mastery (what Freud called the "ego-instincts") which dissolve interpersonal unity.

Civilization, in Freud's view, is born out of this conflict of Eros and death.[26] For Freud, human aggressiveness was the "derivative and main representative of the death instinct."[27] Aggression is the result of turning the destructive force of the death instinct away from one's own ego and towards others. It then becomes the task of civilization, through its cultural institutions (church, state, family, systems of law, etc.) to repress this externalized expression of the death instinct, thus creating the conditions in which Eros can flourish and triumph over death. This process, however, turns out to be self-defeating, in that, under the influence of civilization's repressions, aggression is once again internalized, but this time in the form of guilt, since the energy of the repressed aggressiveness is appropriated by the superego and turned against one's own ego. The death instinct is now experienced in the form of guilt and the need for punishment.[28] In trying to make Eros triumph over death, civilization paradoxically succeeds only in bringing people under the domination of the death instinct in the form of guilt. Freud seems to have perceived civilization as St. Paul perceived the Mosaic Law, as an extraneous authority which promised life, but delivered death in the form of guilt (Romans 7:9-10).

This internalization of cultural prohibitions takes place, in the first instance, during the oedipal phase of the child's development. For Freud, the developmental task of this stage was the successful resolution of the Oedipus complex — that complex of feelings which Freud ascribed to the male child of about four or five toward his parents: attraction to the mother as an object of sexual love, and ambivalent feelings of love and hostility toward the father as a rival for mother's love. In Freud's view, when this complex is successfully resolved two things happen: the child renounces the mother as sexual object and his love for her becomes "aim inhibited" tender affection; secondly, the child identifies with the father, confirming his masculinity and introjecting or internalizing the commands and prohibitions of the father. The result of such introjection is the formation of the superego and the beginnings of conscience. In this way the child is able to overcome his hostility for his father by transferring the source of prohibitions and obstacles to instinctual impulses from an external source (the father) to an internal source (the superego).[29]

This internalizing of the authority of the father is the beginning of the process of internalizing civilization's cultural prohibitions, for in this instance the father represents the extraneous authority of culture which decides what is good and bad. As the child grows, the same internalizing of authority will take place in wider forms of communal life beyond the family. Thus the "loss of happiness through heightening the sense of guilt"[30] which Freud sees as the price of such internalizing of authority is continually reinforced.

> Since culture obeys an internal erotic impulse which causes human beings to unite in a closely knit group, it can only achieve this aim through an ever increasing reinforcement of the sense of guilt. What began in relation to the father is completed in relation to the group.[31]

Notice that while Freud agrees that the child arrives at a sense of guilt through contact with the environment, the nature of that contact is entirely different from that suggested by the theology of the sin of the world. In Freud's view, it is not culture's evil influences which foster the sense of guilt in the individual. Rather it is culture's best efforts on the individual's behalf — the effort of one's parents to transmit cultural and moral values and the effort of cultural institutions to lead humanity to the goal of civilization's "erotic impulsion," i.e. the ultimate "unity of mankind" (the kingdom of God?) — which inevitably produce the sense of guilt.

Why must this be so? Why must civilized humanity's noblest efforts be self-defeating? Freud's answer is that the root of the problem is not in humanity's cultural institutions but in individual human nature, i.e. in the instinctual duality of Eros and death. For Freud, the negative destructive impulses exist apart from civilization, just as for St. Paul, sin exists apart from the law. "Sin was in the world before the law was given, but sin is not counted where there is no law" (Romans 5:13). Sin, as a given of human existence, becomes painfully apparent through the transgressions of the law which it inspires. Guilt, therefore, as the painful awareness of sin, is the result of one's encounter with the law. This is in agreement with the Freudian view that guilt is the result of the individual's encounter with civilization's cultural repressions. Both Freud and St. Paul seem to agree that sin, conceived of as a divisive and alienating egoism which opposes that "life" which is the object of both civilized and religious striving, is rooted in the individual human nature, and what is produced by the individual's contact with the cultural and religious environment is not sin, but the consciousness of it, i.e. guilt.

What then is transmitted by "generation"? If by generation we mean the whole process of parenting, nurturing, and educating suggested by Erikson's "generativity," then what is transmitted is a sense of guilt. Now guilt implies personal responsibility, and it is in the transgressions of religious and cultural prohibitions that this responsibility is felt. But at the same time it is recognized that there is an involuntary aspect to the "sin" which inspires such transgressions. This involuntary aspect — this "law in my members" — is an existential given and, therefore, the universal condition of humanity. In any doctrine of original sin, there is a tension between these two elements, universality and personal responsibility. The obvious intent of the Adamic myth is to explain the universality of sin. It could be noted here, in passing, that the Freudian theory of the primal horde may be read as a similar type of myth. As for Christianity every individual repeats the sin of Adam, for Freud, every individual, in the oedipal experience, relives the guilt-producing experience of the primal horde.

In both cases, however, the myth gives expression to a truth of human existence without explaining it in terms of historical causality. If we adopt the eschatological view of original sin mentioned above, then sin becomes the universal condition of unredeemed humanity, or the contradiction between one's present existence and one's essential being which can only be realized in the eschatological fulfillment promised in Christ. This painful experience of the gap between actual existence and essential being is the universal experience of humanity, and it represents the involuntary aspect of sin.

Perhaps, therefore, it is necessary to retain both meanings of the term "generation," as referring both to the event of conception and birth and also to the generative process described by Erikson. To be born is to enter into human existence and to assume, therefore, this alienation from one's essential being which is the mark of that existence. Generation, then, may be taken in the first instance, to refer to the entry of each individual into human existence which for Paul Tillich represents a "fall" from essence to existence, an entry into the finite of one who belongs to the infinite.[32] But generation can also be understood as that process by which each individual becomes aware of his or her real condition, i.e. the religious and cultural process of "eating of the tree of the knowledge of good and evil," of internalizing moral and cultural values. This process, as we have seen, carries with it the sense of guilt and personal responsibility. Both of these interpretations of the term "generation" are in fundamental disagreement with that proposed by the theology of the "sin of the world." Generation as "birth" suggests a personalist rather than a situational understanding of original sin. Sin is seen as a given of individual human nature rather than something assimilated from the environment. Generation, as a process, on the other hand, is seen as a fundamentally different kind of process from that suggested by the concept of the sin of the world. Sin is not the result of harmful environmental influences; sin, or rather our awareness of it, is paradoxically the' result of beneficial environmental influences. Such an interpretation seems to me to be more in keeping with the intent of the Tridentine formula which is to emphasize that sin, in the first instance, is in the individual and not in the environment.

It should be noted, in conclusion, that, as noted above, any doctrine of original sin faces the challenge of reconciling human personal responsibility with the universality (and therefore an involuntary aspect) of sin. In view of the fact that Tillich's interpretation of the fall, to which we have referred, seems to stress the universal and involuntary aspect of sin and, therefore, to suggest a creation which is not good, the following points should be made:

(1) The alternative to Tillich's interpretation would seem to locate the source of evil in human freedom of choice. This option raises the further question of God's autonomy and his sovereignty over creation. Moreover, it fails to adequately account for the universality of sin.

(2) Tillich in no way wants to deny the essential goodness of creation or of human nature. His position is that the condition of our actual existence is one of estrangement from that essential goodness. Sin is this state of separation from God, from others, and from our own essential being.

(3) The goodness of creation in general and of human nature in particular cannot, in my opinion, be understood in a simply static or ontological way. We cannot ask in simple black and white terms, "Is creation good or bad?" To do so fails to take into account the developmental and redemptive qualities of human becoming. Tillich's view seems to suggest that the essential goodness of human nature is not a given but a goal to be achieved through a process of development which includes a redemptive factor. In other words, the essential goodness of human nature represents the goal of human development, but a transcendent goal which is beyond human achievement and can be realized, in the Christian view, only through that grace which is manifest in Christ. To maintain the essential goodness of human nature it is not necessary to believe that that goodness is fully actualized from the moment of birth. Like the rest of creation we are "eagerly awaiting" that degree of fulfillment, and we "groan inwardly" since the fulfillment (salvation) we desire is not an accomplished fact but "something we must wait for with patience" (Romans 8:18-25).

NOTES

1. *National Catholic Reporter* Aug. 20, 1980, p. 2.

2. *Ibid.*

3. Denzinger, 790.

4. The point of the decree on original sin, for example, is that the remission of original sin is only possible through the redemptive work of Christ which is applied to individuals through the sacrament of baptism. The transmission of the "sin of Adam" is referred to only in the relative clause *"quod origine unum est et propagatione non imitatione transfusum omnibus inest"* (Denzinger 790). Likewise, in the same decree, the doctrinal definition of the necessity of infant baptism is followed by an exposition in which the purpose of the church's practice of baptizing infants is explained in the words *"ut in eis regeneratione mundetur, quod generatione contraxerunt"* (Denzinger 791).

5. André Marie Dubarle, *The Biblical Doctrine of Original Sin* trans. by E.M. Stewart (NewYork: Herder & Herder, 1967) p. 238.

6. Denzinger, 791.

7. See Brian O. McDermott, S.J., "The Theology of Original Sin: Recent Developments" in *Theological Studies,* 38:3 (1977), 478-512.

8. *Ibid.,* p. 480.

9. Dubarle, p. 244.

10. *Ibid.,* p. 241.

11. G. Vandervelde identifies Piet Schoonenberg, Darl Rahner, and Heinz Weger with this situational view. See his *Original Sin: Two Major Trends in Catholic Reinterpretation* (Amsterdam: Rodopi, 1975).

12. Louis Monden, S.J., *Sin, Liberty, and Law,* trans. by Joseph Donceel, S.J. (New York: Sheed and Ward, 1965), p. 71.

13. *Ibid.,* p. 72.

14. Sharon MacIsaac, *Freud and Original Sin* (N.Y.: Paulist Press, 1974), p. 115.

15. *Ibid.,* p. 118.

16. Christian Duquoc, "New Approaches to Original Sin," trans. by Joe Cuneen, in *Cross Currents* (Summer 1978), p. 196.

17. *Ibid.,* p. 196.

18. In this connection it is difficult to overlook the wording of the decree on justification which insists that individuals contract their own injustice in the event of conception. Individuals, it insists, born through generation of the seed of Adam, contract through Adam, in conception, injustice as their own *". . . cum ea propagatione per ipsum dum concipiuntur, propriam iniustitiam contrahant . . . ."* (Denzinger, 795).

19. Theodore Roszak, *Where the Wasteland Ends* (Garden City, N.Y.: Doubleday, 1972), p. XXVIII.

20. Karl Barth, *Epistle to the Romans,* trans. by C. Hoskyns (London: Oxford University Press, 1933), p. 242.

21. Seward Hiltner, "The Psychological Understanding of Religion," *Crozer Quarterly,* 24 (1947), 3-36.

22. Erik Erikson, *Childhood and Society* (New York: W.W.Norton & Co., 1963), p. 267.

23. *Ibid.*

24. Sigmund Freud, *Civilization and its Discontents,* trans. by James Strachey (New York: W.W. Norton & Co., 1971).

25. *Ibid.*, p. 69.

26. *Ibid.*

27. *Ibid.*

28. *Ibid.*, pp. 70-71.

29. The obvious bias and one-sidedness of Freud's interpretation of the Oedipus complex (its exclusive application to the male child, the predominant role of the father, and the essentially sexual character of the conflict) have been pointed out by other theorists (e.g. Adler, Jung, Fromm) and should not distract our attention from the essential features of the oedipal stage which are relevant for our discussion, viz., the processes of identification and internalizing of parental commands and prohibitions which are characteristic of this stage of development and which represent the beginning of the development of conscience and the experience of guilt. For an interesting discussion of the question see Eric Fromm's *The Sane Society* (Greenwich, Conn: Fawcett Publications, 1955), pp. 42-51.

30. Freud, p. 81.

31. *Ibid.*, p. 80.

32. Paul Tillich, *Systematic Theology,* Vol. 2 (Chicago: University of Chicago Press, 1957), 29-44.

Brezik, Victor, editor

One Hundred Years of Thomism/Aeterni Patris and Afterwards:

Norte Dame, IN

0-9605456-0-3

University of Notre Dame Press

pa. $9.95/sale $7.95

Keith J. Egan

18 September 1985

THE RETURN TO THE CLASSROOM
OF THOMAS AQUINAS

Keith J. Egan

Pope John XXIII died twenty years ago on June 3, 1963.[1] The intervening years have produced in Catholic circles a plethora of changes and for some these changes have constituted what Philip Gleason has called a "spiritual earthquake."[2] For all, indeed, some fixture or other of Catholic life is not what it used to be. Among the rejects of this era are neo-scholasticism and Thomism. In the words of Bernard Lonergan, ". . . Aquinas no longer is thought of or appealed to as an arbiter in contemporary Catholic thought."[3] Thomas Aquinas no longer stands at the center of Catholic thought. Yet, comfort may be taken from the realization that this rejection of Thomas Aquinas must eventually spend itself. So classical an author as Thomas can never be long ignored by serious scholarship. One can also take heart from the conviction that a genuine scholarly recovery of Thomas will eliminate those aspects of nineteenth and twentieth century Thomism that rendered it suspect to modern scholarship: an over-dependence on commentators whose commentaries usurped the place of a firsthand study of the texts of Thomas, the absence of a dialogue between Thomists and modern science, a disregard for the historical context of this thirteenth century schoolman, an inability to appreciate the character of the genres in which Thomas taught and wrote, a failure to realize the intuitive character of Thomas' doctrine of the *intellectus,* a lack of appreciation for Thomas' role as an expositor of scripture, and finally the imperialism which flaunted Thomas not only as an authority but almost as the sole authority in philosophy and theology.[4] Inevitably a solitary authority becomes no authority at all. A heavy price is now being paid for the over inflation of the authority of Thomas Aquinas. His friends have done him no small disservice.

It may be premature to forecast a thoroughgoing revival of Thomism; yet, expectations may not be so dim as Karl Rahner's words imply: "I do not believe that some spectacular Thomist renaissance is on the point of breaking out in the church."[5] Moreover, in a very real sense the seeds for a renewed understanding of the work of Thomas Aquinas were sown earlier in this century by scholars such as Pierre Rousselot, Joseph Maréchal, Jacques Maritain, Étienne Gilson, and finally by two contemporary theologians whose work has been so deeply affected by their study of St. Thomas, Karl Rahner and Bernard Lonergan. These two theologians are living reminders of the creative power of contact with the texts of Thomas.

Signs of a gradual reclamation of the thought of Thomas have been occurring. Thus the celebration in 1974 of the seven hundredth anniversary of the death of both Bonaventure and Thomas Aquinas included the colloquy in their honor sponsored by the University of Chicago in conjunction with the Catholic Theological Union and the late Jesuit School of Theology at Chicago.[6] Another hopeful sign for a Thomistic revival is the establishment at the University of St. Thomas in Houston, Texas, of the Center for Thomistic Studies, inaugurated in 1980,[7] a center, however, that confines itself to the study of the philosophy of Thomas Aquinas. No one institution can do everything but Thomistic studies have been plagued by a continual bias to the study of Thomas' philosophy to the neglect of his theology. Fortunately, since 1929 there has been a major center that has been open to training and research into both the philosophy and the theology of Thomas Aquinas, i.e., the Pontifical Institute of Mediaeval Studies, Toronto.[8]

Thomas Aquinas will re-emerge as a key theological resource as scholars continue to identify and make use of the classics of the Christian theological tradition. In the meantime a grave lacuna exists in our access to that tradition. This paper restricts itself to one aspect of this lacuna, the absence of the theology of Thomas Aquinas in the undergraduate curricula of Roman Catholic seminaries, colleges, and universities. Quite frankly this essay advocates some degree of Thomistic literacy for future clergy and laity who might be well informed were it not for an ignorance of Thomistic theology. The wholesale rejection of scholasticism and Thomism during the past two decades has created an unfortunate void in our undergraduate curricula, a void, which, in fact, may never have been filled since theology as distinct from religious instruction in so recent an ingredient in Catholic undergraduate programs.[9] Whether undergraduates in the past have ever been truly conversant with Thomas is not the issue. What is at stake is whether or not we can justify the existence of undergraduate programs in theology where our students are not exposed to the theological inquiries of the *Doctor Communis.*[10]

The absence of Thomas Aquinas in undergraduate programs is more than an impression. An inspection of more than 200 published catalogues from 1981-1983 of Catholic junior colleges, colleges, collegiate seminaries, and universities from all fifty states is a sobering experience for anyone who thinks Thomas Aquinas should be more than a token presence in our educational institutions.[11] Here are some of the statistics. Only seven of the above mentioned undergraduate programs, in their departments of theology, religious studies, and the like, list courses dealing exclusively with the theology of Thomas Aquinas. Another twenty institutions offer one or more courses that include Aquinas in one way or the other, e.g., Georgetown University's Theology 140, "The Catholic Tradition in Politics." This inspection reveals no undergraduate course fully devoted to the study of the theology of Thomas Aquinas in a Catholic seminary. To be expected, some twenty eight institutions offer courses devoted exclusively to the philosophy of Aquinas. Another seventy nine of these institutions list courses in philosophy which include Thomas' thought in one form or another. Numbers are used here in a general way. Precise statistical tables are not what is important for our present discussion. What is evident is the general neglect of Thomas' theology in undergraduate programs in Catholic institutions of higher learning. The numbers used are, in fact, a broad indication of the low level of interest in the theology of Thomas Aquinas on the part of those whose responsibility it is to design courses for undergraduate bulletins. Admittedly, the above figures do not indicate the frequency with which the courses on Thomas are taught. Nor do the figures reveal how often the theology of Thomas Aquinas may be taught under a special rubric that allows for a selected theme during a particular semester. It was under such a rubric that I taught a course on the theology of St. Thomas to undergraduates during the spring semester of 1983 at Marquette University.[12]

This colloquium for undergraduates provides the immediate basis for my reflections on the need for further exposure to the theology of Thomas by undergraduates. However, before getting down to the specifics derived from this experience, I want to address an issue that I believe directly impinges on the question of the place of Thomas Aquinas in theological education. I refer to Thomas' identity as a theologian. The situation in American academic institutions where Thomas is more prominent in philosophy departments than he is in depart- of theology reflects the long confusion about the identity of Thomas' work. Father Armand Maurer of the Pontifical Institute of Mediaeval Studies, Toronto, has ably traced the discussion about the identity of medieval scholasticism as philosophy or theology carried out during the nineteenth and twentieth centuries.[13] The discussion begins with Victor Cousin who concluded that scholasticism was not philosophy but theology. The opposite was soon asserted and not only held sway but was consecrated as a commonplace of Catholic thought in 1879 with the publication by Leo XIII of his encyclical *Aeterni Patris*.[14] The most influential modern historian of medieval scholasticism, Étienne Gilson (d. 1978) espoused and intensified the conviction that scholasticism and Thomism constitute a Christian philosophy. However, with his characteristic passion for truth, Gilson came at age seventy five in his autobiographical account of his intellectual development, *The Philosopher and Theology*, to a new conviction: St. Thomas and other medieval scholastics were first and foremost theologians whose philosophy was always at the service of their theology.[15]

I cite Father Maurer's research and Gilson's conversion not to dismiss the philosophical importance of Thomas Aquinas. Only a fool could make such a superficial judgment. Thomas Aquinas obviously is one of the great philosophers of Western civilization. Our age, too little inclined toward philosophical inquiry, would do well to attend to his philosophy not less but more. What is crucial here is to determine what it was that Thomas was doing and what he thought he was doing. To his contemporaries Thomas became professionally *magister in sacra pagina*, master of the sacred page.[16] Thomas' principal duty as a master was to lecture on the bible. As James Weisheipl has said: "Throughout the entire Middle Ages the basic text of the master's classes was the Bible — always the Bible."[17] Thomas' task was to explain, *exponere*, the meaning of the bible, directly in his now much neglected commentaries on scripture or indirectly in his other works. In the prologue to his masterpiece, the *Summa theologiae*, Thomas describes himself as *catholicae veritatis doctor*, teacher of catholic truth, and refers to his task as "briefly and very lucidly treating those things which pertain to sacred doctrine" — the task which today is called theology. Thomas Aquinas was a theologian who searched for the meaning of the Word of God, often by way of philosophical inquiry, increasingly so as he further mastered the thought of his philosophical mentor, Aristotle. Thomas immeasureably enriched western philosophy, but his central identity was and is as a theologian who primarily *taught* theology just as the Fathers of the Church had primarily preached their doctrine. Thomas' doctrine cannot be identified and understood as primarily a philosophy. As Gilson has stated: "A theology cannot be interpreted as if it were a philosophy. . . ."[18] Thomas Aquinas was a teacher of theology whose doctrine has become classical in the Christian tradition. Within that tradition the Roman Catholic Church has designated Thomas as one of its very special teachers when in 1567 it named Thomas Aquinas a Doctor of the Church.[19] Since that time, especially in the last century the Catholic Church has repeatedly endorsed the doctrine of St. Thomas,[20] even to the point, unfortunately, where Thomas has been made to appear as a partisan teacher of Catholic doctrine.[21]

The classical theological doctrine of Thomas Aquinas, Doctor of the Church, can be ignored only at the impoverishment of the Catholic tradition of theology. If undergraduates are to study theology in Catholic schools, then at least the more gifted and the better motivated should have some firsthand contact with this theology of Thomas Aquinas. Can the laity or the clergy be theologically literate if they have no familiarity with the thought of the man whom Paul Tillich has referred to as ". . . the classical theologian of the Roman Church . . . ."?[22]

What do we pass on to these undergraduates from the extensive corpus of Thomas' writings? While it is important for students to become familiar with the conclusions and the content of Thomas' theology, it is even more crucial, I think, to expose students to the process of Thomas' inquires, to ask questions with him, to explore the meaning of the Christian message in the company of a master explorer. Without this exposure, there might be a return to the days of making an idol out of Thomas Aquinas. Thomas is adamant in his opposition to teaching theology from an authoritarian model:

> . . . if a master determines a question exclusively by means of

authorities, a certain listener (student) will be persuaded that a matter is so, but he will acquire no knowledge (*scientia*) nor understanding (*intellectus*) and he will go away empty-headed.[23]

Thomas perceives the reponsibility of the master to be that of leading the student to knowledge and understanding. No matter how authoritative some of his positions have become, surely Thomas would not countenance the handling on of his doctrinal positions as merely an exercise of the memory. Of course, setting as a goal, not the acquisition of answers but rather the wrestling with the texts of Thomas on his own terms limits severely how much of Thomas' writings can be covered in a course. This goal certainly trimmed my sails in the colloquium on Thomas of this past semester. Yet, the students and I found the goal and what we accomplished satisfying. In this regard I am encouraged by the imagery of Bernard Lonergan, who in the epilogue to *Insight* acknowledges the rewards he gained by wrestling with the texts of St. Thomas:

> After spending years reaching up to the mind of Aquinas, I came to a twofold conclusion. On the one hand, that reaching had changed me profoundly. On the other hand, that change was the essential benefit. For not only did it make me capable of grasping what, in the light of my conclusions, the *vetera* really were, but it also opened challenging vistas on what the *nova* could be.[24]

This reaching up to the mind of Aquinas involves more than learning by rote, and the consequences of reaching are exciting, indeed. According to Lonergan,

> . . .it is only through a personal appropriation of one's own rational self-consciousness that one can hope to reach the mind of Aquinas and, once that mind is reached, then it is difficult not to import his compelling genius to the problems of this later day.[25]

At this point, I would like to share some of the specifics which I take away from the experiment of teaching the theology of Thomas Aquinas to undergraduates. Several years ago when the historical section of the Department of Theology at Marquette University proposed some new courses on classical figures from the Christian tradition, namely, Augustine and Martin Luther, the section demurred at proposing a course on the theology of Thomas Aquinas for undergraduates because it was feared that students were not, in the present academic environment, ready to tackle such demanding and foreign material. It was agreed, however, that the department should look for an opportunity to teach St. Thomas Aquinas as soon as possible. This opportunity arrived when the Mellon Fund made it possible to experiment with a course on the theology of Thomas.

The course rubric was Theology 197, Colloquium: The Theology of Thomas Aquinas. It was considered an introduction to the theology of Aquinas. The emphasis was on the study of the texts of St. Thomas. Secondary literature was recommended only when it was necessary to provide background for the reading of Thomas' texts. After some initial lectures on the times and life of Aquinas in the fashion of intellectual history and biography,[26] in so far as these disciplines contributed to an understanding of Thomas' doctrine, attention was given to Thomas' lectures on two epistles of the New Testament.[27] This exercise was intended to highlight Thomas' role as an expositor of scripture and to familiarize the students with Thomas' manner of understanding scripture. The students also studied *Summa theologiae* I^a, q. 1, a. 10, in order to situate Thomas' significant contribution to the medieval theory of the four senses of scripture, especially his espousal of the historical or literal sense of scripture as the only valid sense for arguing to a theological position.

The class also investigated Question One of the First Part of the *Summa theologiae* to determine the meaning for Thomas of *sacra doctrina* and therefore the meaning of theology for Thomas.[28] Question Thirteen of the same part of the *Summa theologiae* was studied to ask with Thomas about the possibility and the extent of theological language. Were I to teach this course again, I would have the students also study Question Twelve: "How God is known by creatures," as a prelude to Question Thirteen. Thomas so builds on one premise after the other that it becomes diffcult to omit any question, though it is necessary to omit many. The class also studied Thomas' prologue to the *Summa theologiae* as well as several other prologues within this *Summa*[29] because of my conviction that medieval writers took quite seriously the composition of prologues. It has beome clear to me that a study of medieval prologues is instructive and provides helpful insights in the interpretation of what follows the prologues. Thomas is a master of the concise and enlightening prologue.

Two themes in Aquinas' writings were given special attention during this course: faith and Eucharist. Faith, of course, is basic to all theological reflection. Moreover, a study of the virtue of faith reveals Thomas Aquinas at his best, analyzing the human person and the human response to divine action in human life. This topic also allowed for an appreciation of the evolution of Thomas' thought in regard to faith from the time of his *Commentary on the Sentences of Peter Lombard* (the *Scriptum*) until his treatment of faith as the basic virtue in the Second Part of the *Summa theologiae*.[30] So too with the Eucharist one can follow the development of Thomas' thought throughout his life.[31] Both of these topics permit one to witness Thomas' growing appreciation of the dynamism of the intersection of divine and human life. In his reflections on faith we can perceive the dynamic relationship of the human mind and God, and in his inquiries into the Eucharist we can understand the dynamism of the relationship between the believer and the sacramental reality of the Eucharistic presence. Faith and Eucharist are personal favorites from Thomas' theology, and I felt that I could use them to help the students obtain a glimpse of Thomas' brilliance.[32] Numerous other themes similarly reveal Thomas' creative theological mind. The well of his wisdom seems near inexhaustible.

The students were assigned brief reflective papers throughout the course, no more than three typed pages. Each paper challenged the student to seek an understanding of a particular theme in a text of St. Thomas without direct recourse to secondary literature. These papers were opportunities to discover what Thomas did when he explored a theme and how he carried out his inquiries. A final assignment consisted in a reflective reading and report on a theme in the texts of Thomas that corresponded to an interest of the student. This assignment gave each student an opportunity to become more personally involved in the study of Thomas Aquinas, while at the same time it provided the experience of working against an anachronistic reading of his theology. This assignment suggested to the students how Thomas might expand their intellectual horizons on a pertinent issue. Yet, at the same time they were to guard against forcing Thomas to speak to a reality which he did not encounter or envision. Thus, one student explored Thomas's doctrine on the just war to prepare her to understand the tradition as she moved on to study the new issues involved in the discussion of nuclear warfare. This assignment and other aspects of the course alerted the students against using Thomas as an answer machine to reenforce prior convictions.

The students were urged to read regularly from the writings of St. Thomas, daily as an ideal — *nulla die, sine pagina (is)*. They were also invited to compile during the progress of the semester a personal glossary of terms used by St. Thomas. Scholastic categories, unfamiliar to modern students, required special and continual attention. Yet, the rehabilitation of terms whose meaning emerges only after continued struggle proved to be one of the quite rewarding aspects of the course. The discovery and re-discovery of the meaning of terms like *esse, essentia, materia, forma,* etc., were stimulating for students and teacher alike. An attempt was made to work with these terms in Latin in order to free them from associations in English that deprive them of the meaning that they have in the texts of St. Thomas. The students were in agreement that they would have benefitted greatly if they knew some Latin. Background lectures tried to convey what went on in the medieval lecture hall, what the *lectio* was, the nature of the *articulus,* that literary genre that reveals the processes of both *lectio* and *disputatio.*[33]

A *vade mecum* for the course was Thomas Gilby's compilation of *Theological Texts.*[34] Its selections are arranged according to theological themes. The great variety of selections on specific themes enables one to realize the many places where Thomas treats a particular theme. One objective of the course was to alert the members of the class to the peril of looking at a topic in only one place in the writings of St. Thomas. The passing of time, differing genres, philosophical growth, spiritual insight, contact with Greek theology, all made an impact on Thomas' approach to and his understanding of a particular theme during the progress of his intellectual journey.

Members of this class made both oral and written responses to a questionnaire concerning their experience of studying the theology of Thomas Aquinas. Some of their responses have already been incorporated into this paper. All of the students[35] said that they had benefitted intellectually from their study of Thomas. Some mentioned that this study had resulted in spiritual growth and a strengthening of faith.

The proposed method of the class was the seminar approach which did not materialize often enough because none of the students had previous background in the history of the Middle Ages and only two had been exposed in a limited way to the philosophy of St. Thomas. The students all concurred that they would have profited much more from the colloquium if they had taken a course like Marquette University's Theology in the Middle Ages, which, in fact, I had taught the previous year but which none of the students in this colloquium had taken. The students also felt the difficulty of ridding themselves of preconceived notions about Thomism.

All of the students were convinced that there should be available to undergraduates a course on the theology of Thomas Aquinas. Almost all of the students thought that this course should be a seminar in style so as to allow for personal direction and interaction. During the same semester I also taught a graduate course on the theology of Thomas Aquinas. This latter experience allowed for a comparison of the study of Thomas' theology on differing levels of learning. The graduate students in their replies to a questionnaire corroborated the sentiments of the undergraduates. They too felt that select, bright, and hard-working undergraduates would greatly benefit from the study of Aquinas' theology.

A long-time interest in the theology of Thomas Aquinas and the recent opportunity to experiment with the teaching of this theology to undergraduates have been the bases for comments already made in this paper. Since this essay, moreover, has been written to foster a greater attention to the theology of Thomas Aquinas in the undergraduate programs of Catholic institutions of higher learning, I wish to conclude with some specific recommendations.

1. In each undergraduate program of any appreciable size there should be at least one course on the theology of Thomas Aquinas, designed for intellectually alert and avid students. Seminaries have a special responsibility to implement this recommendation.

2. Graduate programs in theology need to offer courses in the theology of Thomas Aquinas. If they do not, there will be no teachers to pass along this important segment of the Christian theological tradition.

3. Faculties of theology should discuss the place that the theology of Thomas Aquinas and that of other classical authors have in their programs. In this age Thomas Aquinas cannot be the sole authority in Roman Catholic theology. However, his work and that of other classical theologians can be spurned only at a great loss to the theological task at hand.

4. Departments of theology and philosophy ought to discuss the relationship of their disciplines and in particular the relationship between the philosophy and theology of Thomas Aquinas, not in a polemical fashion but in a genuine dialogue about this relationship. When this relationship is not understood, the meaning of Thomas' philosophy and theology is skewed.

5. Teachers of undergraduate theology would do well to become familiar with the thought of Thomas Aquinas on a number of themes that occur in their courses, not in search of "proof texts" but as a way of alerting their students to explorations into religious questions that have been made by one of Christianity's most creative thinkers. Other authors deserve like attention, e.g., Origen, Augustine, Luther, Calvin, Newman, etc. I would add that Bonaventure makes an especially good complement to Thomas. No one can be expected to have access to all the great religious thinkers. Yet, our students deserve through their teachers to have available to them a generous sampling of the theologies of Christianity's great minds.

NOTES

1. This paper was presented on the anniversary of the death of Pope John, 3 June 1983, at the annual convention of the College Theology Society. Research for this paper was made possible by the Andrew W. Mellon Fund for Excellence in the Humanities, allocated through Marquette University.

2. Philip Gleason, "In Search of Unity: American Catholic Thought, 1920-1960," *The Catholic Historical Review* 65 (1979), 185.

3. B.F. Lonergan, "The Absence of God in Modern Culture," *A Second Collection*, ed. William F.J. Ryan and Bernard J. Tyrrell (Philadelphia: The Westminster Press, 1974), p. 110.

4. For a discussion of the deficits of neo-scholasticism and neo-Thomism see Lonergan, "The Future of Thomism," ibid. pp. 47-49; Karl Rahner, "On Recognizing the Importance of Thomas Aquinas," *Theological Investigations* 13, trans. David Bourke (London: Darton, Longman, and Todd, 1975), pp. 9ff; Gerald McCool, *Catholic Theology in the Nineteenth Century the Quest for a Unitary Method* (New York: Seabury Press, 1977), chapter 10 and Epilogue; Gerald McCool, "Twentieth-Century Scholasticism," *Celebrating the Medieval Heritage a Colloquy on the Thought of Aquinas and Bonaventure*, ed. David Tracy, *Journal of Religion* 58, Supplement (1978), S200ff. On the restoration of Thomism and the context of the encyclical *Aeterni Patris* which had so crucial a role in the revival of Thomism in the nineteenth century, see James Hennesey, "Leo XIII's Thomistic Revival a Political and Philosophical Event," in *Celebrating the Medieval Heritage* . . . , pp. S185-S197, and Leonard Boyle, "A Remembrance of Pope Leo XIII: the Encyclical *Aeterni Patris,*" *One Hundred Years of Thomism, Aeterni Patris and Afterwards, a Symposium*, ed. Victor B. Brezik (Houston: Center for Thomistic Studies, University of St. Thomas, 1981), pp. 7-22.

5. Karl Rahner, "On Recognizing . . . Thomas Aquinas," p. 12.

6. The presentations were published in *Celebrating the Medieval Heritage* . . . .

7. *One Hundred Years of Thomism* . . . , pp. 165-172; Victor B. Brezik, "A Living Thomism," *Homiletic and Pastoral Review* 83 (1983), 54-62; *Graduate Philosophy Catalogue, Center for Thomistic Studies*, University of St. Thomas, Houston TX 77006; and forthcoming article by Rev. Leonard Kennedy on Thomism in *Canadian Catholic Review*.

8. Laurence K. Shook, "Étienne Henry Gilson (1884-1978)," *Mediaeval Studies* 41 (1979), XI-XII.

9. Philip Gleason, "In Search of Unity . . . ," pp. 195-204.

10. P. Mandonnet, "Les titres doctoraux de Saint Thomas d.Aquin," *Revue Thomiste* 17 (1909), 597-608.

11. Sr. Mary Jane Kreidler, Graduate Student in the Department of Theology, Marquette University, with the support of the Mellon Funding mentioned in note 1 above, compiled the statistics on undergraduate programs from the "College Catalog Collection on Microfiche," published by Career Guidance Foundation, 8090 Engineer Rd., San Diego, CA 92111.

12. *Marquette University 1982-83 Bulletin, Undergraduate*, p. 339.

13. Armand Maurer, "Medieval Philosophy and its Historians," *Essays on the Reconstruction of Medieval History*, ed. Vaclav Mudroch and G.S. Course (Montreal and London: McGill-Queen's University Press, 1974), pp. 69-84.

14. For English text of *Aeterni Patris* see *One Hundred Years of Thomism* . . . , pp. 173-197. On the absence of a title in the original encyclical and of the phrase, *philosophia Christiana*, in the text of the encyclical see James A. Weisheipl, "Commentary," *One Hundred Years of Thomism* . . . , p. 24.

15. Étienne Gilson, *The Philosopher and Theology*, trans. Cecile Gilson, (New York: Random House, 1962), pp. 96-97.

16. On Thomas' role as *magister* see M.-D. Chenu, *Toward Understanding Saint Thomas*, trans. A-M. Landry and D. Hughes (Chicago: Henry Regnery, 1964), pp. 242-249; Chenu, *St. Thomas D'Aquin et la theologie* (Paris: Editions du Seuil, 1957), p. 34: James A. Weisiheipl, *Friar Thomas D'Aquino his Life, Thought, and Work* (Garden City, New York: Doubleday, 1974), pp. 110-129. Corrections and additions to this important intellectual biography of Aquinas are contained in the German translation: James A. Weisiheipl, *Thomas von Aquin, Sein Leben und seine Theologie* (Graz, Vienna, Cologne: Verlag Styria, 1980). Catholic University of America Press is scheduled to bring out a new edition of the out of print Doubleday edition.

17. Weisiheipl, *Friar Thomas D'Aquino*, p. 110.

18. Gilson, *The Philosopher and Theology*, p. 97.

19. J.J. Berthier, *Sanctur Thomas Aquinas, Doctor Communis Ecclesiae*, I (Rome: Editrice Nazionale, 1914). pp. 97-99. On the meaning of doctors of the church, see Keith J. Egan, "The Significance for Theology of the Doctor of the Church: Teresa of Avila," *The Pedagogy of God's Image: Essays on Symbol and the Religious Imagination*, ed. Robert Masson (Chico, CA: Scholars Press, 1982), pp. 153-171.

20. Ibid., (Berthier) *passim;* W.A. Wallace and James A. Weisheipl, "Thomas Aquinas, St.," *The New Catholic Encyclopedia* 14: 109-110.

21. Anthony Kenny, *Aquinas* (New York: Hill and Wang, 1980), p. 27.

22. Paul Tillich, *A History of Christian Thought*, ed. Carl E. Braaten (New York: Simon and Schuster, 1972), p. 180.

23. *Quaestiones de quodlibet*, IV, a. 18, *Questiones quodlibetales*, ed. P. Mandonnet (Paris, 1926), p. 155, cited by M.-D. Chenu, *Nature, Man and Society in the Twelfth Century*, ed. and trans. Jerome Taylor and Lester K. Little, (Chicago and London: University of Chicago Press, 1968), p. 292, n. 50; translation mine.

24. Bernard Lonergan, *Insight; a Study of Human Understanding* (London and New York: Longmans and Philosophical Library, 1958), p. 748.

25. Ibid.

26. Especially helpful is Weisheipl's intellectual biography of Aquinas, see n. 16 above.

27. Because of its availability in paperback the following text was used: Thomas Aquinas, *Commentary on Saint Paul's First Letter to the Thessalonians and the Letter to the Phillipians*, trans. F.R. Larcher and Michael Duffy (Albany, New York: Magi Books, 1969).

28. Thomas Aquinas, *Summa theologiae, I: The Existence of God, Part One, Questions 1-13*, ed. Thomas Gilby (Garden City, New York: Doubleday Image, 1969); James A. Weisiheipl, "The Meaning of *Sacra Doctrina* in Summa Theologiae I, q. 1," *The Thomist* 38 (1974), 49-80; Thomas C. O'Brien, " 'Sacra Doctrina' Revisited: the Context of Medieval Education," *The Thomist* 41 (1977), 475-509.

29. E.g., Prologues to *Pars Prima Secundae, Secundae Secundae*, and *Pars Tertiae.*

30. Particularly helpful was Tad W. Guzie, "The Act of Faith according to St. Thomas: a Study in Theological Methodology," *The Thomist* 29 (1965), 239-280.

31. An excellent guide: Gary A. Macy, "The Development of the Notion of Eucharistic Change in the Writings of Thomas Aquinas," Unpublished M.A. Thesis, Marquette University, 1973.

32. Weisiheipl, *Friar Thomas D'Aquine* . . . , p. 315: " . . . Thomas' discussion of the Eucharist, questions 72-83 [Pars Tertia], is among the most sublime and most perfect treatises produced in the Middle Ages.

33. See Chenu, *Toward Understanding Saint Thomas*, chapter two; Otto Bird, "How to Read an Article of the *Summa,*" *The New Scholasticism* 27 (1953), 129-159.

34. Thomas Aquinas, *Theological Texts,* selected and trans., Thomas Gilby (Oxford: Oxford University Press, 1955; reprinted: Durham, NC: The Labyrinth Press, 1982).

35. There were six students in the undergraduate colloquium and ten in the graduate course.

CONTRIBUTORS

DIANE APOSTOLOS-CAPPADONA teaches courses in religion and the arts at George Washington University, Georgetown University, and Mount Vernon College. The author of articles on the synthesis of artistic and spiritual modes of being, she is the editor of *Art, Creativity and the Sacred: Readings in Religion and Art* (1983) and *The Sacred Play of Children* (1983). She is presently engaged in a study of the spiritual dimensions of the art and philosophy of Isamu Noguchi.

J. PATOUT BURNS, S.J. is associate professor and chair of theology at Loyola University of Chicago. He is author of *The Development of Augustine's Doctrine of Operative Grace* (1980). He edited Bernard Lonergan's *Grace and Freedom* (1971), *Theological Anthropology* (1981), and *The Holy Spirit* (1984). His research interests center on Latin theology of the ancient and medieval periods, particularly the theology of grace.

EWERT H. COUSINS is professor in the theology department of Fordham University. He is a specialist in early Franciscan mysticism and theology. He is general editor of *World Spirituality: An Encyclopedic History of the Religious Quest* and also chief editorial consultant for the 60-volume series The Classics of Western Spirituality and translator and editor of the Bonaventure volume (1978). Since 1974 he has been consultant to the Vatican Secretariat forNon-Christians. In contemporary religious thought, he has specialized in Teilhard de Chardin and process theology. From 1975-1980 he was director of the Graduate Program in Spirituality at Fordham and is visiting professor at Columbia University.

KEITH J. EGAN, professor and chairperson of the department of religious studies, Saint Mary's College, Notre Dame, Indiana, and adjunct professor of theology at the University of Notre Dame, taught historical theology and spirituality at Marquette University from 1969 to 1983, and was co-director of the Institute for Ecumenical Spirituality in America (1970-1980). A past vice-president of the College Theology Society, several of his articles have appeared in the Society's annual volumes. He has published widely in the area of Carmelite spirituality, especially on Teresa of Jesus, and is the first recipient of the Dehon Fellowship (1983-1984).

JAMES FORSYTH is an associate professor of religious studies at the University of Ottawa, Canada. He has been primarily interested in the area of religion and psychology with particular focus on the dialogue between theology and psychology. He has published articles on these topics in *Dialog, Religion in Life, Encounter,* and *Soundings,* as well as the C.T.S. annual publication (1979).

MICHAEL J. GALLAGHER, a native of Philadelphia who was educated at St. Mary's Seminary and University in Baltimore and at the Catholic University of America, is assistant professor and chairperson of the theology department at Trinity College, Washington, D.C. His interests are ecclesiology and ecumenism, and he has written for *The Religion Teacher's Journal* and the *Delmarva Dialogue.*

MONIKA K. HELLWIG is a professor of theology at Georgetown University where she has taught since 1967. Her numerous publications include *The Eucharist and the Hunger of the World* (1976), *Death and Christian Hope* (1978), *Understanding Catholicism* (1981), *Sign of Reconciliation and Conversion* (1982), *Whose Experience Counts in Theological Reflection?* (1982), and (1983) *Jesus the Compassion of God.*

JANE KOPAS, editor of this volume is associate professor of theology at the University of Scranton. She received her doctorate from the Graduate Theological Union. Her interests include theological anthropology and spirituality form a process relational perspective. Among the journals where her articles have appeared are *Horizons, Process Studies,* and the *Journal of Psychology and Theology.*

ALICE L. LAFFEY is currently assistant professor of Old Testament in the department of religious studies at the College of the Holy Cross, Worcester, MA. A Sister of Mercy, she received her A.B. from Carlow College in Pittsburgh, PA. She has done graduate work at Catholic University, Villanova, St. Louis University, and Pittsburgh Theological Seminary. In 1981, she was awarded a doctorate in Sacred Scripture from the Pontifical Biblical Institute in Rome, Italy. Her publications include articles in *The Bible Translator: Technical Papers, Hospital Progress,* and *Religious Education and the Bible.*

WILLIAM P. LOEWE, with a doctorate in religious studies from Marquette, teaches systematic theology as an associate professor in the department of religion and religious education at the Catholic University of America. His research interest in soteriology has led to journal essays in the *Catholic Biblical Quarterly, Anglican Theological Review, The Thomist,* and *Horizons.*

GARY MACY is an associate professor of religious studies at the University of San Diego. He recieved his doctorate from the University of Cambridge where he specialized in medieval theology. His most recent work in this area, *Theologies of the Eucharist in the Early Scholastic Period,* will appear from Oxford University Press in 1984.

GARY A. PHILLIPS holds a Ph.D. from Vanderbilt University and is an assistant professor of religion at Holy Cross College in Worcester. His interests include biblical studies, hermeneutics, literary criticism, semiotics, and structural criticism. His articles have appeared in *Semiology and Parables* and *Semeia.* He is presently writing *Matthew: Gospel Voice and Scribe* for Crossroad.

Bernard Lonergan

Insight: A Study of Human Understanding.

Volume 3 of the Collected Works of

Bernard Lonergan. Toronto: University

of Toronto Press, 1997. Originally

published 1957.

[Longmans, Green 1957. 785 pp.]

Insight. Edited by Frederick E. Crowe

and Robert M Doran. 5th ed. rev.

+ aug. 1992. U of T Press, 1992 875 pp.

INDEX OF PERSONS

Still Available
Back Volumes from the CTS Annual Publication Series

That They May Live, edited by George Devine

A World More Human: A Church More Christian, edited by George Devine

Does Jesus Make a Difference?, edited by Thomas M. McFadden

Liberation, Revolution and Freedom, edited by Thomas M. McFadden

America in Theological Perspective, edited by Thomas M. McFadden

Critical History and Biblical Faith, edited by Thomas J. Ryan

From University Press of America, Lanham, MD 20706

Essays in Morality and Ethics, edited by James Gaffney

From Paulist Press, Ramsey, NJ 07446

The Bent World: Essays on Religion and Culture, edited by John R. May

The Journey of Western Spirituality, edited by Albert W. Sadler

The Pedagogy of God's Image, edited by Robert Masson

Foundations of Religious Literacy, edited by John V. Apczynski

From Scholars Press, Chico, CA